Colonialism and Psychiatry

Colonialism and Psychiatry

Edited by
Dinesh Bhugra
Roland Littlewood

OXFORD
UNIVERSITY PRESS

OXFORD
UNIVERSITY PRESS

YMCA Library Building, Jai Singh Road, New Delhi 110001

Oxford University Press is a department of the University of Oxford. It furthers the University's objective of excellence in research, scholarship, and education by publishing worldwide in

Oxford New York
Athens Auckland Bangkok Bogota Buenos Aires Cape Town
Chennai Dar es Salaam Delhi Florence Hong Kong Istanbul
Karachi Kolkata Kuala Lumpur Madrid Melbourne Mexico City Mumbai
Nairobi Paris Sao Paolo Shanghai Singapore Taipei Tokyo Toronto Warsaw

with associated companies in

Berlin Ibadan

Published in India
By Oxford University Press, New Delhi

ISBN 0 19 565286 X

Typeset by Excellent Laser Typesetters, Pitampura, Delhi 110034
Printed in India at Rashtriya Printers, Delhi 110032
and published by Manzar Khan, Oxford University Press
YMCA Library Building, Jai Singh Road, New Delhi 110 001

Contributors

Dilys R. Davies
Secretary
Section of Psychotherapy
Quorn
Leics, UK

Dinesh Bhugra
Lecturer
Department of History
Case Western Reserve University
Ohio, USA

Gerard Leavey
Research & Development Director
Royal Free & University College School of Medicine
St Ann's Hospital
London, UK

Jock McCulloch
School of Social Inquiry
Deakin University
Pigdons Road
Geelong, Australia

Joop de Jong
Professor & Director
Transcultural Psychosocial Organisation
Keizersgracht
Amsterdam, Netherlands

Milton J. Lewis
Senior Research Fellow
Department of Public Health and Community Medicine
University of Sydney
Sydney, Australia

Perminder Sachdev
Professor of Neuropsychiatry
University of New South Wales &
Director Neuropsychiatric Institute
Prince of Wales Hospital
Sydney, Australia

Poonam Bala
Department of History
Case Western Reserve University
Ohio, UK

Roland Littlewood
Director
Department of Anthropology
University College Centre for Anthropology
University College
London, UK

Vieda Skultans
Department of Mental Health
University of Bristol
Bristol, UK

Contents

1

Colonialism and Psychiatry

Roland Littlewood

INTRODUCTION

Given the enormous interest in the history of psychiatry which has emerged over the last thirty years following the work of Michel Foucault, and the recent post-imperial interest in the actual procedures of everyday colonial practice, it is surprising there has been little work on the practice of colonial psychiatry (Ernst's *Mad Tales from the Raj*, 1991, perhaps excepted but that is largely concerned with the European insane). How much did psychiatric theory and practice really buttress the administration of Europe's empires? What were the similarities in different situations? How does the experience of the interned compare in different colonies? In this book, we attempt a modest start on these and related questions.

By the beginning of the twentieth century, the medical discipline of psychiatry began to extend its practice to the peoples of the colonial empires. Many local patterns which suggested novel types of mental illness had been previously recorded by travellers, missionaries and colonial administrators, sometimes indeed as illnesses but often as examples of the criminal perversity of native life or just as picturesque if rather troublesome oddities. Most notable among these was *amok*, a Malay word, which has passed into English for indiscriminant and unmotivated violence against others. In one of the first discussions of the problems of comparing psychiatric illness across societies, German psychiatrist Emile Kraepelin, after a trip to Java during which he collected accounts of *amoks* and also observed hospitalized patients, suggested that the characteristic symptoms of a particular mental illness—those which one could find everywhere in the world—were the essential biological ones which directly reflected its physical cause. Yet, as he noted, 'Reliable comparison is of course only possible if we are able to draw clear distinctions between identifiable illnesses'. This proved difficult given the variety of local patterns, together with the intention, which Kraepelin enthusiastically shared, to fit them into the restricted number of categories already identified in European hospitals.

It was only when they took these diagnostic systems with them to their colonies at the beginning of the twentieth century that psychiatrists first recognized some difficulties. Dysphoric moods and unusual actions were locally recognized in Africa or Asia, not necessarily as something recalling a physical illness but often as part of totally different patterns of experience and order—as spirit possession or rituals of mourning, or as events in the course of initiation, sorcery and warfare. Those patterns that recalled the psychoses of the West seemed generally recognized as unwelcome but not always as akin to sickness. Yet, when colonial doctors turned to writing reports and academic communications, local understandings of self and illness, which might now seem to us as analogous to psychiatric theories, were described, not as self-contained, meaningful and functional conceptions in themselves, but rather as inadequate approximations to Western scientific knowledge. At times, however, the local understandings of small-scale rural societies, like the more recognizably medical traditions of India and China, cut dramatically across European experience. Anthropologist C. G. Seligman, who was trained as a doctor, reported that there seemed to have been nothing in New Guinea which could be said to resemble schizophrenia before European contact. As cases analogous to schizophrenia have later been identified by psychiatrists, he has been criticized for what is know as 'the Seligman error'—missing a universal illness because local understandings and social response did not allow it to appear objectivized through social extrusion as in a Western hospital but rather incorporated it into some shared institution where it lay unremarked by the medical observer. And similarly, Amerindian and circumpolar pattern of healing, religious inspiration and leadership, in which election to the shamanic role might be signalled by a sudden illness, accident or other troubling experience, were said to mask underlying schizophrenia.

Patterns like *amok* or *pibloktoq* ('arctic hysteria') were initially taken as rather odd—generally simpler—variants of the psychiatric disorders described in Europe. Mental illness in Java, said Kraepelin, showed 'broadly the same clinical picture as we see in our country... The overall similarity far outweighed the deviant features'. Individuals locally regarded as *amoks* were thus really demonstrating epilepsy or perhaps catatonic schizophrenia. But what were to be taken as these 'deviant features', and what was being compared with what?: presumably what psychiatrists termed the form of the illness, the basis for categorization of the pattern as some clinical entity. The assumptions made by Kraepelin in his studies in Java remain the dominant paradigms in comparative psychiatry: how similar do patterns have to be before we can say that we are talking about the same pattern? How do we distinguish between those features which appear to be generally the same from those which vary? And what are our units of categorization going to be when deciding sameness and difference, form and content, normality and pathology? Does something similar to 'depression' occur everywhere? Or perhaps just a less specific experience such as 'distress'?

Psychiatric textbooks have generally argued that locally recognized patterns like *amok* are 'not new diagnostic entities: they are in fact similar to those already known in the West'. This equivalence has often been extraordinarily optimistic. One pattern which attracted interest because of its exotic salience is *windigo*, the 'cannibal-compulsion' syndrome of the North American Ojibwa and Inuit tribes, that was locally described as a near mythical individual becoming possessed by a cannibalistic vampire, who then attacked other people in an attempt to devour them. *Windigo* was identified by psychiatrists confidently but quite variously with patterns as disparate as depression, schizophrenia, hysteria and anxiety. Similarly, *amok* was explained not only as the local manifestation of either epilepsy or schizophrenia, but as malaria, syphilis, cannabis psychosis, sunstroke, mania, hysteria, depression, disinhibited aggression and anxiety. *Latahs*, women of the Malay Peninsula who uttered obscene remarks when startled and who parodied the speech and actions of others apparently without intent, were identified as demonstrating a 'psychosis [or] hysteria, arctic hysteria, reactive psychosis, startle reaction, fright neurosis, hysterical psychosis [or] hypnoid state'. Identifying symptoms rather than the local context meant that *amok* and *latah* have generally been regarded not as autonomous cultural institutions, but simply as erroneous Malay explanations which shaped one single universal disease, although the psychiatric observers disagreed radically as to which disease this might be. The extent to which such patterns could be fitted into a universal schema depended on how far the medical observer was prepared to stretch a known psychiatric category, and thus fitted on the preferred theoretical model. By the 1970s, Weston La Barre and Georges Devereux, psychoanalysts who were much less attached to purely biomedical arguments, had gone further in including as instances of schizophrenia a wide variety of local institutions—possession states, shamanism, prophecy, millennial religions and indeed, for La Barre, social change in general. They argued not just that schizophrenia might typically appear in these social institutions as in the 'Seligman error' critiques, but that the institutions exemplified the schizophrenic experiences from which they originated: everyday culture in non-Western societies could be understood, as it were, as insanity spread out thin.

If psychiatrists of the colonial period remained puzzled about the cultural encrustations they saw adhering to the essential symptoms, they could be struck by the opposite: the 'barrenness of the clinical picture... In more primitive cultures, schizophrenia is ' a poor limitation of European forms' (Ari Kiev as late as 1972). Culturally obscured, or simply a primitive variant, in neither case did culture determine anything but rather acted as a sort of indeterminant soup which passively filled in or distorted the biological matrix. And yet 'culture' itself could be a proxy for biological 'race'.

Categorizations of illness, professional or popular, are adjacent to other social classifications—those of character, ethnicity, gender, the natural world and historical experience—on which they draw and which they plagiarize. The distinction, and indeed opposition, between the form of the illness and its content (a distinction still used) had depended on a fairly clear distinction between universal biology and the variant culture which constrained it. Yet, by the end of the nineteenth century, descriptive psychiatry was increasingly influenced by social Darwinist ideas of racial biology in which, while humans were eventually agreed to have once had a common origin, neurological, psychological, social and moral variations were all considered as reflections of each other at a particular level on the linear scale of 'development'. Allan Young has recently proposed the term 'the normalization of pathology' for the Victorian topology (associated particularly with neurologist Hughlings Jackson and thence found in Herbert Spencer, W. H. R. Rivers and Sigmund Frued) in which the central nervous system, like the colonial order, was organized in a series of levels of control in which the 'higher' could generally override the 'lower'. (Jackson's analogy was a rider and a horse). Hysteria was recognized as dysfunctional at the 'lower' level, and Kraepelin explained the unusual symptomatology of mental illness among the Javanese as reflecting their 'lower stage of intellectual development'. Variations in (what doctors called) the 'presentation' of illness in different societies have been attributed until recently not just to particular historical and political experiences, as we might have expected from the 'pathoplastic' model, but to the existence of a fairly uniform primitive mentality (more nature than culture) which was shared with European children and with the 'degenerate', 'deviant', 'regressed' or 'retarded' European adults, governed by impulse and deficient foresight, and which manifest symptoms characteristic of a loss of higher control: 'hyperidic states', 'catastrophic reactions', 'malignant anxiety', 'simple responses available to psychologically disorganized individuals' and 'primitive reactions corresponding to outbursts of psychopathic persons in developed countries' (Kiev again). Not altogether unrelated physiological explanations attributed *piblokto* and *kayak angst* to the undeveloped mind reflecting on 'the stillness and the sense of impending doom that are so characteristic of the Arctic climate' (*ibid.*).

This topological psychology of linear development, put together with the assumption that symptoms observed in Europe were somehow more real and less obfuscated by cultural values, led to the common argument, that depression did not yet occur in non-Europeans for its essential Western characteristic of self-blame (which is often seen as a result of a mature selfhood) was not observed. The absence of depression was sometimes directly attributed to a less evolved brain where the 'primitive layers' predominated, an idea which could have had (but didn't) implications for the Colonial Office when it considered the possibility of independence for colonial Africa, as recommended to it by J. C. Carothers, and ridiculed by Frantz Fanon. Guilty self-accusations of the type found in clinical depression in the West had in fact been identified in colonial Africa by Margaret Field in the 1930s, not by doctors in the colonial hospitals but by an anthropologist looking at witchcraft and the distribution of shrines. Reactions which recall Western depression are now frequently described in small-scale and non-industrialized communities, but the issue depends not only on the frequency with which people with less socially disturbing problems come to the hospital to be treated and thus studied, on medical failure to empathize with another's experience, nor on a rather cursory epidemiology based on colonial hospital statistics, but on what one means by 'depression'. Is it something like the misery which we might identify in various situations of loss or bereavement, or is it the pattern of rather physical experiences such as loss of interest, waking up early, and poor appetite, which are recognized as clinical depression (and which appear likely to be universal), or else is it some more specific expressed sentiment of Judaeo-Christian guilt, the entrepreneurial self and a wish to die? Greater psychiatric familiarity with the experience of personal distress in the former colonies has suggested that 'depression' may be simply a local variant of widespread patterns of what one might term dysphoric mood which, in depression, is represented through a particularly Western moral psychology which assumes an autonomous self as the invariant locus of experience, memory and agency. When looking across societies, a more common experience of everyday distress than 'depression' (which figures a phenomenological sinking downwards of the once active self into an inertia for which we remain responsible) may be one of depletion and the loss of something essential which has been taken out of the self—a pattern well—glossed in various Latin American idioms of 'soul loss'.

Patterns like *kuru* or the restricted abilities of senescence, or such apparently motivated patterns as homicide and rape, the deliria of malnutrition or alcohol intoxication, or the use of other psychoactive substances have been regarded as characteristic of a particular society but are seldom described as 'culture-bound' because they appear potentially available in any society or else do not immediately recall European 'mental illness'. Yet, if these patterns persisted—like alcohol abuse, *anomic depression* and suicide consequent on the relocation of Native Americans onto reservations—they were taken as manifestations of 'American Indian culture', ignoring the political relationship between the settler and the native, and thus the context of the psychiatric observation. 'New illnesses' identified by more sophisticated epidemiological techniques in urban populations or through the expansion of psychiatric observation to a wider population have been termed 'culture-change' or 'acculturation illnesses' exemplified by the *brain-fag syndrome* identified in West African students.

In part, the continuing problem of 'culture' for psychiatrists has laid in its double-edged connotations. 'Culture' was still a valued commodity, that constraint on nature which distinguished human from animal, educated European from the primitive (and which is thus often referred to 'high culture' alone). Yet, for Western psychiatrists establishing their discipline as a medical speciality, 'culture' remained secondary to scientific biological reality. As frank biological racism became disreputable after the Second World War and the unifying idiom of 'development' separated out into the distinct fields of child psychology, economics and technology, the psychological differences between the European and the non-European could again be perceived only in rather uncertain 'cultural' terms: as a medical proxy for the other's 'difference' (or even for the lingering idea of biological 'race') and which still immersed the individual in some undifferentiated "other", now less their biological level than their way of life. As medicine had little idea of how to deal with 'culture', it drew on other disciplines, particularly psychoanalysis and social anthropology, which claimed to be able to relate the interests of medicine to the inter-subjective social world in a more empirical and humanistic way than evolutionary medicine. The new cultural psychiatrists generally held appointments in Western university departments, away from the poorly-funded and intellectually marginal concerns of colonial psychiatry, which still remained close to popular Western ideas of race. Psychoanalysts and anthropologists interested in providing a 'cultural psychiatry' or local patterns in British Africa based on intensive fieldwork in local communities were seldom interested in examining hospital statistics, unlike the epidemiologists associated with the World Health Organization who until recently have preferred to stick with the presumed biomedical universals, and thus with the idioms of hospital psychiatry.

The evolutionary schema did offer one mode of comparison by placing societies (or illnesses) as states of transformation along a historical spectrum driven by certain processes and thus 'normalizing' pathologies as emergent stages.

Few social anthropologists, some sociobiologists, Freudians and Marxists perhaps excepted, would now subscribe to the idea of unilinear human development through which local institutions and mentalities are to be understood as determined by underlying processes, whether those of evolutionary selection or of the relations of production. Whilst it is still argued that the insights offered by psychoanalysts may provide a useful perspective when trying to understand psychological experience in non-European societies, others have argued that Freud's followers have little to contribute to the critical or social sciences for they offer a moralized version of common-sensical Western assumptions about the inevitability of European rationality with entrepreneurial autonomy as 'health' or 'adaptation'. On the whole, with the exception of a few psychoanalytically orientated anthropologists, the ethnographic monographs written by anthropologists now place little emphasis on the early childhood experiences which the psychoanalysts had argued was significant in generating culture. They take particular patterns of childrearing as the manifestation rather than the cause of social knowledge. The assumption that non-European thought is less rational has been superseded by the recognition that all societies employ both deductive and inductive logic, both concrete and abstract reasoning, but that they do so within limits which are determined by their own social interests.

Societies differ psychologically not in their capabilities but in their modes of thought—through cognitions and categorizations of space and time, the sexes and the natural world, their understandings of causality and individuals, and which are encoded in their systems of representation, particularly language. What was once regarded as primitive (magical) thinking on the origins of sickness or misfortune appears now as a focus on the moral 'why' rather than the technical 'how', for societies differ in the focus of their immediate interests and practised knowledge. Indeed, in terms of the everyday understanding of sickness, Western medicine is less efficacious in relieving distress through its emphasis on the proximate mechanisms of misfortune, leaving the individual with chronic or serious illness with little help in answering 'why me?'. In the case of severe mental illness we might note that psychiatry remains unable to offer its patients any understanding, technical or moral, in terms of everyday knowledge (or, indeed, of biology).

To recognize some other's pattern as especially 'cultural' is to assume a privileged perspective concerning it, whether colonial hubris or academic analysis. (As Pascal had put it, we have truth but they have customs). By the mid-1980s, culture-specific illnesses had been recognized by critics as psychiatry's 'twilight zone', or 'what other people have, not us'. Medical interest in isolated and disembodied exotic patterns was seen to have directed attention to more immediate questions of economic development, poverty, exploitation and nutritional diseases, besides providing yet another justification of the otherness of non-Europeans. It also ignored the role of Western medicine, once in facilitating imperial expansion and now, in the global marketing of untested pharmaceutical drugs.

How directly relevant had psychiatry been to imperialism? Did either theory or practice enhance the process of colonial administration? Both evidently developed in the same period. It is true they shared certain modes of reasoning: we might note, for instance, some affinities between the scientific objectification of illness experienced as disease and the objectification of people as chattel slaves or a colonial manpower, or the topological parallels between the nervous system and the imperial order. Both argued for an absence of 'higher' functions or sense of personal responsibility among patients and non-Europeans. The extent, however, to which any elaborated set of ideas, which might be termed 'imperial psychiatry', provided a specific rationale for colonialism in British Africa or India is debatable. With remarkably few exceptions, the small number of colonial psychiatrists barely participated in the debates I have briefly outlined above. Segregated facilities, of course as Bhugra and McCulloch show here; used prejudice and neglect, undoubtedly; but hardly practicable ideologies for perpetuating racial or cultural inferiority. (Indeed, we might more plausibly argue the case of contemporary psychiatric practice in Britain). One possible exception was the common medical (and anthropological) assumption in the 1940s that too rapid social change (that is, access to schools and waged labour) was causing an increase in African psychiatric illness, but this increase was often explained by others as a better access to hospital services. I am doubtful whether this argument was taken seriously in London or any other colonial metropolis; it could of course be turned on its head by arguing that it was colonization, not 'change', that was pathogenic. Whilst the few British colonial psychiatrists were quite tangential to the making of the Colonial Office policy (and were themselves rather 'marginal' individuals within both British and colonial society), in the francophone colonies and in Haiti, local Black psychiatrists developed radical critiques of European domination to argue for a distinct 'African identity' as against the settlers, and one which was couched in terms of the Haitian idea of 'ethnopsychiatry'. Ethnographers like W. H. R. Rivers, Bronislaw Malinowski and Margaret Field, aspects of whose work developed into what was to become medical anthropology, whilst they relied on missionary evidence and Colonial Office support, did not significantly influence British policy in Africa or elsewhere. If diseases in the colonies were of any political interest to the metropolis, the concern was not madness but the acute infections which threatened to deprive the imperial administration of its labour force, or else the psychological health of the colonists themselves.

Anthropologist Evans-Pritchard, for example, was commissioned to examine the role of prophets in inciting anti-British resistance among the Nuers of colonial Sudan. In what became a classic text in anthropology (with photographs supplied by the RAF bombing crews) we can note that on a couple of occasions he refers to some of them as 'psychotic' but this is nowhere developed as any sort of racial or medical theory. Whilst colonialism took for granted a difference between 'higher' and 'lower' levels of civilization, this was not linked to any neurological topology beyond the isolated speculations of the colonial doctors, Vint, Carothers and Tooth. By contrast, in the United States, psychiatry was deployed extensively during the nineteenth and twentieth centuries to justify what we may term the internal colonization of Amerindians and African-Americans.

In the early stages of imperial expansion, domination is explicitly economic or military, and any necessary justification rests simply on evident technical or administrative superiority, sometimes manifest destiny, security of trade or the historical requirements of civilization; only when dominated peoples 'inside the walls' threaten to achieve some sort of equality do apologies appear couched as a discourse on primitive pathology or biological inferiority. To an extent we may argue that Europe prepared to abandon her settlements well before equality threatened (except for the significant instances of Kenya, Algeria and the French Caribbean) and before colonial administrations had established institutions much beyond a basic mental hospital for the native criminally insane. In North America, arguments in favour of the emancipation of slaves had appeared by the time of Independence only to be countered by medical justifications for continued servitude which invoked such novel diseases as *drapetomania* (the impulse to escape) (Brigham in 1832) or arguments put forward by Benjamin Rush (1799), that African ancestry was itself an attenuated disease; justifications which became even more necessary for White supremacy after emancipation. Among Native Americans, for whom collective political action was impossible after they were dispersed on reservations beyond the boundary of a European state, twentieth-century administrators and medical officers developed increasingly psychological—and thence psychopathological—explanations to explain their high rates of suicide, alcoholism and general failure to participate in national life: the 'internalization of the frontier' as Andreas Heinz has put it.

Why the English/French difference? Perhaps because French colonialism tended to a model of cultural and biological assimilation, while the English argued more for cultural segregation. French psychiatry was (and is) a more intellectual profession than its pragmatic British counterpart, and medical students from Martinique or Senegal, when studying in Paris, were more likely to be exposed to political and philosophical debate than they would have been in a London medical school.

In this volume, McCulloch proposes that there was a fairly unified body of European knowledge which he calls 'ethnopsychiatry' in colonized Africa in the twentieth century. As he notes, psychiatric facilities developed fairly late in the history of settlement and then, largely to serve the needs of the European settlers. As the career of J. C. Carothers indicates, colonial psychiatry was, however, fairly haphazard and unplanned. His opinions developed those outlined above—that the African was at a state of development corresponding to a lobotomized European.

On the other hand the dilemmas of the contemporary psychiatrist using the categories of the 'inter-cultural' classification, to search for the hidden origins and metaphors involved in the category of depression, the current medical notion are a part stemming from diverse sources, Hippocratic and ecclesiastical, and conceptually overlaps with such idioms as melancholy, fatigue and stress. It could be argued that psychological depression is a quintessentially Western-European term and experience. Little surprise that it was not identified in India or Africa. In a detailed study, Bhugra shows how the British in India neglected, indeed disdained, an already well-developed theoretical and practical local psychiatry. The cost was a gross disparity between the treatment of European and Indian patients. He argues that Indian psychiatry is still, fifty years after Independence, firmly in the British style and has still to develop a relationship with Indian tradition and knowledge.

Lewis's account of Australian psychiatry is largely concerned with the white population rather than the aboriginal community. Psychiatry in Australia largely follows a line similar to Britain (though with closer ties between the medical and penal systems at psychiatry's early development in the nineteenth century). Lay and 'moral' treatment was superseded by the late nineteenth century turn to Darwinism and biological pessimism. As early twentieth century turned to community psychiatry and the late confrontations with libertarian anti-psychiatry, the British influence faded, without any development of a characteristically 'national' school. By contrast, Sachdev considers the still continuing conflict between the Maoris and the Whites in New Zealand. Difficulties in doctor-patient communication stem not only from pure 'cultural' differences but from an imbalance of power. Local initiatives such as 'culture brokers' (*pukenga*) go some way in making Western psychiatry acceptable to the Maoris and in educating the *pakeha* (Whites). Purely cultural differences must be read through still vital questions of inequality and neglect.

The legacy of colonial administration and Western psychiatry in the economically poorer nations is explored by de Jong, with particular reference to Africa. He argues that neurotic conditions, essentially ignored by imperial psychiatry, are probably still better treated by local healers whose idioms are more congenial to the locals (and they are more accessible than Western trained doctors). By contrast, local patterns of understanding and treating the more serious psychiatric disorders are less successful than biomedical services, even though these are often rudimentary through poverty and post-independence military conflicts.

Skultan's chapter on Latvia is different, both in its method and subject—the effects of the Soviet occupation on individual lives. Though psychiatry was used for coercive dealing with dissidents, her main focus is on how neurasthenia as an ambiguous psychiatric category was a way of making sense and of resisting Soviet power. Where past life experiences could not be directly conceived of in a political way, resulting dysphoria and dissatisfaction could be conceptualized as neurasthenia, a diagnosis which allowed some personal negotiating space for the individual as well as a disavowal of personal responsibility.

Leavey and Davies also compare what we may term a form of more internalized colonialism. Despite the apparently easy assimilation of Irish people into British society, the high rates of mental illness among Irish migrants cannot simply be explained by their relatively lower economic position, and Leavey argues that we have to reach further back to the nineteenth century stereotypes of the Irish to find the roots of a still continuing pattern of discrimination. This has recently been reinforced by continuing disputes over the status of Northern Ireland which have occasionally spilled over into Britain. Starting from the relative paucity of Welsh language psychotherapy available in Wales, Davies draws widely from phenomenology and personal construct theory to post-colonial (subaltern) theory to provide a psychological view of Welsh double consciousness. Her model is relevant not only for Latvians and Irish but for all situations where the colonizers instituted patterns of an internalized colonial identity which persist parallelly with a related subdominant identity. And this, we might argue, is true for most post-colonial settings.

The editors are aware that this first collection does little more than scratch the surface. What we hope for is that out of this first foray, more practicable questions might emerge. What were the considerations by which the colonizers first considered local facilities—decorum, humanitarianism or the consolidation of imperial authority? How did the first organized Western-style services deal with the question of local healers? Were these sanctions against local practice or did the imperial authorities gladly leave part of their burden to the despised traditional practitioners? Are there significant differences between the fate of more professionalized types of local practice (*Unani*, *Ayurveda*) and the less institutionalized forms of local healing of the mentally ill? If colonial and post-colonial psychiatry often seem to follow European models (say in the shift from penal institutions to asylums and thence to 'community' based facilities), are there any significant local contingencies which have affected this picture? Have new local practices embodied a critique of colonialism? How have notions such as 'culture' or 'race' been understood by Western psychiatrists in the countries they once colonized? Did colonization do anything more than re-lable local deviances; can we say that in itself it was pathogenic in any empirical sense?

2

The Impact of Colonialism on the Mental Health of the New Zealand Maori: A Historical and Contemporary Perspective

Perminder Sachdev

Te maatauranga o te Pakeha	The knowledge of the Pakeha (European)
He mea whakatoo hei tinanatanga	is propagated
Moo wai ra?...	For whom?...
Hei patu tikanga	To kill customs
Patu mahara	To kill memory
Mauri e	To kill our sacred powers.

(Tuini Ngawai, Ngaati Porou composer, c. 1950)

The Maoris of New Zealand present an excellent example of the interaction of the fourth world people with a first-world colonizing power and its institutions, and the impact this has had on their health. Prior to contact with European settlers, the Maoris had a pre-scientific health system with its accompanying healing practices. In the nineteenth and early twentieth centuries, this was largely replaced by Western scientific medicine and psychology, at least in most observable domains. This change was at times brought about by the active suppression of traditional practices. The old, however, maintained a dynamic tension with the new, and traditional Maori concepts and practices continued to influence health-seeking behaviour of the Maoris and their interaction with the Western health system. The background socio-economic and political factors had a major influence on this interaction. The current assessment of the Maoris' mental health suggests that the promise of first-world medicine has not produced the desired results, with the Maori community faring poorly on most indicators of positive health in comparison with the non-Maori (*Pakeha*). The last two decades have seen a re-appraisal of Maori health needs and the appropriate health care delivery system, with an emphasis on the empowerment of the Maori community in bringing about change.

ETHNOHISTORICAL BACKGROUND

The Maori[1] are the indigenous Polynesian people of New Zealand who attribute their presence in *Aotearoa* ('the Land of the Long White Cloud') to waves of migration in the early part of the second millenium. The Europeans first contacted the Maori in the late eighteenth century when the country was explored by British naval officer James Cook, paving the way for colonization.[2] The Maori in this period were agriculturists, and had reached a high point in the arts of warfare, canoe construction, weaving and building. The Maori society was divided into groups called *iwi* (tribes),[3] which consisted of a number of *hapu* (sub-tribes), and in turn, a number of *whanau* (extended families). A comprehensive account of Maori society before and since colonization can be obtained from standard works by Best (1924), Buck (1950), Firth (1959) and Metge (1976).

James Cook estimated the Maori population to be between 100,000 and 300,000 towards the end of the eighteenth century (Schwimmer, 1974), but the reliability of this estimate has been questioned (Pool, 1977). There is general agreement that the numbers dropped sharply in the first century of European settlement

[1] The word Maori, like many other Maori nouns, is currently used as both singular and plural.

[2] The first documented European to arrive in New Zealand was Abel Tasman, a Dutch sailor, in 1642.

[3] William's (1975) 'A Dictionary of the Maori Language' is used as the standard reference for the Maori words used.

to an estimated less than 50,000 by late nineteenth century (Pool, 1977). In 1846, Dr Isaac Featherston, a surgeon and later a Member of Parliament, is reported to have said, 'A barbarous and coloured race must inevitably die out by mere contact with the civilised White; our business, therefore, and all we can do, is to smooth the pillow of the dying Maori race' (quoted in Miller, 1958, p. 104). While this view may seem extreme, it was held widely, and the extinction of the full-blooded Maori was presented as a Darwinian outcome of the struggle between the two races. Reasons for the decline in population were the rapid spread of contagious diseases such as tuberculosis, measles, influenza (*rewharewha*), typhoid fever, whooping cough and scarlet fever to which the Maoris had little resistance, the introduction of the musket to warfare with its lethal potential, and the wider socio-economic and environmental changes which included alienation from the land.

Maori life was profoundly affected by colonization. A capitalist economy affected the whole material basis of life. In the early nineteenth century, many Maori people moved from the hilltop sites to coastal areas for trade with settlers or new jobs. Not only were the new settlements poor in amenities, they led to a more sedentary way of life. Christianity cut across sanctions and prohibitions, thus altering the social fabric, which was further modified by new beliefs and pursuits. After the British formally assumed control of the country following the Treaty of Waitangi[4] in 1840, the Maori waged a series of wars against the colonists which resulted in the loss of enormous tracts of Maori territory and further disruption of the Maori society. The loss of land (*whenua*) has been identified by many Maoris as the cornerstone of Maori disempowerment and loss of *mana* (prestige or status). Land sale by the Maori to the *Pakeha* (White person or European) was actively encouraged by the government through legislation to

[4] The Treaty of Waitangi was negotiated between Britain's designated consul and lieutenant governor William Hobson and many North Island chiefs, and was signed at the northern settlement of Waitangi on 5–6 February 1840. The treaty purportedly transferred sovereignty over the Maori people to the British Crown (Kawharu, 1989). The motives behind the treaty, the manner of its execution, the adherence to it by later governments, and its current status are all shrouded in controversy, and the treaty has often been a rallying point for Maori activism who accuse the British Government of fraud.

overcome collective Maori resistance and encourage individualization of title (Parsonson, 1981).

The decline in the Maori population was reversed in the twentieth century and this has been a remarkable period of continuing readjustment. Maori participation has been a major factor in this recovery and growth, as I will discuss later. Sociocultural change in the Maori society has been rapid in the twentieth century. Massive urbanization of the Maoris occurred during the first three decades of the second half of the twentieth century. This resulted in increased participation of the Maori in the industrialized economy, and increased cultural contact with the *Pakeha*, leading to intermarriage, as well as disruption of extended family networks traditional for the Maori. By the end of the twentieth century, the Maori population was larger and probably healthier than it had ever been before. The 1991 National Census estimated the Maori population at a little over 0.5 million. Maori life expectancy is 68 years for men and 72.9 years for women (Department of Statistics, 1993).

The recovery has not, however, gone far enough, and the Maori continue to compare poorly with the *Pakeha* on most indices of health and socio-economic status. The Maoris remain on a lower rung of the social ladder, although a sprinkling can be seen at all levels, and their participation in government is significant. The educational achievement of most Maori children is below that of the non-Maori (62 per cent of Maoris leave secondary school without passing at least one subject of school certificate, compared to 28 per cent of non-Maori; only 9.5 per cent qualify for university entrance 34 per cent non-Maoris). The unemployment rate in the Maori youth is more than twice that in the non-Maoris. The indicators of physical and psychological health again show the Maoris at a disadvantage, as do indicators of social instability such as domestic violence, broken marriages, court appearances, and dependence on social welfare.

TRADITIONAL MAORI MENTAL HEALTH CONCEPTS

There is general agreement that the Maori definition of health encompasses four basic components: spiritual (*te taha wairua*), psychic (*te taha hinengaro*), physical (*te taha tinana*) and family (*te taha whanau*) (Te Hui Whakaoranga, 1984). The spiritual component has been stressed as the most important and basic requirement. This spirituality is in essence an awareness of one's relationship with other living beings and the environment. There is particular emphasis on the link with the land which augments one's spiritual strength. A similar continuity with the spiritual world is provided by the spirits of the deceased relatives. The Maori encourage the expression of thoughts and emotion and much of this expression is ritualized on the *marae* (meeting place). Integrative and holistic thinking is valued over analytical thought, and group well-being takes precedence over personal ambition, the free expression of the latter being considered a sign of ill-health. The third component, physical health, emphasizes a number of ritualized procedures concerning bodily function. The preparation and consumption of food, the cleansing of the body and the disposal of excrement are governed by the laws of *tapu* (discussed later), which had an extremely important role in traditional society and continue to be important determinants of Maori health. The fourth component—the family (*whanau*)—has a much wider dimension in Maori culture than in the *Pakeha*. The family in the Maori sense denotes the extended kinship system. It is said to include the *whanau te rito*, or the immediate relatives, and *whanui* or the tribal component where a common *whakapapa* links the person to a large group of people. Family or tribal affiliation is a core construct in Maori personal identity, and obligations to the family get precedence over individual needs. When a Maori attempts to describe himself or another Maori, he or she begins with the tribal affiliation and the lineage (*whakapapa*). Maori children are nurtured by the elders and other tribal kinsfolk, and the care of the aged is a major Maori concern. A telling example of the difference between the Maori and *Pakeha* approaches to health is that Maori elders, when asked to list important health problems affecting the Maori people, are most likely to highlight the pollution of food sources and the health of children than diseases like diabetes, gout, hypertension, carcinoma of the lung and psychiatric illness on which the Maori fare worse than the *Pakeha*.

Three Maori ethnopsychological constructs—*mana*, *tapu* and *noa*—are important for the understanding of the Maori views on aetiology and management of illness, the mechanisms of social organization and control, and the behaviour of individuals. *Mana* is most commonly used to convey 'influence, power or prestige', but it is a spiritual power or force, originating from the *atua* (gods) and spoken of in relation to persons, spirits or inanimate objects and never in isolation. Much of it is inherited depending upon the seniority of descent, birth order, sex and the *mana* of the ancestors, but it can also be earned by great achievement, especially in traditional spheres, by direct contact with the supernatural, the acquisition of land, marriage and some other means. Its maintenance needs continued endorsement by others and it can be lost by failing to live up to their expectations, by greed or covetousness, or defeat and humiliation. High *mana* would entail positive functioning in all spheres of health discussed earlier. *Tapu* has been variously translated as 'under religious or ceremonial restriction', 'holy or sacred' or 'forbidden'. Its modern usage is in the sense of 'sacred', but without the ethical connotations of 'moral righteousness' implied in the New Testament. A person, place, thing or action can be *tapu* and, in this sense, is removed from the influence of the profane and common and enters that of the sacred. It is imbued with the influence of the *atua*, and the *tapu* state, and the person or object in it, needs to be treated with respect or caution. This is because the influence of the gods, or its withdrawal, could be beneficial or harmful. *Tapu* has the property of spreading by contagion and likeness, and it can be ritually instilled. Because of this, its influence was quite pervasive in conservative Maori society, and a large number of activities, especially the ones concerning war, disease, death, power over others, religion, food and procreation, were influenced and greatly regulated by virtue of being *tapu*. This served a useful purpose of maintaining order, ensuring sanitation, protecting food resources, reducing cross-infection (without an explicit concept of contagious infection being present), etc. The obverse of *tapu* is *noa* which is commonly used to mean 'free from *tapu* or any other restriction'. A person, object, place or action is *noa* when it is quite removed from the influence of the gods. Though in the domain of the common and profane, a *noa* state had the advantage of lacking the restrictions that went with being *tapu*. *Tapu* and *noa* had a dynamic interaction, and movement from one to the other could occur to meet material, psychological or spiritual needs. A *noa* object could be made *tapu* in special circumstances by the imposition of a *rahui*.

While there was some recognition of natural causes, e.g. accidents or combat (*mate tangata*), illness in most instances had a supernatural causation in Maori society (*mate atua*). The concepts were no different for physical and mental disorders although supernatural causation could more obviously be implicated for the latter, and such beliefs have, to some degree, persisted to the present. Impairment of health was attributed to the malevolent behaviour of a supernatural agent such as a spirit, a demon or a god, the *atua*. The Maori personified sickness, and so spoke of being afflicted by *Whiro*, *Maiki-nui*, *Maiki-roa*, etc. Many *atua* were considered malignant and forever disposed to attack man. The direct cause of this attack was either an infringement of the law of *tapu* or the performance of sorcery, the former being the most important. The offence against *tapu* (called *hara*) could be deliberate or accidental, and considering the ramifications of *tapu* restrictions, such an offence was not difficult for a *tohunga* (healer or priest) to find. Examples of *tapu* violation include the profane handling of genealogies, violation of burial grounds, improper observance of *marae* etiquette, etc. The diagnosis and treatment usually depended upon the *tohunga*, although a person could appeal directly to an *atua*. Illness was also often attributed to the covert action of an envious, affronted or malicious human being who used sorcery or *makutu*, either himself or with the help of a *tohunga*, to injure his victims.

A skilled *tohunga*, after making the correct causal attribution, used healing incantations and rituals for treatment. Water was a common ingredient of the rituals, both for cleansing as well as preparing a person for a *tapu* ritual. Incantations were sometimes skillfully combined with practical measures, e.g. the incantation for treating a person choking on a bone blamed him for being greedy, accompanied by vigorous slapping on the back. Some physical remedies, derived from leaves, berries or fruit were used for local application, and occasionally for internal ailments. A few accounts of minor surgical procedures, such as cauterization, myringotomy and bloodletting are available. In keeping with the theories of illness causation, much of the healing practices were spiritual rather than physical.

The Current Status of Maori Health

The health status of the pre-colonial Maori is difficult to assess because of a lack of reliable documentation. Accounts of early explorers suggest that the Maori was a healthy and robust community. However, based on skeletal studies, the average life span was estimated to have been no more than 30 years (Houghton, 1980, pp. 147–8). The current status of Maori health is generally discussed in comparison with the *Pakeha* and is almost uniformly assessed to be relatively poor (Rose, 1960; Pomare, 1980; Pomare and de Boer, 1988; Kokiri, 1993). The Maori continue to lag behind the non-Maori on most indices of health, and have higher rates of many common disorders. About twice as many Maori in the age group of 25–44 years die of ischaemic heart disease as their non-Maori counterparts. Overall rates of cerebrovascular disease, respiratory diseases such as pneumonia and bronchial asthma, diabetes mellitus and gout are consistently higher in the Maori (Pomare and de Boer, 1988), after accounting for effects of social class. Maori children have a high incidence of rheumatic fever, and in some communities these rates are comparable with the third world (Neutze and Clarkson, 1984). Life expectancy for the Maori is 5–7 years less than the *Pakeha*, and infant mortality rates are 50 per cent higher. While this is a great improvement over the situation even 30 years ago, there are some disturbing trends in relation to cardiovascular diseases, lung and breast cancer, etc.

While many causes have been identified for the excess morbidity and mortality in the Maori, several reviews (Pomare, 1980; Smith and Pearce, 1984; Sachdev, 1990) have implicated behavioural factors to a major extent. These include adverse lifestyle factors such as smoking, alcohol abuse, overnutrition and accidents. According to the analysis by Smith and Pearce (1984) for the period 1974–8, the proportions of the excess mortality in the Maori aged 15–64 years that could be attributed to behavioural factors were: obesity, 5 per cent for both sexes; smoking, 15 per cent for males and 16 per cent for females; alcohol (excluding alcohol-related accidents), 10 per cent for males and 2 per cent for females; and accidents, 17 per cent for males and 8 per cent for females. The authors also reported an excess, not related to social class, of five times or more for Maori mortality due to rheumatic and hypertensive heart diseases, nephritis, bronchiectasis, diabetes and tuberculosis, all diseases for which there are effective treatments, thereby suggesting either a poor delivery to or an ineffective use by the Maori population of the health care facilities (Hyslop *et al.*, 1983).

The data on psychiatric morbidity are from secondary sources as no population-based survey of the Maori has been conducted. These data suggest that the Maori have a slightly greater risk of psychiatric hospitalization than the non-Maori (Sachdev, 1989a). First admission and readmission rates for schizophrenia are higher for the Maori. First admission rates for major affective illness are roughly comparable with the non-Maori, and those for neuroses and neurotic depression are lower in the Maori. Rates of admission for alcohol abuse, alcohol dependence and personality disorders are much higher for the Maori male aged 20–40 years, and this group is at the greatest risk of psychiatric hospitalization. The Maori have shown an increase in first psychiatric admission rates since the 1950s, with rapid increases in the early 1960s and the 1980s (Sachdev, 1989a). The rates for psychotic disorders have been relatively constant, and the most significant changes have been for alcohol abuse, alcohol dependence and personality disorders. A larger proportion of Maori are admitted involuntarily, especially under the Criminal Justice Act as special patients. In 1986, 67 per cent of special patients were Maori while they comprised only 12 per cent of the population (*Psychiatric Report*, 1988). There has been only one major review of psychiatric disability in the Maori, conducted by the Maori Trustee (Mason, 1991). This report suggested that the Maori were over-represented in the psychiatrically disabled individuals, whether living in institutions or in the community.

Psychiatric morbidity among the Maori cannot be considered to be alarming, but the unfavourable statistics have excited many debates in the health professions and in Maoridom in general. Particular attention has been focused on the increase in psychiatric hospital admission rates in the last four decades. These changes have been related to socio-economic and politico-cultural factors, in particular the stress of rapid urbanization (Sachdev, 1989a). The figures have also been argued to suggest that the Western health care system, especially psychiatric treatment, did not seem to be particularly effective for the Maori (Kokiri, 1994). The data must, of course, be examined in the light of other sociocultural aspects of the modern Maori, including the socio-economic disadvantage, lower educational and occupational status, ethnic minority status and the perspective of Western health institutions not being sympathetic to cultural differences.

THE MEDICAL ESTABLISHMENT IN NEW ZEALAND

The medical establishment in the country is part of the Western scientific tradition which can be traced back to the early post-contact years with the arrival of European settlers to the colony. Social security was introduced in 1938–40 which made a free public health system accessible to everyone. What has emerged since then is a 'dual' system comprising state-funded public provisions and state-subsidized private or voluntary provisions. General practice and other primary care belongs to the latter category. The general (or family) physicians are the point of first medical contact except in emergency situations. Consultation with a general physician is highly subsidized by the state but the patient still has to pay a small amount, which may be significant for families on low income. Eighty per cent of hospitals are state hospitals, which are free, and the remaining 20 per cent subsidized by the state. Psychiatric patients occupy 42 per cent of all hospital beds although this situation is changing because of a move toward de-institutionalization. The country spends approximately 8 per cent of the GNP on health. There are a few other systems of medicine like naturopathy, osteopathy, acupuncture, etc. which complement the main system to a small extent but do not compete with it.

HOW DO THE MAORI INTERACT WITH THE CONTEMPORARY HEALTH SYSTEM?

Colonization brought with it a number of diseases which the Maori had not been exposed to and had little resistance against. The Maori *tohunga* had a limited repertoire of therapies and 'the disease spirits of the white man would not obey his exhortations to leave' (Buck 1950: 409).[5] A number of factors led to the adoption of Western medicine by the Maori. One of these was the rapid fall in the Maori population due to wars and *Pakeha* diseases. Another was the realization that *Pakeha* medicine was the only effective cure in

[5] There were evidently no endemic or epidemic diseases in New Zealand in the pre-European days. Typhoid, tuberculosis, measles, and venereal diseases were all introduced by the European (Buck, 1950). Since the natives lacked immunity to these diseases, the effect was devastating.

many cases. Contact with the *Pakeha* and the adoption of Christianity weakened the hold of *tapu* and *makutu* on the populace, making a naturalistic explanation of disease more acceptable. The accessibility of medical attention was another factor. The governmental stance that health care should be based on Western principles was clearly enunciated in the Tohunga Suppression Act 1907, which had the support of some Maori leaders.

The twentieth century has seen an interplay of Maori health aspirations and the health goals of the State. Not infrequently, the two have been incompatible or even in direct conflict. For most of this period, the Maori have seen the health system as an imposition because of its narrow approach to health care and the shifts in priorities entailed by political realities. The Maori response to this will be discussed later. On the other hand, the health bureaucracy had, until recently, taken for granted the acceptance of the '*Pakeha* health system' by the Maori. If the Maori have the same access to the health system as the *Pakeha* and yet perform poorly on most health indicators, is it possible that their help-seeking behaviour is different, leading to a suboptimal usage of the facilities? This question has been partially addressed empirically. At the primary care level, studies suggest a higher rate of medical contact for the Maori compared to the non-Maori (West and Harris, 1980; Davis, 1986), although this may still fall short of the estimates based on illness burden (Davis, 1986). The hospital data lead to a similar conclusion (Mitchell and Borman, 1986). In case of psychiatric illness, for the years 1981–3, the patient or a relative was the source of referral for psychiatric admission in 12.5 per cent Maori and 10.3 per cent non-Maori psychiatric admissions, thus suggesting that the Maori are not particularly averse to bringing themselves to a hospital. The research evidence, therefore, suggests that the Maori do use the *Pakeha* health system.

The more difficult question to address in a research study is whether they use the system effectively, and for the right reasons. Informed comment exists that the Maori do not usually seek help voluntarily for problems like obesity (Murchie, 1984) or alcoholism (Awatere *et al.*, 1984). Other commentators have outlined various reasons why the Maori are uncomfortable with *Pakeha* hospitals and doctors (Walker, 1982; Marsden, 1986). The major factor identified is the monocultural nature of these institutions that dismisses the obvious, and certainly the subtle, cultural differences and expectations that the Maori brings to them. Furthermore, Maori commentators have stressed that the Maori concept of health is different from that of the *Pakeha*, and what a *Pakeha* may view as unhealthy may not be so in Maori eyes and vice versa. Neglect of one aspect of health by the health care system may well lead to the neglect of other aspects as well.

SOME POSSIBLE REASONS FOR THE INEFFECTIVE USAGE OF THE HEALTH CARE SYSTEM BY THE MAORI

The problems in the interaction of the Maori with the mainstream health system have attracted considerable scholarly interest and comment (Durie, 1977; Older, 1978; Jacobsen, 1983; Broughton, 1984; Hui Whakaoranga, 1984; Pomare, 1986), but little anthropological investigation. Maori attitudes to Western medicine, problems in the communication between *Pakeha* health professionals and Maori patients, the inflexibility of the health system to accommodate the cultural differences of the Maori, and relics of traditional Maori beliefs and practices have all been suggested as reasons why the Maori have been unable to fully exploit the benefits of modern medicine. The power equation, too, must not be ignored. It is true that the health system is controlled by the *Pakeha* and the Maori is not only an under-represented minority but also a socio-economically disadvantaged one. It is certainly likely that some Maori will see the *Pakeha* insistence on the Maori utilization of the system as another instance of control by a dominant group whose values are sometimes unacceptable and in conflict with Maori values. This resentment has historical roots and is openly expressed in Maori forums (Walker, 1982; Hui Whakaoranga, 1984). The view commonly expressed by the Maori is that the health status was intimately related to tribal land ownership or *mana whenua*. Dispossession of Maori land was seen as the symbol of Maori disempowerment and their lack of control over their affairs, which included management of health. This loss of *mana* was a major factor in the Maori antipathy towards *Pakeha* institutions.

Another difficulty the Maori face is related to problems in effective communication with *Pakeha* health professionals, and the cross-cultural differences in illness and help-seeking behaviours.

The following reasons can be identified for the failure in communication).

INADEQUATE USE OF LANGUAGE

Even though all Maori people, except perhaps a rare elderly person in a rural area, speak English, their command over the language and their use of metaphor and sophisticated nuance have often been demonstrated to be poorer than the *Pakeha*, and at times quite limited (Bray and Hill, 1974). Durie (1984), a Maori psychiatrist, reported that about half of his general psychiatric Maori patients reported feeling inadequate in their usage of English although seeming fluent to the staff members. About half of this group welcomed a chance to discuss their problems in Maori.

USE OF NON-VERBAL COMMUNICATION

The Maori emphasize the 'body language' more and verbalization less than the *Pakeha* (Metge and Kinloch, 1979). It is not uncommon to hear the Maori complain, albeit exaggeratedly, about the *Pakeha* who is 'forever talking' but is 'deaf to what others have to say (mostly non-verbally)'. There are also cross-cultural differences in the interpretation of some signs which can create difficulties. The Maori patient tends not to look at the professional in the eye in deference to the latter's authority (Metge and Kinloch, 1979).

ATTITUDE TO AUTHORITY

A number of authors have commented on the Maori's deference to the authority of the health professional, especially the doctor (Durie, 1984; Mackay, 1985). This deference has been traced to the early relationship of the common man with the *tohunga* who was a man imbued with great *mana* (power, prestige) and, therefore, worthy of great respect and awe. A doctor is, therefore, approached only warily and few demands are made on him or her. This attitude may extend to nurses, physiotherapists, etc. (Rostenburg, 1981).

DECISION MAKING AND RESPONSIBILITY

A modern medical practitioner expects the patient to make a number of choices and be responsible for these choices (Mechanic, 1978). These role expectations vary with culture (Segall, 1976) and are different for the Maori who are reportedly more passive in the therapeutic encounter (Durie, 1984). They tend to deliberate a great deal on any issue and seek the opinion of others before 'making up their minds' (Metge and Kinloch, 1979). In addition, the Maori are, in general, unlikely to freely express themselves until a personal affective rapport has been formed (Ritchie, 1963) and this is true about their interaction with health professionals (Walker, 1982). They are likely to leave decisions to the 'expert' and seek advice rather than participate in a one-to-one interchange (Tipene-Leach, 1978). This kind of 'illness behaviour' has also been described in other cultures with a strong emphasis on kinship and affiliation rather than individuality and differentiation (Neki, 1976).

INVOLVEMENT OF FAMILY

There is great emphasis on the involvement of the *whanau* (family group) with the ill person, and a tendency for a large number of family members to stay with him or her lest the patient think that he or she has been forsaken. The family is involved in decisions about treatment, providing practical help to the patient's immediate dependants, and in nursing him or her back to health. This can easily be misunderstood by the *Pakeha* as an intrusion rather than a culturally appropriate and desirable response (Durie, 1984).

TRADITIONAL MAORI CUSTOMS AFFECTING THE UTILIZATION OF THE MODERN HEALTH SYSTEM

A number of Maori traditions, although having been influenced greatly by the long contact with the *Pakeha*, continue to influence the daily life of the Maori (Dansey, 1978). Some of these traditions affecting the interaction between the Maori and the health system can be summarized as follows.

LAWS OF TAPU

The pervasiveness of *tapu* in traditional Maori society has been referred to above. Since disease, death, and healing were intensely *tapu*, the Maori relates to illness, doctors, and hospitals with some anxiety and awe. Modern health institutions are secular and professedly egalitarian, but the Maori often complains of lack of 'spirituality' in the modern hospital (Pomare, 1986). Not uncommonly, therefore, while accepting the Western treatment, the Maori is simultaneously exploring his own and his family's circumstances to find 'the real cause' (Durie, 1977: 484) of the *mate atua*. Other *tapu* rules may make some of the practices in hospitals unacceptable to the Maori. One of these is the mixing of *tapu* and *noa* things. The most common example given is the mixing of things connected with food or cooking (*noa*) with things connected with the body, especially the head (*tapu*) (Dansey, 1978). The head, and by extension the hair, is particularly *tapu* and should be treated with respect. Since hair (and nail) clippings are extensions of the body and can be used in *makutu* to the detriment of the original owner, their proper disposal is considered important. Prior to surgery, some patients welcome the idea that their relatives be allowed to shave their bodies (Durie, 1985).

USE OF *TOHUNGA*

Since a number of Maori patients have an 'unspoken and unconscious fear' (Durie, 1977: 484) of some infringement of *tapu*, families may seek the services of a *tohunga* in their search for the *hara* (infringement), at the same time as they participate in *Pakeha* medicine, and especially if the latter fails. Following the enactment of the Tohunga Suppression Act in 1907, Maori healers were forced to go underground, and their methods were not reliably transmitted to future generations. While a few *tohunga* remain, a Maori elder (*kaumatua*) with knowledge of *Maoritanga* (Maori cultural values) often fulfils the role in modern times. Most often, the *tohunga* complements rather than replaces the doctor, and Maori leaders have argued for a degree of cooperation between the two systems (Hui Whakaoranga, 1984). Some *Pakeha* doctors sensitive to cross-cultural issues have advocated a respect for use of the *tohunga* except in life-threatening emergencies (Jacobsen, 1983).

CHILDBIRTH

The traditional Maori viewed birth as a transit into this world from the realm of the gods (Smith, 1974), the place to which the *wairua* (spirit or soul) would return after death. All customs associated with childbirth were *tapu* and occurred either out in the open or in a specially constructed *whare kohanga* (nest house) (Heuer, 1972). One concern of the modern Maori of relevance to this discussion is the disposal of the placenta. Since the baby brings the afterbirths along with it, these are associated with the *atuas* and are *tapu*. Thus the need to dispose the *whenua* (placenta) by burying it in a place where it would not be trodden upon (Buck, 1950: 351). The family of the Maori woman who has given birth in hospital often demands the placenta and the umbilical cord, and this practice is prevalent even in urban areas (Beagley, 1984). Hospital staff are expected to cooperate in this (Rostenburg, 1981).

DEATH

The customs surrounding death (*tangihanga*) are some of the most important Maori traditions. These demand that the body of the deceased be placed on the *marae*[6] (the Maori community meeting place) as soon as possible because, when the visitors arrive, the absence of the body may lead to accusations of negligence on the part of the family. As the *wairua* is not considered to depart immediately upon death but hovers around the body for some time, it is addressed by the mourners and watched over until the time of the burial. Considerable anxiety is caused to the family by a delay in the handing over of the body by the hospital authorities, especially where a post-mortem needs to be performed (Durie, 1977).

SOCIOPOLITICAL AND HEALTH INITIATIVES TO IMPROVE MAORI HEALTH

Maori leaders in the early part of the twentieth century realized the value of many aspects of Western medicine and made efforts to increase its acceptance amongst their people, but they had to

[6] The *marae*, or the Maori meeting place, has been the focal point of the Maori community for centuries. Almost every Maori community has its own *marae*, and *marae kawa* (protocol) varies from one to another. The *marae* is considered by the Maori to be *waahi rangatira mana* (place of greatest *mana*), *waahi rangatira iwi* (place that heightens people's dignity) *and waahi rangatira tikanga Maori* (place in which Maori customs are given ultimate expression). For a modern description of the *marae* functions, see Tauroa and Tauroa (1986).

work against considerable resistance and prejudice (Buck, 1950: 411). There was a recognition that any change necessitated leadership to spring from within the community. What was controversial was the form the response should take, i.e. whether the Maori should move toward autonomy and self-determination, or should work within the prevalent Western framework. The former was best evidenced by the opening of *Paremata Maori*, or the Maori Parliament, in 1892. Even though there was no explicit health agenda in this development, it was influential in the official passing of the Maori Councils Act 1900, which had a number of public health functions. The other approach, that of working within the current legislative framework, was best exemplified by leaders like Maui Pomare and Peter Buck, both medical doctors, who were aware of the value of medical officers with Maori blood and familiarity with *Maoritanga* who could interpret Western medicine to the Maori in their own idiom. The establishment of a Division of Maori Hygiene within the Department of Health, with Peter Buck as Director, was a major advance for Maori aspirations. Pomare and Buck, because of their *mana*, and links with Maori leaders, were influential in increasing Maori participation in health practices and lifting the morale of the community. The decline in Maori numbers had been halted and even reversed, but this optimism declined by the 1930s with the abolition of Maori Councils and the Division of Maori Hygiene. There was a move away from Maori participation in health planning, with the Maori delegated to supportive roles.

The period from the 1930s to the 1970s saw only minor gains. There was a gradually increasing number of Maori health professionals including some who rose to important positions, but this did not entail any major shift in official policy. The most important grass-roots work was performed by two women's organizations, the Women's Health League and the Maori Women's Welfare League. These organizations had political, social and health agendas and were instrumental in raising the Maori voice calling for legislative change.

The year 1975 is often seen as a watershed year for Maoridom with the passing of the Treaty of Waitangi Act 1975. The Treaty of Waitangi 1840 had been intended as a partnership between the Maori people and the colonial settlers. The 1975 Act re-established the validity of the Treaty and made it the basis for future legislation that affected the Maori people. It was the beginning of the general acceptance of Maori cultural differences, and this flowed soon into the health domain. Modern Maori leaders reiterated that improving the health of the Maori community needed a response from the community itself, so that Western medical technology could be adapted to Maori cultural needs and expectations (Hui Whakaoranga, 1984). In the last few years, a number of efforts have been made in this direction. The main approaches are discussed below.

THE TREATY OF WAITANGI AND MAORI HEALTH

With direct recognition of the fact that health of a people could not be separated from sociocultural and political realities, the Standing Committee on Maori Health recommended in 1985 that the Treaty be regarded as a foundation for good health. Accepting this call, the New Zealand Board of Health (1988) recommended that 'All legislation relating to health should include recognition of the Treaty of Waitangi'. This Treaty was entered into in 1840 between the British Crown and some Maori chiefs and provided for a transfer of sovereignty to the Crown in exchange for the continuation of property rights and citizenship rights for the Maori. Health concerns were seen as being one of the factors motivating the Treaty. Ever since its signing, however, the Maori have had a number of grievances about its lack of application. Its official acceptance by the government as the 'founding document of New Zealand' prompted calls for its implications for the poor state of Maori health. What resulted was a move to make health delivery bicultural, and initiate reform in public health to address the disparities in the different ethnic communities.

A BICULTURAL APPROACH TO HEALTH

A reappraisal of cultural biases in the health system was expedited by two key reports in the 1980s: the *Puao-te-ata-tu* and *Te Urupare Rangapu*. The first was a an Advisory Committee Report (1986) to the Minister claiming that the Department of Social Welfare practised institutionalized racism in its policies for Maori youth. The second was a Department of Maori Affairs Report (1988) which made it clear that all government departments would need to respond to the needs of the Maori, including the Department of Health. A number of initiatives followed these reports.

Biculturalism was seen on a continuum for acknowledging a Maori perspective to health to active Maori involvement in health delivery, including parallel and at times independent Maori institutions complementing the existing public health system. Maori issues and networks would thus receive a clear focus and outcomes, judged from a Maori perspective. Some examples of the initiatives are as follows.

EDUCATING THE HEALTH CARE GIVERS IN *MAORITANGA*

An effort has been made to educate *Pakeha* doctors and other health professionals in those aspects of *Maoritanga* that are likely to impinge on their diagnosis and management of Maori patients. Efforts have also been made to include aspects of *Maoritanga* in the Behavioural Science courses and projects in the two medical schools in the country. Auckland Medical School established a *marae* on its premises in 1977 due to the links formed with the *Te Rawara* and *Te Aupori* people. There were weekend exchange visits during which issues of importance to Maori people and medicine were discussed at *hui (*gathering held on *marae* according to protocol). A voluntary tutoring scheme for Maori and Pacific Island children was established by the medical students. Similar programmes were developed at the Otago Medical School and the clinical schools in Christchurch and Wellington. Nursing training courses introduced Maori cultural awareness programmes. Similar efforts have been made by other health-related disciplines, e.g. psychology, occupational therapy, and physiotherapy. At least two major psychiatric hospitals catering to large Maori patient populations—the Tokanui Hospital near Hamilton and the Carrington Hospital in Auckland—have organized meetings (*waananga*) with a focus on the psychiatric health of the Maori with both Maori and *Pakeha* participation. Unfortunately, much of this interaction has been a part of Psychiatry and Behavioural Science programmes and has not penetrated the largely monocultural institutions of Medicine and Surgery, thereby diluting its impact.

TRAINING AND EMPLOYMENT OF MORE MAORI AS HEALTH PROFESSIONALS AND PLANNERS

The Maori are under-represented in most professions, including health (Older, 1978). The Division of Nursing of the Department of Health estimated in 1984 that 3.6 per cent of the total nursing workforce was Maori (and 1 per cent other Polynesian). There has been a move to increase this percentage with more Maori enrolment in technical institutes, new pre-nursing courses for Maori secondary school students, greater sponsorship of nursing trainees and establishment of more scholarships. The Otago Medical School has maintained a preferential entry plan for Maori (and other Polynesian) students which, until 1974, allocated two places each year for this purpose. In 1974, this number was increased to six (out of a total intake of 150–200), although a considerable proportion of the openings has not been filled. There are only a few Maori in the mental health profession—such as psychiatric social workers or professional counsellors—and an appeal has been made for greater recruitment. The results of the efforts to increase participation have been slow to come. Older and Jensen (1976) traced this to a generally poorer performance of the Maori population in higher education and the lack of a flexible and accommodating response of the educational institutions in the country.

Maori professionals often have to meet demands over and above their non-Maori peers. Not only are they called upon to advise the non-Maori professionals on *taha Maori*, but they become natural choices for leadership roles in their community. Their knowledge of *taha Maori* has, therefore, to be more than bicultural literacy, and rigid programmes developed for the *Pakeha* may not be sufficient for them. In some cases, their involvement in the communal activities may give them the necessary basis. In other situations, special programmes aimed at the Maori professional, such as the one developed by the School of Social Work in Auckland, may be necessary.

BICULTURAL INTERMEDIARIES

There has been an attempt to enlist the services of Maori individuals of high status in the community who are also versed in *Pakeha* culture to act as cultural interpreters for the *Pakeha* health professionals and the Maori patients. In addition, there is an attempt to train Maori paraprofessionals who would take Western medical practices to their people, either in the hospitals or the community. Some examples of this are as follows.

Kaumatua or Pukenga as Voluntary Counsellors

A number of psychiatric hospitals have enlisted the support of Maori *kaumatua* or *pukenga* (those steeped in Maori culture) to act as counsellors for Maori patients, and assist and advise the staff with regard to management. Maori ministers, especially those from the Ratana Church, have been particularly involved. The four psychiatric hospitals in Auckland have lists of local *tohunga* who can be approached for consultation and referral.

At the Cherry Farm Psychiatric Hospital in Dunedin, the author studied the involvement of a *pukenga*, who visited the hospital once a week but was available on other days. Some of the functions served were as follows: (a) obtaining background cultural information from the patient which would assist in management; (b) liaising with families of these patients, who were often residing in distant areas; (c) assisting staff in the management of hostile, aggressive or non-compliant patients, principally by winning support and trust of the patient; (d) acting as counsellor for the patient, usually from a cultural perspective; (e) providing a link between the hospital staff and the Maori community, so as to build the community's trust in the services provided; and (f) organizing *hui* and *hakari* (feast) on the hospital grounds, thereby educating the *Pakeha* staff in *taha Maori*. An informal survey conducted on the staff working on the ward indicated a uniformly positive response towards their work. The dynamics of the relationship between the elder and the patients were examined using content analysis of the audio-visual record of the interviews. The results of this analysis were used to construct a theoretical paradigm of the Elder-Patient Transaction, which is presented elsewhere (Sachdev, 1989c).

Maori Health Co-ordinators

As part of the increasing involvement of the Maori in health care, the Department of Health in Wellington supported the appointment of Maori Health Liaison Officers or Maori Health Coordinators to general hospitals. These individuals were selected from the local Maori community, and usually had a social work background although formal training was not always necessary. They underwent a short induction course, and subsequently, two-day workshops were held for ongoing training and sharing of experiences. The author observed the functioning of one such coordinator in a general hospital in Rotorua in the North Island, and the multiple functions she was called upon to perform were obvious.

Marae-based Health Programmes

The *marae* has a central place in Maori culture; a place to which the Maori belongs, a place he visits regularly and feels at home, and a place that has high *mana*. It was for this reason that the suggestion that health clinics and other activities be based at the *marae* had a receptive audience as it was considered the best way to combine the Maori and Western traditions. A number of such activities now take place.

Marae health Clinics

There is governmental support for their development, as part of the distribution of the health resources into Maori hands. The clinic is usually set up with a grant from the Department of Health (about $ 100,000 in some cases) which is distributed through the Area Health Board. The purpose of the clinic is to complement the community health services already in place. The author visited one such clinic in Rotorua.

TUMAHAURANGI MARAE CLINIC

This clinic was set up in January 1988 by the Te Arawa Trust. It has one full-time community health worker and a number of part-time volunteers from the community. There is a part-time secretary who also acts as the receptionist and typist. Domiciliary nurses and social workers from the hospital are present from time to time: they give advice, conduct groups and deliver educational lectures. A day programme is coordinated by the health worker in which a number of *marae*-based activities are included. The main purpose of the clinic has been health promotion and follow-up of patients after discharge from hospital.

Health Programmes

These initiatives emphasise activities that have an appeal for the Maori clientele, and the stress on physical health is not paramount.

Three such programmes have been prominent: Waiora, Rapuora and Tipuora.

WAIORA PROGRAMME IN OTARA, AUCKLAND

This was started in 1977 by the Catholic Maori Society of Otara and Otahuhu, two suburbs in the south of Auckland with a large Maori population. The efforts were renewed in 1984. There are a number of *marae*-based programmes, with an attempt to train young people, often those with a history of psychiatric disorder. Programmes include: bone-carving, wood-carving, jewellery-making, calligraphy, sewing, catering, hospitality, building, and hairdressing. Participation in Maori cultural activities is usual and the *kaumatua* visit regularly, thus combining job training with enhancement in the pride in being Maori. Polynesian, and occasionally, *Pakeha* youth also attend.

BICULTURAL MAORI PSYCHIATRIC UNITS

The trend of increasing psychiatric hospitalization and rehospitalization of the Maori led to a push towards the development of special psychiatric units which were truly bicultural, i.e. they followed Maori *kaupapa* (value systems), had Maori staff, were bilingual in their communication, but were designed to provide Western psychiatric care.

The first such unit was set up in Tokanui Hospital situated in Te Awamutu, about 30 km from Hamilton, in the heart of the rich dairy country of Waikato, and was called *Whai Ora* (Maori health unit). A twenty-bed ward was used for this purpose, staff members steeped in *Maoritanga* and involved with the Maori community were employed, and a nurse with high *mana* was appointed as the Unit Manager. The daily routine was run strictly according to Maori *kawa*. There was a *Karakia* (ritual incantation) before each meal and at bed time. The ward meetings followed the protocol of the *hui*. Visitors were accorded a formal Maori welcome. Each patient was encouraged to become familiar with his or her Maori roots and identify himself or herself in reference to the ancestors. Instructions were imparted in the Maori language. Egalitarianism was identified as a strong guiding principle, in part as a reaction to the perceived hierarchical structure of the usual psychiatric ward. There was, therefore, a greater tolerance of differences. Psychiatric symptomatology received little discussion, and there was a premium on normal functioning. The psychiatric resident on the ward also happened to be a Maori at the time I visited this unit, although this was not originally intended because of marked dearth of Maori doctors. At the time the unit was set up, the Medical Superintendent of the hospital was also a Maori, something that is extremely unusual.

Following the example of the above unit, many other psychiatric hospitals across the country set up bicultural units, with similar aims but sometimes with different structures. Some of the units, for example the ones set up in Carrington Hospital in Auckland (*whare paia* and *whare hui*) attempted to move a bit too far out of mainstream psychiatry, thereby causing a great deal of political debate. Most units, however, were successfully able to function within the constraints of modern psychiatry.

OTHER HEALTH INITIATIVES

The *Hui Whakaoranga* (1984) argued for the training of *Ringa Awhina* (cultural interpreters). Walker (1982) advocated the adoption of the 'barefoot doctor' concept from China. A number of forums (see Mackay, 1985) have recommended the training of Maori community health workers. One of the models offered is that of the Aboriginal Health Worker Training Program (Cawte, 1987) successfully used in Australia, apart from the other models which were available. The Maori Women's Welfare League advocated the training of what it called Maori Community Health Assistants with a certificate and a salary. A community-based health education scheme in Auckland, called *Te Koputu Taonga*, trains community health workers who educate Maori families on health matters. Groups like the *Te Ropu Rapu Oranga* (Group holding out Good Health) have sprung up all over the country. An attempt to deal with the problem of 'street kids' and solvent abuse was made by setting up *whare manaak*i (houses of caring), often run by a caring couple with community support. The success of many of these ventures, along with sociocultural and educational projects like *Rapu Mahi*, *Kokiri*, *Kohanga Reo*, *Matua Whangai*, etc. has been acclaimed (see *New Zealand Official Year Book*, 1986–7).

ADMINISTRATIVE CHANGES

Most of the above proposals could not have occurred if the health bureaucracy was totally inflexible. In the last two decades, many changes at both the national and local bodies, levels have taken place or been proposed. Some of the important ones are as follows.

Policy Statement (Partnership Response 1984) (Te Urupare Rangapu)

In this policy statement, the government reaffirmed its major objectives with regard to the interests of the Maori: to honour the principles of the Treaty of Waitangi; eliminate the gaps which exist between the educational, social, economic and cultural well-being of Maori people; provide for Maori language and culture to receive an equitable allocation of resources and a fair opportunity to develop; and promote decision-making in the government machinery in areas of importance to Maori communities.

A number of proposals were made: (a) measures to restore and strengthen the operational base of *iwi* (tribe) by moving toward the development of the *Iwi* Authorities by 1994 based on Maori self-reliance on their own terms; (b) to develop a new Ministry of Maori Affairs (in 1989) with a similar role and status to that of Treasury and the State Services Commission. It will review and comment on all governmental proposals where it believes a Maori perspective is essential. The Ministry will also ensure that all government agencies are aware that policy proposals should be consistent with the Treaty of Waitangi and the government's seven principal objectives in the area of Maori affairs; (c) the transfer of the Maori Land Court's servicing to the Department of Justice (1989); (d) an *Iwi* Transition Agency (for a 5-year period) to help *iwi* develop their operational base; (e) an independent review of the Maori Trust Office; and (f) disbanding of the Maori Affairs Board. The above proposals are revolutionary in that the Maori have been given much power to determine their own strategies to deal with their problems, and to incorporate the Maori perspective into legislative activities. It will not be until later that the success or failure of these initiatives will be judged.

Maori Participation in Area Health Boards

The fifth annual Maori Health *Waananga*, hosted by Te Roopu Awhina o Tokanui, was held at Tokanui Hospital on November

23 and 24, 1985. A major focus of discussion at the *hui* was ways of ensuring adequate Maori participation in the decision-making of Area Health Boards. The *waananga* affirmed the idea that a Regional Maori Health Board (RMHB) should be established in each area. It should adopt a broad Maori view of 'health' and should be composed primarily of the representatives of Maori health initiative groups active in the area. The final name, composition, and *kawa* (protocol) of each RHMB should be determined by the Maori people in each area. Progress in this has been satisfactory.

Resurgence of other Maori Health Institutions

Maori leaders recognise three principal institutions, traditionally regarded as critical determinants of good mental health: *whenua* (land), *whanau* (family) and *reo* (language) (Durie, 1985). The importance of land to the Maori has been recognised by the *Waitangi Tribunal* with an increased emphasis on honouring some aspects of the Treaty of Waitangi. Aspects of the *whanau* have already been discussed. A brief mention will be made here of *reo* and the new initiative *Kohanga Reo*.

From the end of the 19th century, the Maori language suffered a gradual decline, to a large part due to the educational policy of using English exclusively in schools, and the neglect of Maori by the government. The Maori people recognise their language as one of their *taonga* (treasures) that need to be preserved. The most important attempt made by the Maori themselves to save their language is embodied in the *Kohanga Reo* movement. Under this scheme, a number of day centres have been established for pre-schoolers that exclusively use the Maori language for everyday communication. The intention is to create truly bilingual people who retain a pride in their own language.

FINAL COMMENTS

The Maori experience highlights the larger issue of the interaction of a minority ethnic group with mainstream Western medicine in the context of colonization and disempowerment. Like many other ethnic groups, the Maori have their own particular concepts of disease and illness, including the presentation, classification, and aetiology of symptoms, and beliefs and attitudes toward health and illness. Since their illness experience is also somewhat different from the majority Anglo-Saxon community in New Zealand, their needs have to be specially defined. Further, their interaction with mainstream health professionals and organisations is different, and their utilisation patterns of hospitals and clinics so determined. The Maori share these aspects with other ethnic minorities expected to obtain medical care from a mainstream health system that is universal and yet monocultural. What makes the situation special for the Maori is their historical and cultural background. The health institutions of the country were developed on the models imported from the colonizing culture with little input from the Maori population. Their own health practices were either actively discouraged or otherwise allowed to become impoverished. Furthermore, the current health statistics were seen by the Maori as signifying a failure of the *Pakeha* health system to meet the needs of the Maori, and another indicator of their powerlessness and subjugation.

At the same time, the Maori leaders recognised that they could not return to a pre-colonial conceptualization of illness and modes of treatment. They recognised the power of modern medicine and identified that its exploitation was a two directional process: not only did the individual Maori have to become more aware of the system, the latter had to be more adaptive to the particular needs of the former. The emphasis in the past had been on the first part of this equation, which had not produced the desired results and had led to Maori resentment. The key deficiencies were therefore recognised and a need for the following identified: the health institutions had to become bicultural without necessarily compromising on the scientific basis of the practice of medicine; the health professionals had to become more aware of the cultural and behavioural aspects of the Maori patient including the general styles of interaction, attitudes toward authority figures, ways of expressing emotion, illness attribution, health concepts, sex-role allocation, and help-seeking behaviour; more Maori individuals had to be trained to become health professionals; and key individuals had to be identified and appointed who could mediate between the two cultures such that the less acculturated Maori or *Pakeha* could interact with a professional or other individual from the other culture. Many of the initiatives I have discussed as part of the Maori response are particular instances of these main objectives.

These developments could not have occurred in the absence of a political will and climate for change. A unique set of circumstances was therefore necessary: a social awareness of the health status of the population, a political leadership in the country that was receptive to calls for change, and the presence of leaders in the Maori community and a process of discussion that produced viable alternatives. Politically, the change had indeed become necessary because of a significant and visible Maori population that now lived in cities was vocal in its demands and could not be ignored from a political perspective. Issues of land rights and equal opportunity in employment provided the backdrop for action in the health sector. The change was economically rational since it was not that the Maori did not already use the health services but that their use was not producing the expected results. None of the measures introduced was particularly expensive and their cost-effectiveness could easily be established. It was, therefore, a major effort at acculturation by the majority system in the other direction to what had been traditional, with the recognition that it had to change rather than expect the Maori to meet the *Pakeha* expectations or suffer.

The Maori experience has relevance for minority ethnic communities elsewhere, especially those from aboriginal cultures that have similarly encountered colonial powers. Considerable literature exists on the encounters of Australian Aboriginals (Cawte, 1987; Cawte *et al.*, 1976), Navajo Indians (Kunitz and Levy, 1981), and other ethnic groups with mainstream Western medicine. The Maori response to their special problems may usefully serve as a model in the other settings. The major lesson from the Maori experience is that the primary initiative has to come from the minority community itself, and that sociopolitical conditions have to be created for the change to occur. The disadvantaged community has to be given the sense of empowerment to bring about the change, and the mainstream health system should see such a change as adaptive, rational, and even cost-effective.

REFERENCES

Awatere D., S. Casswell, and H. Cullen (eds) (1984). 'Alcohol and the Maori people'. Auckland: Alcohol Research Unit, School of Medicine, University of Auckland.

Beagley M. J. (1984). 'Maori health: treatment of Maori patients'. *Behavioural Science Project*. Dunedin: Department of Psychological Medicine, University of Otago Medical School (unpublished).

Best E. (1924). *The Maori*, vols I–II. Wellington: Board of Ethnological Research.

Bray D. H. and C. G. N. Hill (1974). *Polynesian and Pakeha in New Zealand Education*. Auckland: Heinemann Educational Books.

Broughton H. R. (1984). 'A viewpoint on Maori health'. *New Zealand Medical Journal*, 97: 290–1.

Buck Sir Peter (Te Rangi Hiroa) (1950). 'The Coming of the Maori'. Wellington: Maori Purposes Fund Board.

Cawte J., M. V. Kahn, and J. Henry (1976). 'Mental health services by and for Australian Aborigines'. *Australian and New Zealand Journal of Psychiatry*, 10: 221–8.

Cawte J. (1987). 'Aboriginal mental health'. *Australian Aboriginal Studies*, 1: 100–9.

Dansey H. (1978). *Maori Custom Today*. Auckland: Shortland Publications.

Davis P. B. (1986). 'Office encounters in general practice in the Hamilton health district'. II: Ethnic group patterns among employed, 15–64. *New Zealand Medical Journal*, 99: 265–8.

Department of Maori Affairs (1988). *Te Urupare Rangapu: Partnership Response*. Wellington: Department of Maori Affairs.

Department of Statistics (1993). '1991 Census of Populations and Dwellings: Iwi Population and Dwellings'. Wellington: Department of Statistics.

Durie M. (1977). 'Maori attitudes to sickness, doctors and hospitals'. *New Zealand Medical Journal*, 86: 483–5.

——— (1984). 'Maori referrals to a general hospital psychiatric unit'. Presented to the RANZCP 9th Annual Symposium, Social and Cultural Section, Royal Australian and New Zealand College of Psychiatrists, held in Rotorua, New Zealand (Unpublished).

——— (1985). 'A Maori perspective on health'. *Social Science and Medicine*, 20: 483–6.

——— (1994). *Whaiora: Maori Health Development*. Auckland: Oxford University Press.

Firth R. (1959). *Economics of the New Zealand Maori*, 2nd edition. Wellington: Government Printer.

Heuer B. (1972). *Maori Women*. Wellington: Reed.

Houghton P. (1980). *The First New Zealanders*. Auckland: Hodder and Stoughton.

Hui Whakaoranga (1984). *Maori Health Planning Workshop*. Wellington: Department of Health.

Hyslop J., J. Dowland, and J. Hickling (1983). *Health Facts New Zealand*.

Wellington: Management Survey and Research Unit, Department of Health.

Ihimaera W. (1986). *The Matriarch.* Auckland: Pan Books.

Jacobsen C. T. (1983). 'Family medicine in a Maori community'. *New Zealand Family Physician*, 10: 182–5.

Kokiri Te Puni (1993). *He Kakano: A handbook of Maori Health Data.* Wellington: Ministry of Maori Development.

——— (1994). 'Trends in Maori Mental Health—A discussion document'. Wellington: Ministry of Maori Development.

Kunitz S. J. and J. E. Levy (1981). 'Navajos in A. Harwood' (ed.). *Ethnicity and Medical Care*, pp. 337–96. Cambridge, Massachusetts: Harvard University Press.

Mackay P. (1985). *The Health of the Maori People.* Whangarei. New Zealand: Northland Community College.

Mason K. (1991). '*Atawhaitia:* The Maori Trustee Report on the last of Maori under the Protection of Pensional and Property Rights Act 1988 and Part X of the Maori Affairs Act 1953'. Wellington: Maori Trustee.

Marsden M. (1986). 'Maori illness and healing'. *Seminar on Mental Health—A case for reform. Legal Research Foundation Seminar.* Auckland: (Reprints available from the Mental Health Foundation, Box 37438, Parnell, Auckland, New Zealand).

Mechanic D. (1978). *Medical sociology: A selective view*, 2nd edition. New York: The Free Press.

Metge J. (1976). *The Maoris of New Zealand: Rautahi.* London: Routledge and Kegan Paul.

Metge J. and P. Kinloch (1979). *Talking Past Each Other.* Wellington: Victoria University Press.

Miller J. (1958). *Early Victorian New Zealand.* London: Oxford.

Mitchell E. A., B. Borman (1986). 'Demographic characteristics of asthmatic admissions to hospital'. *New Zealand Medical Journal*, 99: 576–9.

Murchie E. (ed.) (1984). *Rapuora—Health and Maori Women.* Wellington: The Maori Women's Welfare League Inc.

Neki J. S. (1976). 'An examination of the cultural relativism of dependence as a dynamic of social and therapeutic relationships'. *British Journal of Medical Psychology*, 49: 1–10.

Neutze J. and P. Clarkson (1984). 'Rheumatic fever: An unsolved problem in New Zealand'. *New Zealand Medical Journal*, 97: 592.

New Zealand Board of Health (1988). 'Priorities for New Zealand Health Services'. Weliington: New Zealand Board of Health.

New Zealand Official Year Book 1986–7. Wellington: Department of Statistics.

Older J. (1978). *The Pakeha Papers.* Dunedin: John McIndoe.

Older J. and D. Jensen (1976). 'Maoris and Medicine in Contemporary New Zealand'. Dunedin: University of Otago Medical School. (unpublished paper)

Parsons T. (1951). *The Social System.* New York: The Free Press.

Parsonson A. (1981). 'The pursuit of *Mana*' in W. H. Oliver (ed.) *The Oxford History of New Zealand.* Wellington: Oxford University Press, pp. 163–5.

Pomare E. W. (1980). 'Maori Standards of Health: A study of the 20-year period 1955–1975'. Medical Research Council of NZ Special Report series 7. Auckland: Medical Research Council of New Zealand.

———(1986). 'Maori health: New concepts and initiatives'. *New Zealand Medical Journal*, 99: 410–11.

Pomare E. W., G. M. de Boer (1988). '*Hauora*—Maori standards of health'. Special Report, series 78. Wellington: Department of Health.

Pool D. I. (1977). *The Maori Population of New Zealand, 1769–1971*, pp. 48–51. Auckland: Auckland University Press.

Psychiatric Report (1988). Committee of Inquiry Report to the Minister of Health. Wellington: Government Press.

Ritchie J. (1963). *The Making of a Maori.* Wellington: Reed.

Rose R. J. (1960). 'Maori-European Standard of Health', Special Report no. 1. Wellington: Department of Health.

Rostenburg M. (1981). 'Aspects of the Maori patient'. *New Zealand Journal of Physiotherapy*, 9: 7–9.

Sachdev P. (1989a). 'Psychiatric illness in the New Zealand Maori'. *Australian and New Zealand Journal of Psychiatry*, 23: 529–41.

——— (1989b). '*Mana, Tapu, Noa:* Maori cultural constructs with medical and psychosocial relevance'. *Psychological Medicine*, 19: 959–70.

——— (1989c). 'Maori elder-patient relationship as a therapeutic paradigm'. *Psychiatry*, 53: 393–403.

——— (1990). 'Behavioural factors affecting physical health of the Maori'. *Social Science and Medicine*, 30: 431–40.

Segall A. (1976). 'The sick role concept: understanding illness behaviour'. *Journal of Health and Social Behaviour*, 17: 163.

3

The Colonized Psyche: British Influence on Indian Psychiatry

Dinesh Bhugra

INTRODUCTION

India has suffered invasions by several aggressors over the centuries. Occasionally, these have influenced her culture and thinking. The influence of the last and most powerful invader, the British, has been far-reaching and persists to the present day. The British and the Indians have had an ambivalent relationship ever since the days of the Raj. Even now, although Western medicine holds sway in the country, it is in patches. Bhardwaj (1975) reported that in four villages in the Punjab, *Angrezi* (English) medicine and allopathic doctors were generally preferred to the *desi* (indigenous) medicine and its practitioners. This was in marked contrast to earlier studies by Marriott (1955), Lewis (1965), and Fonaroff and Fonaroff (1966).

During the prolonged period of colonization, although the British rulers had allowed certain cultural practices (i.e. religion and certain aspects of government) to continue alongside British

Acknowledgements: The author is grateful to Dr R. M. Mallett for her help in shaping the manuscript. Grateful thanks and appreciation are also due to Drs G. Berrios, S. Jadhav, and Professors R. Littlewood and W. Bynum for their comments on earlier drafts of this paper. Sincere thanks to Mrs Maureen Trott for her secretarial skills, help and patience.

implanted practices, the colonization of traditional medical services was almost complete and, while assertive nationalism has been the hallmark of all post-independence Indian governments, Western medicine has remained an important part of health services.

The gradual colonization of the medical system is almost complete. This chapter sets out to look at the British influence on Indian psychiatry, not only in terms of developing new 'services' at the expense of existing norms, but also in training and the way in which, like all other branches of Indian traditional medicine, it has been subordinated to Western medicine.

The influence of the British on the development of psychiatry in India can be divided into three main areas: the role of the Indian Medical Service, the development of asylums, and the influence of the Royal Medico-Psychological Association. After a brief introduction to the historical development of mental illness and its treatments in the Ayurvedic system, dating from several centuries BC to the nineteenth century, I will focus on each of these areas in turn.

HISTORICAL DEVELOPMENTS

AYURVEDA

Ayurvedic texts describe various kinds of mental illness. An interaction of personality, food, and other extraneous factors, including the position of stars, was responsible for various kinds of madness and distress. The Hindu texts date several hundred centuries BC (Bhugra, 1992). *Charaka Samhita* remains the primary exposition of Ayurveda, the science of life. It is the science of the causes and symptoms of diseases, of their medication, and of the maintenance of health. It also deals with the origin of medical science, the fundamental causes of conception and birth, and of physical deformities (Ray and Gupta, 1980).

Ayurveda has eight branches of which *bhuta-vidya* (psychiatric knowledge) is one. The details of Ayurvedic system are available elsewhere (see Ray and Gupta, 1980; Haldipur, 1984; Bhugra, 1992). The role of the physician was clearly defined. Any person could aspire to become a physician provided he had a clear idea of the duties and obligations about the profession. Besides an austere and celebate life, the aspiring physician had to possess good health, a capacity for sustained effort, and a single-minded devotion to the science. The student could choose the subject and the teacher. The teacher would assess the abilities and merits of the student, including his mental outlook before taking them on as students. All instruction was free and the disciple lived with the teacher like a son or apprentice till the training was complete, and had to follow a rigid timetable. The classificatory system in *Charaka Samhita* on Ayurvedic physiological systems and diseases was a marked feature.

The asylums and mental institutions are said to have existed up to around AD 300. Burdeth (1891) blames the decay of these institutions on Brahminical supremacy. Isolated samples of other psychiatric institutions exist (Rao, 1975). Thus, the British were not the first to introduce the concept of asylums. Their impact was fundamental in changing the practice of psychiatry from traditional methods to the Western methods.

Ayurvedic texts described evil spirits as responsible for possession and mental disorder. These spirits would enter the body unnoticed, as an image enters a mirror. In addition to various types of management in different texts, *mantras* (religious verses), yoga and *mula* (roots of herbs) formed the basis of treatment. The practitioners who were proficient in *bhuta-vidya* (study of evil spirits) were called *narendra* and could counteract or destroy the evil spirits by using *mantras*, or tying roots to the wrists (Sharma, 1972).

The *Sidha* system of medicine developed in parallel with the Ayurvedic system, but came into its own in the post-Vedic period (Raina, 1991). The *sidhars* sought ways to stop degeneration through yoga and personal discipline and searched for drugs that, unlike herbs, could be stored indefinitely without losing their potency. In addition, *natyasastra* (which deals with drama and dance) covered psychological, social, and cultural practices in different regions of the country. The basic premise here was the correlation of psychological states with clear determinants and consequences. Song, dance and music played an important role in therapy. These systems are still practised in India.

HOSPITALS

The establishment of *arogyashalas* (literally, places for health) are well known in Ayurvedic texts. In one of the ancient scriptures reference exists to the endowment for hospitals with trained physicians and the 'pious men who erect such hospitals' (Raina 1990). The Ayurvedic texts refer to special hospitals for surgery, medical diseases and disorders of the brain. A Chinese traveller to India (Fahien, AD 405–11) described charitable dispensaries in North India as:

> ...the nobels and householders of this country have founded hospitals within the city to which the poor of all countries, the destitute, the diseased may repair. They receive every kind of requisite help free. Physicians inspect their diseases, and according to their cases order them food and drink and medicines, or decoctions, everything in fact that may contribute to their ease. When cured, they depart at their convenience.

In later periods, references to hospitals constructed in the tenth, twelfth, and thirteenth centuries are well known (Raina, 1990).

The attitudes of the public towards the mentally ill have been described to be that of compassion and a desire to help without sense of fear, frivolity, and prejudice (Somasundaram, 1987). In a temple in South India where patients were treated as well in the ninth century, there appears no mention of segregation of psychiatric patients (Subba Reddy, 1971).

Although Bala (1991) argues that the professional practice of Ayurvedic medicine is debatable, Indian medicine in the ancient and medieval periods was in a dynamic process of change in the direction of a 'profession'. Medical training remained lengthy (up to 7 years) and, in addition to prestige and status, the medical practice was formalized as compilations originating from religious orthodoxy sources.

During the Muslim rule, Arabic medicine took the form of the Unani system. Un Hammod (AD 1222) described seven varieties of mental illness and a mental hospital was said to have been established in central India between 1436 and 1439 (Somasundaram, 1987) (for a detailed review see Bala, 1991). As a result, by the nineteenth and twentieth centuries, the traditional beliefs and practices of Ayurvedic physicians were beginning to change from those ascribed to the classic texts and were deeply influenced by the Unani system (Leslie, 1976). In India today, Ayurvedic practitioners, Unani practitioners, practitioners of syncretic medicine of traditional culture, cosmopolitan practitioners of the Western system, allopathy, and homoeopathic practitioners coexist and many practitioners use a mixture of methods of clinical practice.

COLONIAL INFLUENCES

The British contact with India started at the beginning of the seventeenth century when the East India Company came into existence on 31 December 1600. Even though the Portuguese had reached India in 1498, as did other Europeans like the French, the Dutch, and the Danes, it is the British that were destined to leave a lasting imprint. Following the formation of the East India Company, interestingly enough, it was a British doctor who was responsible for getting its first trading rights.

For the first quarter of the seventeenth century, the islands of the Malay Archipelago rather than continental India were the chief aim and the seat of the Company. As folklore has it, following a successful cure of the daughter of the Mughal emperor, Shah Jahan, her doctor was asked to name his own reward. He asked for and obtained liberty for his masters, the East India Company, to trade in Bengal—on the east coast. The first medical officers in the employment of the East India Company were surgeons on board the ships. Later, with the expansion of the trading rights and establishment of various factories, one medical officer was allocated to each permanent factory. The Bengal Medical Service came into existence in 1763 when its constitution was formed. However, it was not till the middle of the eighteenth century that the British found it necessary to employ surgeons with troops as well as at their factories; or indeed to employ troops at all other than the small standing garrisons maintained at each factory.

Arnold (1989) observes that the involvement of the military in the medical interventionism of the imperial period is one of its most striking and significant features. In part, it reflected the prominence of the army in the establishment and maintenance of the imperial regimes in general, as well as the extent to which the health of the military remained one of the prime incentives behind wider medical action. The imperialists were prepared to commit resources to the protection of the army's health and sanitation to an extent unthinkable for civilian populations.

With the establishment of the East India Company, the coexistene of a new medical system with multiple old systems lasted only a short time. The European doctors were often presented to the courts of the royal and princely families in India. However, these rulers were forbidden to use the term 'Royal' because in the British mind there was only one Royal, i.e. Queen Victoria. At the same time, the prime ministers of various princely states could not be called prime ministers because in the British eye there was only one Prime Minister, who resided at 10 Downing Street (Lynton and Rajan 1974). The acceptance of Western methods of treatment in preference to the traditional *hakims* and *vaids* by the ruling classes was bound to influence the choices of the masses. However, it will become apparent that this choice was becoming increasingly limited.

The main tenets of revivalist ideology evolved early in the nineteenth century in a conflict between British orientalists and Anglicists. The Anglicists wanted the East India Company to establish an English language school system with the practical purpose of training Indian men for jobs in British enterprises. The orientalists, on the other hand, were cultural pluralists advocating that reforms be undertaken by utilizing indigenous institutions (Leslie, 1976), but the Anglicists won the day. The purpose of the British rulers was 'to seek every practicable means of effecting the gradual diffusion over European knowledge' (Mukhopadhyaya, 1926). The political decision was worked out in different phases and after setting the state for a showdown of European supremacy, Ayurvedic classes were gradually abolished (Gupta, 1976). However, while a considerable number of foreigners were appointed to the Indian Medical Service in the eighteenth century, including French, Dutch, and Portuguese doctors, the appointment of natives of India (a native was a son of parents of whom either one or both were of pure unmixed native extraction) as commissioned officers in the Indian Medical Service was strictly forbidden by the court. In spite of the order against their admission, a few men who were officially called natives of India were appointed. However, since they had European names, it seems likely that they were either Indian-born Europeans or Eurasians (Crawford, 1914).

In 1858, the Government of India was transferred from the Company to the Crown. This period of transition affected not only medical care but also medical education. In order to placate the natives, a subordinate medical service gradually developed whose members were taken in as apprentices in the hospitals under British doctors (DGHS annual report, 1955). The arrangements were inadequate and expensive (Dutta, 1988a).

In the closing years of the nineteenth century (the period during which the asylums started to appear on the subcontinent), medicine had become a demonstration of the superior political, technical, and military power of the West, and hence a celebration of imperialism itself (Arnold, 1989). As Arnold goes on to emphasize, this gave expression to Europe's faith in its own innate superiority, its mastery over man as well as nature. Medicine had to reflect the imperial determination in order to organize the environments of the ruled, and had to fashion indigenous societies and economies in the light of its own precepts and priorities. The regime believed that all health problems could be solved by using scientific methods and resolutions to overcome any local opposition and dissent and the beliefs of the individual and the rationality of the indigenous medicine were simple obstacles to be conquered. Medical intervention, therefore, was allowed to assume 'an unprecedented right' over the health and bodies (and minds) of its colonized subjects.

THE INDIAN MEDICAL SERVICE UNDER THE RAJ

The first Western style medical school opened in Calcutta in 1822, and the native medical institutes were abolished in 1835. Initially, all doctors had to register with the General Medical Council in London. Indian registration did not start until 1933 when the Medical Council of India came into being. The Indian Medical Association was formed in 1928 (Dutta, 1988b). The first branch of the British Medical Association had been formed in 1865 in Bengal and was initially well received. However, following the reading of a paper advocating the use of homoeopathy, there was so much dissension that the branch went into a non-active nominal existence and lasted only a few years. The closing down of the branch showed that the hold of the establishment over medical services was gradually tightening and no dissension was tolerated at all. The models of diagnosis and treatment were those transmitted from England, and all local cultural, social-political dimensions were totally ignored. As Fisher (1985) points out: 'In colonial society, debilitating comparisons made between colonizer and colonized cause the former to command the respect of the latter, at the expense of the latter's self-esteem'. As Fanon (1963) noted, even though eventually the colonized came to see through the hoax of 'a portrait of wretchedness (that) has been indelibly engraved' (Memmi, 1965), the regeneration of the colonized may take a very long time to come about. Thus, the impact of colonization on the practice of medicine as well as psychiatry cannot be underestimated.

The contribution of the British to the development of psychiatry is difficult to isolate from their contribution to the whole medical service. Certainly, initially there was little distinction among medical specialists. Psychiatry as a speciality evolved much later. Qvarsall (1985) argues that the establishment of psychiatry was a long, complicated process involving the introduction of the new discipline to the universities and medical schools (which were set up much later in India); the formulation of a classification scheme for mental diseases (ignoring completely the pre-existing classificatory schemes); and publication of text books (which in the days of the Raj, and even now to a certain degree, came from Great Britain). The psychiatric textbooks of the period made no mention at all of the indigenous aetiological factors and treatment methods. Any illness that did not fit in the Western classification was bizarre, exotic, and esoteric, thereby sowing the seeds for culture-bound syndromes.

It is only relatively recently that the psychiatrists in India have gone back to the traditional Ayurvedic teachings to deal with neuroses (Vahia *et al.*, 1966; Neki, 1973, 1974). Various researches have shown that a proportion of neurotics are reported to get better through religious ceremonies (Somasundaram, 1973; Satija, *et al.*, 1981), and more recently, proposals have been put forward to use indigenous systems of treatment as one of the methods for assuring mental health for all by the year 2000 under the Alma Ata Declaration (Sethi, 1981).

THE SERVICE

Before 1919, the Viceroy or Governor General (in Council) was the supreme head of the Government of India in every sphere of government activity and the central government could dictate to the local government. British India was divided into three 'presidencies'—Bengal, Bombay and Madras—each governed by a Governor (sent from England) and his legislative council; six 'provinces' (excluding the Indian state which constituted one third of the subcontinent), each administered by a Lieutenant Governor selected from the Indian Civil Service and his legislative council; and certain dependent territories. The medical issues were managed by the Director General of the Indian Medical Service (IMS) as head of the service and adviser to the central government along with three Surgeons-General, one in each Presidency, and six Inspectors-General of civil hospitals. With gradual development of hospitals, the hospital or medical boards were constituted. These boards were responsible for the running of the hospitals.

Founded in 1764 as an expansion of the initial Bengal Medical Service, the IMS allowed its officers to hold commissions as combatant officers in addition to their warrants. As stated earlier, natives were not appointed to the service though they could join one of the subordinate medical services, i.e. the military or civil subordinate medical services as military or civil hospital assistants and civil apothecaries. A hierarchy of services, with clearly laid down line of command, was thus falling into place. The colonial nature of the administrative services and power structure demanded that the natives were good enough for the assistantships and pharmacies but not for the Indian Medical Services.

During 1860–1864, no recruits were admitted to the Indian Medical Service and regular uncovenanted medical officers seem to have come into existence gradually during the second quarter of the nineteenth century. The Indian government made the local appointments. Every officer of the IMS was posted to military duty on first entering the services and was required to do two years military duty before becoming eligible for civil employment. The military service was more attractive because it paid more and it was not strenuous work. The civil employee starting at the bottom was posted to the poorest and worst-equipped hospitals.

In 1901, the Army Medical School in England was made responsible for probation of the Royal Army Medical Corps (RAMC) and the Indian Medical Service (IMS). Following selection, the recruits to the former were sent to Aldershot, and the latter to Nettley for two months. Until 1905, Professorship of Military Medicine was held at Nettley by a retired officer of the IMS and was partly paid for by the Government of India. With the introduction of an entrance examination, entry to the IMS was controlled even further.

The majority of men in civil employment did the work of the ordinary district civil surgeon. According to Crawford (1914), the civil surgeon's first duty in the morning was to visit his jail of which he was the superintendent as well as medical officer. Depending upon the type of jail, additional staff were available. From the jail, the civil surgeon would go on to the hospital 'where he will most likely have another hour's work at the least, it may be two or three hours; sometimes, in time of pressure, even more. The time spent in hospital, however, depends a good deal on a man's own enthusiasm and fondness for the work' (Crawford, 1914).

Where the civil surgeon was a superintendent of a lunatic asylum, or of the vernacular medical school, additional allowances were made available. Even in those days Crawford (1914) highlights 'The professorships in the medical colleges are perhaps the appointments most sought after. They were by no means well paid, considering that they were supposed to attract the very best men in the Service, but lead to professional reputation', and unlike the present time, the professorships carried with them a very large private practice. Doctors in the IMS were often free to do other things, indulge in their hobbies full-time as well as take on other careers—most commonly, businesses. IMS officers also held posts in botany departments, the mint, sanitary departments, bacteriological departments, etc.

Noting various structural and administrative problems of the medical service, McDowell (1897) laid the blame squarely on the medical superintendents who were 'almost invariably non-resident, engaged in private practice and other important and exacting official duties'. The pay was poor and the duties harassing. It was only in the early part of the twentieth century that the adverse publicity given to the state of the asylums produced a major change along with a new crop of superintendents.

ALIENISTS

The recognition of specialists in mental illness as full-time officers in the hospital was the most positive step (Shaw, 1932). With the establishment of the Alienist Department of the Government, there was a forlorn hope that working conditions and status would improve, and not surprisingly it did not come about.

The professionalization of alienists in India followed a similar pattern to Britain, but occurring a century or so later. The meetings were annual, as they were in Britain, and the scientific journal took a long time to take off (Scull, 1979). As in the patriarchal tradition of both India and Victorian Britain, the alienists were almost exclusively male, certainly at the medical superintendent level. The first superintendent, Ewens (1900–14), was described by Lodge Patch, himself a serving medical superintendent at Lahore, as the greatest author and alienist to practise in the East. No doubt humane, Ewens, like his contemporaries, was prone to make bold, generalized statements like: 'There is no hysteria in India'.

As the very first conference of alienists held in India (for the Indian division of the Royal Medico-Psychological Association) at the Punjab Mental Hospital, Lahore, on 23 of January 1939, Lodge Patch concluded: 'The motto of our association is: "Let wisdom guide", and we can carry out that conjunction by propagating knowledge regarding the true nature, the prophylaxis, and treatment of insanity; we can make an effort to abolish or alleviate the existing abuses both in our own institutions and in patients still at large. We can at least see that the practice of psychiatry remains at a reasonably high level', (Lodge Patch, 1939).

According to Shaw (1932), the chief obstruction to progress in psychiatry in the mid-1930s was the freedom movement and its leaders (especially Gandhi). Gandhi's preference for Ayurvedic and other indigenous methods that in the style of the ruler, Shaw argued, was not modern and... '[these methods] even more out of date than that of Galen.'

THE GROWTH OF ASYLUMS IN INDIA

Although there is an occasional mention of asylums in ancient India, the last known asylums existed in the ninth century AD in Madras (Somasundaram, 1987).

The (modern) history of psychiatry in India is argued to be the history of establishment of mental hospitals and an increase in their accommodation from time to time as the exigencies of time demanded (Varma, 1953). Although the Western style hospitals and medicine were introduced in India by the Portuguese, it was the British who founded the asylums. Not surprisingly, the practice, ideas, and concepts dealing with mental illness were thus similar to those that were prevalent in Western Europe. The early establishment of mental hospitals in the Indian subcontinent is said to have reflected the needs and demands of European patients in India (Sharma and Varma, 1984).

The growth of asylums paralleled the historical turmoil in India that was occurring with the decline of the Mughal empire, a marked resurgence of nationalist Sikh and Maratha movements, and the fight for supremacy between the British and the French in South India. Sarkar (1932) argues that this political instability was linked with the psychological and social turmoil. Therefore, the siting of initial asylums was important. Initially, these were in Calcutta, Madras and Bombay—the cities that were growing with British influence and expertise.

Bynum *et al.* (1985) suggest that the history of policy towards the insane during the past two hundred years was a response to the phobias of the polite and the propertied (i.e. the powerful). The same principle can be extended to the colonies, where the European power elite (i.e. the rulers) dictated policy. The asylums were built in India for the same reason as other countries—to protect the community (Shaw, 1932). The segregation of mentally ill people away from the community was due to popular demand, Shaw notes. However, he does not clarify the origins of such a 'popular demand'. Scull (1979) proposed that madhouses originated in at least two distinct ways: for the pauper lunatics, or for the affluent classes. In the colonies, read ruling classes for affluent classes. The dichotomized response was institutionalization for the natives going mad, whereas the Europeans were 'segregated' and 'sent home'.

In the heyday of imperialism in the nineteenth century, the people of Europe and North America saw themselves as a superior race and they observed no reason as to why they should not maintain this control forever. Official activities in the colonized countries were inspired by an intent to promote the interests of the imperial power in every sphere. However, British expansion in India did not result in hastening industrialization; in fact it was deliberately retarded with the results that even the existing economy did not function normally (Gopal, 1980). The doctor's race, sex, and demeanour could matter as much as the therapies he proffered. Physical contact between doctor and patient could be one of the most direct and traumatic aspects of the colonial encounter (Fanon, 1979).

Döerner (1981) argues that the building of a house of correction allowed the bourgeoisie to move about freely without scandal. However, in India, the rulers had separate estates and even towns called cantonments where natives were usually not welcome, except as servants. While in Britain, the bourgeoisie were showing the citizens to interiorize an attitude that made them moral and working citizens, in India, this direct contact was limited. Thus, this interiorization, if it occurred, must have been through the ruler–ruled dyad. He also argues that mental illness was the product of industrial economy, though no such distinct economy existed in the vast majority of the country. Hence this control could be seen as an extension of the ruler privilege.

Doerner emphasizes that the interiorization of restraint was the order of the day—the principle of self-esteem went beyond that of fear although both principles are celebrated as freeing the patient from external physical restraint. Among the colonized, the fear would be more prominent and self-esteem did not count. Therefore, the interiorization among the insane at least may not be as clearly applicable as Doerner claims.

Shaw (1932) held a very strong view that Europeans and persons of European habits should not, as a rule, be treated in the same mental hospitals as Indians; not on any grounds of sentiment (sic) but because the accommodation and amenities necessary for the one are unsuited to the other. Thus, the use of asylums and the ideas pertaining to such a segregation were brought in by the colonizer. Foucault (1971) has suggested that in Western Europe the first houses of confinement appeared in the most industrialized parts. However, in India it was obvious that the initial siting of asylums was to do with the needs of the rulers and not those of the ruled.

The segregation of the European mentally ill from the native mentally ill was to continue till the British left. To save money on the running costs of the asylums, it was recommended that:

'Insane patients should not be detained longer than was absolutely necessary in India but should be sent home at once', (IOR, 1820). The patients were then sent back to Pembroke House in Hackney. Noting this practice in 1925, Overbeck-Wright warned that large shipping companies were likely to refuse transfer of the insane to England.

The building and supervision of asylums were clearly of entirely British conception. A self-acknowledged expert on layout and construction of mental hospitals in India, Shaw (1932) advocated a suitable 'pavilion' or 'block' arrangement of buildings. These asylums were constructed away from the cities with high enclosures, in either dilapidated barrack-like buildings left by the military men or sepoys (Sharma, 1990), or in old prisons. The government asylums were started to treat European soldiers employed by the East India Company, and as Burdett (1891) observed, were on the same footing as dispensaries and hospitals. These were based on British models and did not take into account local geographical or climatic factors.

A private asylum was noted to exist in 1787 in Calcutta, which took care of the European mentally ill while they were in India. The Calcutta asylum was not recognized by the Medical Board and subsequently another asylum was opened and rented out to the East India Company. The dates when various asylums opened in the subcontinent are shown in Table 3.1.

In 1793, the proposals for the establishment of a lunatic asylum in Madras were put forward and the asylum opened a year later. The whole asylum was rebuilt after 1816. From 1841 to 1867, 'harmless idiots' were kept separately to avoid overcrowding the asylum. Smaller asylums also opened in two other sites in Madras State as the East Indian Company gradually established its hold in South India. Though the Bombay asylum was said to be functioning in 1745, it was only in 1817 that a note of the prevalent conditions was made. The excited patients were being treated with morphia, opium, hot baths, and bloodletting at this time (Sharma and Varma, 1984).

Following the acquisition of imperial power by the British Crown from the East India Company, the first Lunacy Act was enacted in 1858. This Act set out the procedures for admission of mental patients as well as the guidelines for establishing mental asylums. Under the 1858 Act, the police were empowered to arrest

Table 3.1: The Establishment of Lunatic Asylums in the Indian Subcontinent

Year	Site
1774	Bombay
1787	Calcutta
1794 (expansion 1799, 1807)	Madras
1795	Monghyr (Bihar)
1806	Colaba, Bombay
1840	Lahore, Punjab
1854	Benares (UP)
1858	Agra (UP)
1862	Bareilly (UP)
1865	Colaba, Poona, Dharwar, Ahmedabad, Ratnagiri, Hyderabad (Sind)
1866	Jabalpur, Brar (CP)
1871	Waltair, Trichinapally (Madras)
1874	Berhampur, Bhawanipore, Dulanda; Dacca (Bengal) Patna (Bihar) Cuttak (Orissa)
1876	Tezpur (Assam)

all wandering lunatics and all persons who were complained of as dangerous. They were brought before a magistrate who would order their removal to an asylum if the Civil Surgeon certified such persons as insane. Alternatively, they could be discharged to the care of relatives. In cases where there was a doubt about the insanity of the patient, the magistrate could order their detention for 10 days (extendable to 14 on a medical certificate) in an asylum. In Presidency towns, an insane person could be received under an order signed by a relative supported by two medical certificates. A board of visitors to the asylum was responsible for inspection and release of any insane patient if three of them agreed (Ewens, 1908). However, one visitor had to be a medical person.

It is difficult to ascertain the actual number of the insane during this period. Available figures are low, and some nineteenth century and early twentieth-century authors such as Wise (1853) cautioned that numbers quoted are an underestimate. Table 3.2 gives a comparison of returns from three different geographical areas.

Table 3.2: A Comparison of Returns from Three Different Geographical Areas (Wise, 1853)

Country	Population	Lunatics in treatment	Probably actual number	%
Island of Ceylon	1,009,008	125	450	0.00446
Dacca Circle	9,891,484	1575	2000	0.00202
England & Wales	17,905,831	13,400	13,400	0.00754

McDowall (1897) had observed that according to available statistics, there was one insane person per 70,000 in India compared to three per 1000 in England and Wales. He raised the question, 'Where are the others?' He also observed that of 4311 persons in asylum 1154 were criminal lunatics. Thus, criminal lunatics represented a more visible, violent class of insane.

Ewens (1908) also noted that the number under treatment was excessively small, and argued that these patients were of an excessively dangerous and troublesome class. He noted that an ordinary, quiet, insane person would not come to an asylum and was looked after by the family. He does not expand on his definition of ordinary, quiet, insane person. Ewens went on to hypothesize that the greater simplicity of life, effect of the climate, tradition and training rendered, fatalistic and patient people, and the conservatism and dislike of hustle and high mortality among the insane were responsible for the differences in committal numbers between England and India.

Bearing in mind the colonial views such as 'Hindoos are perhaps in a lower state of mental development than even the rudest savage' and 'I never knew of a well-educated native becoming insane' along with attitudes towards 'superstitious idolatry' and 'unnatural fanaticism so closely allied to insanity' (Ewens, 1908), it is not surprising that the insane natives kept away from their masters.

On 1 January 1889, the 21 institutions on the Indian subcontinent had a capacity for 3668 lunatics with 3246 patients (Burdett, 1891). Table 3.3 shows the movement of the insane population in various asylums. Table 3.4 shows the data on in-patients including the number of criminals.

The average cost per patient for the year 1888 is shown in Table 3.5. Assam asylum, which does not figure in the table, had an average cost of Rs 98 per year per patient. The gross anomaly of

Table 3.3: Movement of Insane Population in Various Asylums across all Presidencies (Modified after Burdett, 1891)

Movement	Bombay			Bengal	Madras			Central Provinces	Burma			Assam			Punjab (1889)			Ceylon
	M	F	Total	Total	M	F	Total	Total	M	F	Total	M	F	Total	M	F	Total	Total
Remaining on 1 January	557	126	683	922	474	153	627	262	211	22	233	61	12	73	201	54	255	–
Admitted	196	46	242	238	129	39	168	51	83	13	96	23	9	32	54	8	62	69
Readmitted	20	4	24	–	–	–	–	3	3	1	4	2	1	3	2	1	3	–
Total population	733	196	929	1160	–	–	–	316	–	–	–	–	–	–	257	63	320	–
Cured	57	15	72	67	43	18	61	15	30	9	39	–	–	–	25	3	28	48
Improved	83	13	96	45	–	–	–	5	12	3	15	–	–	–	8	1	9	6
Discharged— Not improved	19	1	20	13	–	–	–	–	–	–	–	13	2	15	–	–	–	–
Otherwise	–	–	–	4	–	–	21	5	4	–	4	–	–	–	–	–	–	–
Transferred to friends	–	–	–	–	–	–	27	–	–	–	–	–	–	–	–	–	–	–
Escaped	–	–	–	–	–	–	–	–	–	–	–	–	–	3	–	2	–	–
Died	73	13	86	74	24	15	39	19	15	2	17	6	1	7	27	10	37	27
Remaining on 31 December	541	134	675	957	491	156	647	272	236	22	258	64	19	83	193	48	241	–

Table 3.4: Data on Inpatients including Criminals

Government	No. of Asylums	Patients in Asylum at the end of 1895			Number of criminals included in the figures		
		M	F	Total	M	F	Total
Madras	3	475	148	623	142	18	160
Bombay	6	566	141	707	91	10	101
Burma	1	223	30	253	97	5	102
Central Provinces	2	245	69	314	84	8	92
Punjab	2	269	73	342	71	4	75
Bengal	5	726	197	923	408	55	463
Assam	1	83	22	105	18	1	19
N.W. Provinces including Oudh	4	850	194	1044	142	18	160

Table 3.5: The Average Annual Cost of Each Patient

Asylum	Cost per patient in Rupees
Ahmedabad	117.00
Berhampore	74.00
Bhowanipore	598.00*
Calicut	10.04**
Colaba, Bombay	215.00++
Cuttack	120.00
Dacca	83.00
Dellu	118.00
Dharwar	239.00+
Dullunda, Culcutta	114.00
Hyderabad (Sind)	76.00
Jubbulpore	66.00
Lahore	110.00
Madras	10.00** (11)
Nagpore	79.00
Patna	72.00
Poona	145.00
Rangoon	103.00
Ratnagiri	179.00
Vizagapatnam	9.00

Key:
Natives in brackets
* European asylum
** Average monthly cost
\+ High cost due to small number of patients
++ Small numbers and construction of padded cells

cost per patient between the European and the 'natives' is worth noting in Bhowanipore and Madras. This distinction was to do with the environment as well as maintaining a class distinction. The social distance was related to social status of the two kinds of patients as well as the power structure.

Berkeley-Hill (1924), when given details of the Ranchi European Mental Hospital, acknowledged that natives were not eligible for admission to this hospital. Situated on 85.16 acres of land, about 275 miles northwest of Calcutta, the asylum had ten wards and 180 inpatient beds. The amount paid to the hospital by each province was based on the number of patients sent to the hospital from the province. Herein, lie the seeds of market forces and buying services from different hospitals.

The hospital was well staffed with five medical officers, one compounder to prepare the medicines, seven European male attendants, five European nurses, and thirty-five male and thirty-five female Indian attendants. The latter groups had to qualify for a certificate from the Red Cross Society. In spite of its declared custodial function, the treatment included occupational therapy that, Berkeley-Hill acknowledges, was organized according to the information from the USA. Thus, the emphasis arguably was on new fashionable treatments. It is not clear from the records whether similar facilities were offered to the 'native Indians' in other places. At Ranchi, the payments for occupational therapy were made in cash or kind and six categories of occupations were available to either sex. Berkeley-Hill admits to seeing occupational therapy as 'very overrated therapeutic measures', maybe because it came from the USA. The six grades of each occupational therapy are shown in Table 3.6.

Table 3.6: Grades of Occupational Therapy in Ranchi Hospital

Grade	Male	Female
1.	Shorthand, clerical, librarian, instructional	Instruction, high-class needle work
2.	High-class book binding or carpentry, restringing tennis rackets	Lace making, fancy work, high-class knitting
3.	Middle-class carpentry or book binding, signboard painting	Middle-class needlework, ordinary crochet and knitting
4.	Low-class carpentry or metalwork, plain painting	Low-class needlework
5.	Low-class cane work, net making	Net-making
6.	Scraping paint; extracting and strengthening nails, sorting colour beads; winding yarn, coir picking	Cutting up vegetables, winding wool and yarn, sorting colours

In the European hospital, padded cells were unknown and the control of the individual was 'through sympathetic personal control only'. After-discharge, care was non-existent even for the European patients. Berkeley-Hill attempted to contact each discharged patient every six months with a 'welfare enquiry' letter. However, the natives in the Punjab asylum were handcuffed, and Lodge Patch sent two hundred weights of handcuffs, fetters, and other instruments of torture to the local jail.

The principles of moral treatment propounded by Tukes at the Retreat (Digby, 1985) were being used for Europeans whereas the natives were being treated as pauper lunatics living in shabby, dirty accommodation with limited medical input.

Describing a century of psychiatry in the Punjab province in northwest India, Lodge Patch (1939) observed that in 1847, before the Crown takeover, a doctor called Hoginberger, based at the palace of Maharajah Ranjit Singh, used to treat insane patients with hydrotherapy. Following the annexation of the province by the British, Hoginberger handed over the care of his 'twelve epileptics and idiots' (who used to live at the palace) to a Dr Smith—the first civil surgeon at Lahore. Over the next decade, the insane remained at the Maharajah's stables and their number increased from twelve to eighty-five. However, not more than forty could be accommodated in this place. When the numbers increased to 285 by 1863, the conditions 'deteriorated'.

The period between 1863 and 1900 was one of Stygian gloom for the Lahore patients, according to Lodge Patch (1939). He lamented that during this period there was a lot of eyewash with no attention to detail. This may have been due to bad clinical practice, but it is more likely to be the colonial attitude of ignoring the natives. Such apathy and indifference to the plight of the insane is difficult to understand in any terms other than pure colonialism. At the same time, when such methods of treatment were being followed in India, in Britain the humane treatment of the mentally ill was well advanced.

The patients in Lahore were admitted to the *congee* house (the local inn) in 1857, which had been made suitable for the insane by the erection of high walls and small enclosures. The numbers trebled in six years and they were moved again—this time to a *sarai* (a roadside inn) which had been converted into a prison. This parallels the scenes from England only a couple of centuries earlier, where houses of correction generally resulted from an expansion of existing prisons (Doerner, 1981).

The sanitary conditions were observed to be appalling, and in Lahore the death rate was enormous—ninety per annum out of a total of 240 inmates. To make matters even worse, the administrators were asked to reduce the existing expenditure with a reduction in staff to thirty-seven from fifty-six. In one instance, a qualified assistant surgeon (monthly salary Rs 150) was replaced by an unqualified hospital assistant (monthly salary Rs 30). The cost of keeping a patient was thus brought down from Rs 120 to Rs 99 per annum. This was bound to lead to a deterioration in services. Similar suggestions to reduce expenditure in the British asylums were noted by Scull (1979). The escape of one criminal lunatic in 1895 encouraged eight others to follow suit. This led to 'tardy amends'. As a result, food and clothing, quinine and arsenic in medication were made available more liberally. A separate asylum for females was constructed later to overcome the problems of overcrowding. In 1904, the asylum that was constructed a mere 50 years after the original recommendation for such a construction was, according to Lodge Patch, '...a hermaphrodite (sic) of hospital and jail. It was a credit neither to the Punjab nor to the British Empire.'

Possibly due to the First World War and because psychiatry was not seen as a priority, it was not until 1922 that an officer from the IMS could be spared—when Lodge Patch took over as the Superintendent at Lahore. He noted that the sight that met his eyes was horrific. Naked, handcuffed and fettered men, universal seclusion, and a reign of terror were the order of the day in Lahore asylum. The contrast with Ranchi could not be greater. This is an obvious reflection of the British Government's attitude to the psychiatric needs to the native.

THE LUNACY ACT

Under the Lunancy Act of 1912, the husband or wife, or any other relative of the patient could submit an application for a reception order to the magistrate, within whose jurisdiction the lunatic ordinarily resided. If such a petition was presented by anyone else, it had to contain a statement about why it was not submitted by a relative, the connection of the petitioner with the alleged lunatic, and of the circumstances under which the petition was presented. The applicant had to be a major, and should have seen the patient personally within 14 days of presentation of the petition.

Under the Act, the petition had to be on the prescribed form and supported by two medical officers—one a gazetted medical officer and the other an approved medical practitioner. On receipt of the application, the magistrate must personally examine the alleged lunatic and, if satisfied, grant a reception order. Failing this, he must fix a date for the consideration of the petition. If the petition is dismissed, the magistrate must give his reasons in writing. Parallels can be drawn with the subsequent Mental Health Acts of 1959 and 1983 in the UK.

The grounds for certifying a patient and sending him to an asylum was not solely the danger occurring to the patient, or to the public by his remaining at large, but mainly the due care and treatment of the case. The first thing to decide is: 'Is the patient insane?' Then: 'Is the patient a proper person to be detained under care and treatment?' The chief ground for which being: danger to himself or other; disturbance of public peace, inability to care for self or manage himself and his affairs, acute mental symptoms, and amenability to curative treatment that cannot be applied without certification. Then came the fact: 'Facts indicating insanity observed by myself' (i.e., the examining medical officer). The magistrate could authorize the detention of an alleged lunatic in suitable custody under medical observations for a 10-day period with two possible extensions of 10 days each.

According to the Lunancy Act of 1912, ill-treatment of the insane, besides being a reason for confinement in asylum, also rendered those responsible for it liable to heavy punishment (Section 15(2), Act IV of 1912). A boarder received into asylum on personal application could not be detained for more that 24 hours after giving notice in writing to the person in charge of his desire to leave. Non-criminal lunatics could be discharged by three visitors of the asylum (one of whom being a medical officer). Discharge by the relative was possible through the agreement of a medical superintendent.

Any relative or friend of a lunatic could apply to the authority who signed the reception order for their release. The superintendent and the visitors were then asked for the report and following sufficient undertaking from the relative of the lunatic, the discharge could go ahead. Any lunatic escaping could be recaptured and returned by any police officer, or by any officer or servant of the asylum. Except criminal lunaics and European lunatics under the

Army Act, this power did not extend beyond a month from the date of escape. Illegal detention was liable to imprisonment for a term not exceeding two years, or a fine, or both.

In 1987, Indian Lok Sabha (Lower House) passed the Mental Health Bill, which has simplified the procedures for admission and discharge. Compulsory admission is for 90 days, and relatives or friends of the mentally ill are eligible for application with two medical officers agreeing to it. There are more safeguards and the role of the Visitor's Board is well clarified. Treatability has become the major criterion (Sharma, 1990). The Mental Health Act, though different from Lunacy Act of 1912, follows in the same traditions.

Somasundaram (1987), who has charted the progress of various Lunacy Acts since the arrival of the British in India, noted that after the takeover of India by the Crown, Queen Victoria had promised: 'By the blessing of providence, it is our earnest desire to stimulate the peaceful industry of India, to promote the works of public utility and improvement and to administer the Government for the benefit of all subjects'. However, he wondered whether that included the mentally ill. The Indian Mental Health Acts did follow from the English Acts of 1845.

When legal minds contributed to the Lunacy Act of 1890 in England (Jones, 1972), the procedures in India were bound to follow suit. Twenty years later, the Select Committee set out to establish the Lunacy Act with the promise: 'We propose to bring the law in certain important particulars in line with the modern English Act.' Thus, in 1912, the Indian Lunacy Act came into being. The Governor General of Madras, in a far-sighted move, drew the attention of the Committee to the admission procedures for voluntary patients—nearly two decades before voluntary patient admissions were made possible in England and Wales. In 1906, the Government decided to bring all lunatic asylums under a central supervisory system. In 1913, the asylum accommodation was 7243 for a total population of 259,716,306 (Overbeck-Wright, 1925). In 1922, the usage of the term 'lunatic asylums' was replaced by 'mental hospitals' in the Act, though one administrative medical officer opposed it on the grounds: 'Asylums could not be considered hospitals, as no lunatics ever recovered.' Thus, the debate about care versus cure (as noted by Allderidge, 1985; Scull 1979; Foucault, 1971) was beginning, though in very muted tones.

TRAINING

In all the textbooks of psychiatry circulating in the early twentieth century (Overbeck-Wright, 1912, 1925; Ewens, 1908; Lodge Patch, 1934), the symptomatology and treatment was from those in Britain—only some of the aetiological factors varied. Child marriage was seen as a very important aetiological factor in the development of insanity (Overbeck-Wright, 1912). Lodge Patch (1934) acknowledged the importance of marriage among Hindus and advised his colleagues to seek the help of a Hindu physician to stop the mentally ill from getting married. This was due to 'the propagation of the insane' and he suggested that in cases where more than one member has been insane or defective, the marriage should be emphatically opposed.

In addition to child marriages, the next important cause was 'Indian hemp insanity' (Dhunjibhoy, 1930). Overbeck-Wright (1912) reported that a quarter of his male admissions gave a positive history of cannabis abuse. He further argued that it was an established fact that neuroses and psychoses were more common among the Europeans and their descendants in hot climates. He advised the increasingly Westernized Indians and Europeans to change their habits in view of the climatic factors. Overbeck-Wright (1925) also warned the naive medical officer to be wary of native Indians feigning insanity to avoid the results of business transactions.

According to Sharma (1990), the data for 35 years, since 1951, reveal that the number of hospitals increased by 50 per cent from 30 to 45) during this period, whereas the bed strength rose by 100 per cent (from 10,148 to 20,674). However, in the same period, the role of mental hospitals has changed, and Sharma (1990) points out that paucity of funds, inadequate manpower and other scarce resources of these hospitals are important features.

Just before independence, the Health Survey and Development Committee (1946), under the chairmanship of Colonel M. Taylor, surveyed mental hospitals and made recommendations for clinical practice, research, and training. The committee emphasized that the physical and mental health of an individual are interrelated. Thus, no health programme could be considered complete without the promotion of positive mental health and adequate provisions for the treatment of mentally ill patients. The Health Survey and Development Committee (1946) noted a gross inadequacy in medical, nursing, and attendant staff. The majority of mental hospitals were found to be quite out of date and without regard for curative treatment. The existing bed strength for psychiatric patients in 1946 is shown in Table 3.7. The committee noted that the position in India was unsatisfactory and recommended that mental health organizations should be created as part of the establishment under the director General of Health Services, also improvement of existing mental hospitals, improved training for medical and ancillary personnel and establishment of a department of mental health in the proposed new All India Medical Institute. Thus, again, the emphasis was on the Western style of medicine.

Table 3.7: Mental Hospitals in India with their Location and Bed Strength

Province	Location	Number of beds
Assam	Tezpur	716
Bengal	Private institutions	–
Bihar	(European) Ranchi	271
	(India) Ranchi	1380
Bombay	Poona	1227
	Thana	390
	Ahmedabad	267
	Ratnagiri	176
	Dharwar	199
CP & Brar	Nagpur	600
Delhi	Nil	–
Madras	Madras	888
	Calicut	364
	Waltair	164
North West Frontier	Central Prison Peshawar	140
Orissa	Nil	–
Punjab	Lahore	1408
UP	Agra	617
	Bareilly	408
	Benares	331
Sind	Hyderabad	343
Indian State		
Mysore	Bangalore	300
	Total:	10,189

THE ROYAL MEDICO-PSYCHOLOGICAL ASSOCIATION

The establishment of various societies had a variable influence in India, largely due to the vastness of the country and the conflicting interests of Europeans and Indians. As noted earlier, the Indian branch of the British Medical Association lasted only a few years. A similar fate befell the Royal Medico-Psychological Association (RMPA). For a long time, the psychiatric interest of the country lay with the RMPA's Indian Division. However, the membership was only forty and the association was not very active. The division came into existence in 1936 and it took two years before the inaugural meeting could be held at Madras in 1938–9. The RMPA Council had agreed to the formation of the Indian Division in 1936—confirmed at its September 1936 meeting. The division was discussed a few times at the council meetings, but no great amount of activity was observed. The council agreed to the dissolution of the Indian Division in 1948 '...due to the political situation'. The Indian Psychiatric Society was set up after independence following a failure to revive the RMPA's Indian Division. Its first meeting was attended by only thirteen members. At present, it is a thriving society with regular meetings and more than one journal.

CONCLUSION

Curran and Harding (1978) noted that in the year 1978, India, Pakistan and Nigeria were still following the Acts passed in 1912 and 1916, respectively. The Indian Parliament, however, passed the new Mental Health Bill in 1987, leading towards a broader health policy to meet the needs of the people by AD 2000. The mental hospitals in India continue to reflect more of the European and the English designs, ideas, and attitudes rather than the Indian attitudes and aspirations.

Until recently, the models of psychiatric illness, classification, and management have been exclusively British. It is only within the last few years that new models of community care considering local traditions and local needs have been set up (Wig, 1977). These involve using the relatives as helpers on the wards and custodians outside. It is highly unlikely that Indian psychiatry will ever come out of the shadow and influence of British psychiatry but it is hoped that within such an umbrella it will develop new models and ideas specific to local needs.

Until a new generation of psychiatrists establish local and indigenous mental health practices, the fledgling mental health programmes, training of medical and other personnel in the fields of mental health, and the notions of a national mental health service (albeit limited in practice), which undoubtedly owe their origins to the British, will continue to bear the stamp of the Raj.

REFERENCES

Allderidge P. (1985). 'Bedlam: Fact or Fantasy' in W. F. Bynum, R. Porter, M. Shephered (eds), *The Anatomy of Madness*, vol. II. London: Tavistock, 17–23.

Arnold D. (1989). 'Introduction: Disease, medicine and empire' in D. Arnold (ed.), *Imperial Medicine and Indigenous Societies*. Delhi: Oxford University Press.

Bala P. (1991). *Imperialism and Medicine in Bengal*. New Delhi: Sage.

Berkeley-Hill O. (1924). 'The Ranchi European Mental Hospital'. *Journal of Mental Science*, 70: 68–76.

Bhardwaj S. M. (1975). 'Attitude toward different systems of medicine: A survey of four villages in the Punjab—India'. *Social Science and Medicine*, 9: 603–12.

Bhatia J. C., D. Vir, A. Timmapaya, and C. C. Chuttani (1973). 'Indigenous medical practitioners and their attitudes toward the proposed rural health scheme'. *National Institute of Health Administration and Education Bulletin*, 5: 302.

Bhugra D. (1992). 'Psychopathology in ancient Indian texts'. *History of Psychiatry*, 2: 167–86.

Burdett H. C. (1891). *Hospitals and Asylums Around the World*. London: J&A Churchill.

Bynum W. F., R. Porter, and M. Shepherd (1985). *The Anatomy of Madness*, vol. II. London: Tavistock, 1–16.

Chaudhury N. (1988). 'Memsahibs and motherhood in the nineteenth century colonial India'. *Victorian Studies*, 31(4): 517–35.

Chandra B. (1980). 'Karl Marx; his theories of Asian societies and colonial rule'. *Sociological Theories: Race and Colonialism*. Paris: UNESCO, 383–452.

Crawford D. G. (1914). *History of the Indian Medical Service* 1600–1913, vols I and II. London: Thacker and Co.

Curran W. J. and T. Harding (1978). *The Law and Mental Health Harmonizing Objectives*. Geneva: WHO.

DGHS Annual Report (1955). Simla: Govt. of India Press.

Dhunjibhoy J. E. (1930). 'Indian hemp insanity'. *Journal of Mental Science*, 256–64.

Digby A. (1985). 'Moral Treatment at the Retreat 1796–1846' in W. F. Bynum, R. Porter, and M. Shepherd (eds). *The Anatomy of Madness*, vol. II. London: Tavistock, 52–72.

Doerner K. (1981). *Madman and the Bourgeoise*. Oxford: Basil Blackwell.

Dutta G. P. (1988a). 'Medical Council of India'. *Journal of the Indian Medical Association*, 86(8): 201.

——— (1988b). 'Sixty years of Indian Medical Association: a journey of struggle and achievements'. *Journal of the Indian Medical Association*, 86(9): 229.

Ernst W. and D. Kantowsky (1983). *Mad Tales from the Raj: Case Studies from Pembroke House and Ealing Lunatic Asylum* 1818–92. Sweden: Paper presented to Eighth European Conference on Modern South Asian Studies Tallberg, 2–8 July.

Ewens G. F. W. (1908). *Insanity in India*. Calcutta: Thacker Spinks & Co.

Fanon F. (1963). *The Wretched of the Earth*. New York: Grove.

——— (1970). *A Dying Colonialism*. Harmondsworth: Pelican, pp. 104–9.

Fisher L. E. (1985). *Colonial Madness: Mental Health in Barbadian Social Order*. New Brunswick, NJ: Rutgers University Press.

Fonaroff L. S. and A. Fonaroff (1996). 'The cultural environment of medical geography in rural Hindu India'. *Pacific Viewpoint*, 7: 67.

Foucault M. (1971). *Madness and Civilization*. London: Tavistock.

Gopal S. (1980). 'Emergence of modern nationalism' in *Sociological Theories: Race and Colonialism*. Paris: UNESCO, 85–92.

Gupta B. (1976). 'Indigenous Medicine in Nineteenth and Twentieth-Century Bengal' in C. Leslie (ed.), *Asian Medical Systems*. Berkeley: University of California Press.

Haldipur C. V. (1984). 'Madness in ancient India: concept of insanity in Charaka Samhita'. *Comprehensive Psychiatry*, 25: 335–44.

Health Survey and Development Committee (1946), Report. Simla: Govt. of India Press.

Hussain M. F. (1985). 'Islamic principles in psychiatry'. *Hamdard Medicus*, 28(1): 60–71.

IOR 1817; IOR 1820 (1983). Cited in Ernst and Kantowsky.

Jones K. (1972). *A History of the Mental Health Services*. London: RK&P.

Lodge Patch C. J. (1934). *A Manual of Mental Diseases*. London: Baillere Tindall and Cox.

——— (1939). 'A century of psychiatry in the Punjab'. *Journal of Mental Sciences*, 85: 381–91.

Leslie C. (1976). 'The ambiguities of medical revivalism in modern India' in C. Leslie (ed.), *Asian Medical Systems.* Berkeley: University of California Press.

Lewis O. (1965). *Village Life in Northern India.* NY: Random House, p. 265.

Lynton H. R. and M. Rajan (1974). *Days of the Beloved.* Berkeley: University of California Press.

McDowall T. W. (1897). 'The insane of India and their treatment'. *Journal of Mental Science*, 43, 683–703.

Marriott M. C. K. (1955). 'Western Medicine in a Village in Northern India', in D. P. Benjamin (ed.), *Health Culture and Community.* NY: Russel Sage, p. 241.

Marx K. (1969). S. Avineri (ed.), *Karl Marx on Colonialism and Modernization.* NY: Anchor Books.

Master R. S. (1985). *Psychiatry for medical undergraduates.* Poona: Office Management Services.

Memmi A. (1965). *The Colonizer and the Colonized.* NY: Orion.

Mukhopadhyaya G. (1926). *History of Indian Medicine*, 2 vols. Calcutta: University of Calcutta Press.

Neki J. S. (1973). 'Guru-Chela relationship: The possibility of a therapeutic paradigm'. *American Journal of Orthopsychiatry*, 43: 755–66.

——— (1974). 'A reappraisal of the Guru-Chela relationship as a therapeutic paradigm'. *International Mental Health Research Newsletter*, 16: 2–5.

Overbeck-Wright A. W. (1912). *Mental Derangements in India.* Calcutta: Thacker, Spink and Co.

——— (1921). *Lunacy in India.* London: Bailliere, Tindall and Cox.

Qvarsall R. (1985). 'Locked up or put to bed: psychiatry and the treatment of the mentally ill in Sweden 1800–1920' in W. F. Bynum, R. Porter and M. Shephered (eds). *The Anatomy of Madness*, vol. II. London: Tavistock, pp. 86–97.

Raina B. L. (1990). *Health Science in Ancient India.* New Delhi: Commonwealth Publishers.

——— (1991). *Health Science: March Through Centuries.* New Delhi: Commonwealth Publishers.

Rao A. V. (1975). India in J. G. Howells (ed.). *World History of Psychiatry.* London: Bailliere Tindall.

Ray P. R. and H. N. Gupta (1980). *Charaka Samhita.* New Delhi: INSA.

Sarkar S. C. (1932). *A Text Book of Indian History.* Calcutta.

Satija D. C., D. Singh, S. S. Nathawat, and V. Sharma (1981). 'A psychiatric study of patients attending Mehandipur Balaji Temple'. *Indian Journal of Psychiatry*, 23: 247–50.

Scull A. T. (1979). *Museums of Madness*. London: Allen Lane.
Selhi B. B. (1981). 'Mental Health by the year AD 2000'. *Indian Journal of Psychiatry*, 23(3): 191–2.
Sharma P. V. (1972). *Indian Medicine in the Classical Age*. Varanasi: Chowkhamba Publications.
Sharma S. (1990). *Mental Hospitals in India*. New Delhi: DGHS.
Shrama S. and L. P. Verma (1984). 'History of mental hospitals in Indian subcontinent'. *Indian Journal of Psychiatry*, 26: 295–300.
Shaw W. S. (1932). 'The Alienist Department of India'. *Journal of Mental Science*, 78: 331–41.
Somasundaram O. (1973). 'Religious treatment in Tamil Nadu'. *Indian Journal of Psychiatry*, 15: 38.
——— (1987). 'Indian Lunacy Act, 1912: the historical background'. *Indian Journal of Psychiatry*, 29: 3–14.
Taylor M. (1946). *Report of the Health Survey and Development Committee*. Simla: Government of India Press.
Varma L. P. (1953). 'History of psychiatry in India and Pakistan'. *Indian Journal of Neurology and Psychiatry*, 4: 26–53, 138–64.
Vahia N. S., S. L. Vinekar and D. R. Doongaji (1966). 'Some ancient Indian concepts in the treatment of psychiatric disorders'. *British Journal of Psychiatry*, 112: 1089–96.
Wig N. N. (1977). In *Mental Health Services in S. E. Asia:* WHO Project I.C.P.
Wise T. N. (1853). 'Insanity in India'. *Journal of Psychological Medicine and Mental Pathology*, 6: 356–67.

4

The Theory and Practice of European Psychiatry in Colonial Africa

Jock McCulloch

INTRODUCTION

The term ethnopsychiatry was used during the colonial era to describe the study of the psychology and behaviour of African peoples. It occupied a small and uncomfortable niche between psychiatry and anthropology, but in contrast to those two sciences ethnopsychiatry never achieved prominence. Consequently, there has been little historical research evaluating its philosophies or clinical practice.[1] In the mid-1960s, ethnopsychiatry was supplanted

[1] There have been few full-length reviews of the science's past achievements. For example, see Littlewood R. and M. Lipsedge (1982), *Aliens and Alienists*. London: Penguin Books; Ari Kiev, *Transcultural Psychiatry* (1972), New York, Free Press; and Suman Fernando (1988), *Race and Culture in Psychiatry*. London: Croom Helm. In general, monographs on the subject are addressed to specialist issues and to a specialist audience such as Georges Devereux's (1980), *Basic Problems in Ethnopsychiatry*. Chicago: University of Chicago Press. Among the few works which examine the history and politics of the discipline are John Cox (ed.) (1986), *Transcultural Psychiatry*. London: Croom Helm, Megan Vaughan (1991), 'The Madman and the Medicine Man: Colonial Society and the Theory of Deculturation,' in *Curing Their Ills: Colonial Power and African Illness*. London: Polity Press; and Jock McCulloch (1995), *Colonial Psychiatry and the 'African Mind'*. Cambridge: Cambridge University Press. For an anthropology of mental illness in a colonial society, see Lawrence Fisher (1985), *Colonial Madness: Mental Health in the Barbadian Social Order*. New Brunswick: Rutgers University Press. For a guide to the

by a broader transcultural psychiatry that acknowledged the shift in its clientele from colonial subjects to guest workers and ethnic minorities within Europe itself.

Ethnopsychiatry lasted from about 1900 to 1960, disappearing along with the social conditions upon which it rested. Clearly demarcated from mainstream psychiatry, ethnopsychiatry had its own subjects, its own plant, and its own areas of expertise. It was very much a self-enclosed enterprise and what we know of it comes from papers, conference reports, and archival holdings in former colonies. In reviewing the history of the science it is important to remember that colonialism in Africa was itself short-lived. The empires of Britain and France came into being at the end of the nineteenth century, but effective occupation took place only many years later and few peasantries were fully incorporated into either wage labour or comprehensive taxation systems. Apart from the work of missions or programmes to control infectious diseases, few Africans came into contact with European physicians, even fewer saw a European psychiatrist. For indigenous populations, the most important changes came with the new cities and with the urban culture they brought. It was within an urban context that the most intimate contact between White settlers and Africans took place. It was also from that setting that the majority of African psychiatric patients were recruited.

There was little incentive for European psychiatrists to visit colonial regions. Travel was slow, difficult and hazardous, not least because of infectious diseases. The one prominent psychiatrist to come into contact with colonial subjects was Emile Kraeplin.[2] In 1902, Kraeplin visited Java and Singapore where he sought to compare mental illness in Europeans with that found among the Javanese and Chinese. At the Buitenzorg Asylum in Java, Kraeplin found no cases of melancholia and he perceived a lack of religious

---

literatures of both the colonial and contemporary periods, see David Westley (1993), *Mental Health and Psychiatry in Africa: An Annotated Bibliography*. London: Hans Zell Publishers.

[2] See Sashidharan, S. P. (1986) 'Ideology and Politics of Transcultural Psychiatry', in J. L. Cox (ed.), *Transcultural Psychiatry*. London: Croom Helm and E. Kraeplin (1974), 'Comparative Psychiatry' in S. R. Hirsch and M. Shepherd (eds) *Themes and Variations in European Psychiatry*. Bristol: John Wright & Sons.

sentiment or a sense of responsibility among the inmates. Those ideas were to be a recurring theme in ethnopsychiatric research for the next 50 years.

Colonial states expanded slowly and the problems caused by mental illness were far outweighed by the need for public health programmes to control diseases such as malaria and typhoid. When asylums were established in the first two decades of the twentieth century, they were an adjunct to the penal system. As late as 1944 the annual reports on asylums for British West Africa, for example, appeared as a subheading under prisons. On the eve of political independence in the 1960s, no colonial state had a comprehensive mental health system and it was common for a country as large as Kenya to have only one specialist. The most notable physicians who worked in the colonial period were J. C. Carothers and H. L. Gordon (Kenya), Antoine Porot (Algeria), B. J. F. Laubscher and Wulf Sachs (South Africa), Octave Mannoni (Malagasy), J. F. Ritchie (Northern Rhodesia), and J. F. Smartt (Tanganyika). Their ranks included the science's most eloquent critic Frantz Fanon who practised in Algeria and Tunisia.

Physicians such as Carothers were isolated intellectually and in most cases had no colleagues with whom they could share their professional concerns. That so much research was published is testament to the endurance of those men (there were no women in the field) and to the importance they attached to the pathologies of their patients. The authors of this literature worked in disparate settings and the philosophical foundations of their work were heterogeneous. Laubscher, Sachs and Ritchie were Freudians of a sort, Mannoni was influenced by Alfred Adler, while Carothers and Smartt were versed in British eclecticism. Psychiatrists worked independently of each other, they had no professional association, no journals, and we know from Carothers that they did not have access to each other's research.[3] It seems likely that Frantz Fanon was the first practitioner to have read the work of both Francophone and Anglophone specialists.[4]

[3] Interviews conducted with the author at Carothers's home in Havants, England in November 1986.

[4] In *The Wretched of the Earth* and 'Reflexions sur l'ethnopsychiatrie', *Conscience maghrebine*, Frantz Fanon reviewed the discipline and its ruling orthodoxies. However, those reviews were not read widely by practitioners.

The psychiatrists who worked in Africa had no training in anthropology, while psychiatric theory has never formed a routine part of the education of anthropologists. Although each discipline has often behaved as if the other did not exist, major debates have been conducted across their borders—among them are Malinowski's work on the Oedipus complex and Margaret Mead's research into adolescence in Samoa. Social anthropologists have regarded the ethnopsychiatrists with suspicion, pointing to their ethnocentrism and their lack of methodological precision. The most serious criticism of all has been that, unlike social anthropologists, they had little empathy with their subjects.

The interest of European scientists in the lives of primitive peoples preceded by two centuries the establishment of asylums for the treatment of Africans. Through historical accident, the first literature about mental illness among people of African descent was published in the United States. It was only much later that a parallel literature, written from within the continent, was produced.[5] Travellers' narratives, the diaries of missionaries and explorers fed scientific interest in peoples who were believed to be living representatives of Europe's distant past. Those narratives were a precursor of ethnopsychiatry. Francis Galton, for example, who is best known for having invented the term eugenics, made extended visits to the Sudan in 1846 and to southern Africa in 1852. He published an account of his wanderings which included journeys in Namibia and Angola. Like other explorers Galton noted that native peoples appeared impervious to physical pain and were able to bear almost any discomfort without complaint.[6] He also found the women to have no affection either for their husbands or their children, ideas which had been part of the rhetoric justifying

Carothers, who was the best travelled of the ethnopsychiatrists, when interviewed by the author in 1986 was unaware of the existence of Fanon's work. See Frantz Fanon (1967), *The Wretched of the Earth*, translated by Constance Farrington, London: Penguin Books, and (1995), 'Reflexions sur l'ethnopsychiatrie', *Conscience maghrebine*, no. 3, pp. 1–2.

[5] See for example, E. M. Green (1914), 'Psychosis among Negroes: A Comparative Study', *Journal of Mental and Nervous Disease*, 41, pp. 697–708 and John. E. Lind (1913–14), 'The Dream as a Simple Wish-Fulfilment in the Negro', *Psychoanalytic Review*, 1, pp. 295–300.

[6] See Francis Galton (1889), *Narrative of an Explorer in Tropical South Africa*, London: Ward, Lock & Co., p. 137.

the transatlantic slave trade. Galton's narrative was in that sense conventional. However, most European scientists who took an interest in the lives of primitives never visited the continent.

The figure of the primitive was important to successive generations of nineteenth and early twentieth century psychologists and social philosophers, among them Karl Marx, Emile Durkheim, Max Weber, and Freud, for whom the non-West was important as a contrast to the achievements of contemporary Europe. Perhaps the best known among those who, on the basis of second- and third-hand evidence, fashioned a career out of speculating about primitive mentality was the lapsed French philosopher Lucien Levy-Bruhl. According to Adam Kuper, the concept of the primitive offered nineteenth-century Europeans an image of their own society as if in a distorting mirror.[7] It was for that reason that speculation upon primitive society was so influential in a number of disciplines including law, anthology, and psychoanalysis and why it was used by writers as politically diverse as Engels, Freud, Durkheim, and the anarchist Peter Kropotkin.

THE ASYLUMS: MATHARI

Psychiatric services were first established where European populations were the largest and colonial administrations made little effort to set up hospitals or clinics in territories where there were few expatriates. Consequently, the most elaborate facilities were found in South Africa, Algeria, Southern Rhodesia, and Kenya.

In Kenya, the main concern of public health officials was to control the spread of infectious diseases and to cater to the needs of colonial administrators and their families. Before 1910, African lunatics were housed in prisons and indigent Europeans were sent at government expense to South Africa for treatment.[8] Families who could afford to have their sick relatives repatriated to England did so. The first African hospital was established at Fort Hall in

[7] See Adam Kuper (1988); *The Invention of Primitive Society: Transformations of an Illusion*, London: Routledge & Kegan Paul, p. 240.

[8] South African authorities never welcomed this arrangement, as it only added to their own problems in providing adequate mental health care. From April 1931, the South African government restricted the numbers of lunatics and feeble minded patients it would take from neighbouring colonies such as Kenya. 'Memo: "Admission of Patients to Mental Hospitals in the Union"

1909 and in 1910, Mathari Mental Hospital, a small facility offering beds for two European and eight African patients, was opened in Nairobi. However, until 1930 the medical officer in charge of the native and prison hospitals also had the task of supervising the asylum.

In the 1920s, there were high death rates in colonial asylums mainly due to the prevalence of infectious diseases. In Mathari in 1921, there were eighty-eight admissions and twenty-six deaths, and of the 160 patients treated two-thirds were male. Most of the inmates came from Nairobi itself and proximity to the hospital was a major factor in the admission of both Europeans and Africans.[9] African families, especially those living close to major towns, used the asylum as a dumping ground for incurably ill relatives and Mathari came to be filled with patients suffering from organic disorders. The same had happened in Western Europe and North America a century earlier when the newly established asylums soon filled with untreatable patients. However, in Africa the vast majority of the mentally ill were treated by traditional methods and never came to the attention of European authorities. This pattern remained unchanged throughout the colonial period.

Despite the constant growth in the number of patients, Mathari remained a small part of the health system. In 1930, for example, a total of 278 psychiatric patients were treated which was less than one per cent of those admitted to native hospitals. In Western Europe, the majority of asylum inmates were women while at Mathari, as at other colonial asylums, men outnumbered women by two to one.

In 1930, Dr H. L. Gordon was appointed medical superintendent and he succeeded in reducing the mortality rate. Admissions were also cut in order to alleviate the overcrowding and those not admitted were kept in the Nairobi Prison.[10] The prison and asylum

---

from Under Secretary of External Affairs, South Africa, to the Colonial Secretary, Kenya, 20 April 1931'. *Department of Health, File no. PM 49/44*, Kenya National Archive (KNA).

[9] See *Annual Report, Department of Public Health,* KNA 1921, pp. 95–8.

[10] According to Gordon's estimates, the native female wards were overcrowded to the extent of 50 per cent above their intended capacity and the native male wards to 33 per cent. See *Annual Report, Department of Public Health,* KNA 1932, pp. 53, 56.

populations overlapped and a significant proportion of African inmates had committed a criminal offence such as assault, murder or arson. Under Gordon's direction, the physical health of the patients was also improved and serious illnesses were restricted to malaria and tuberculosis. Gordon also carried out the first survey of Mathari's population, initially diagnosing and classifying the male inmates and separating the psychotics from those suffering from organic disorders. One major problem faced by the staff was the need to segregate the civil from the criminal cases.

It was customary to confine lunatics, under temporary detention orders, in local gaols until such time as they recovered spontaneously or could be transferred to Mathari. Kenya is, however, a large country, and there were often long delays in transferring psychotic patients from outlying districts. Besides the problems of distance and transport, there were delays due to a lack of available beds. As early as July 1939, the Colonial Office decreed that prisons were not suitable for lunatics and their use could only be justified as a temporary measure. However, it took almost 15 years before wards in native hospitals were set aside specifically for the temporary accommodation of the insane.

In 1948, Mathari treated a total of 750 patients. Of these sixty-eight were Europeans, sixty-two were Asians, and the rest were Africans. In that same year, the native civil hospitals in the capital treated a total of 21,181 inpatients. In addition, a further 2007 cases were treated at the prisons hospital.[11] Tuberculosis was a constant problem among Mathari's inmates, and the rate of infection was at least four times higher than at hospitals in the UK.[12] Besides mental illness, many of the patients carried self-inflicted injuries and suicide attempts by hanging were common.

The majority of asylum staff were African orderlies who worked under the supervision of a small number of qualified European nurses. Before the 1940s there was virtually no treatment provided in any colonial asylum and the function of such institutions was purely custodial. Occupational therapy was confined to gardening and the maintenance of the hospital buildings and when

[11] See correspondence for the Department of Public Health's *Annual Reports* for the years 1947, 1948, and 1949. KNA File No. TC 787 3/40, pp. 29–31.

[12] Correspondence for Department of Public Health (1949), *Annual Reports*, KNA, p. 39.

formal treatment began it was in the form of electroconvulsive therapy (ECT). At Mathari, in contrast to Ingutsheni, Southern Rhodesia's asylum at Bulawayo, ECT was used sparingly.[13] Pre-frontal leucotomy arrived at Mathari in 1948; when it was used on four patients: one died, and two of the surviving three improved sufficiently to be released.[14] However, the procedure was discontinued because it was too demanding of the hospital's limited resources.

The staff was overworked and underpaid and they had little opportunity to minister to the psychological needs of patients. The hospitals' records indicate that African and European inmates either went into spontaneous remission and were released or deteriorated and spent the rest of their lives in confinement. The asylums did relieve settlers' families of mad relatives but that relief was bought at the price of the stigma attached to mental illness. White communities were small and gossip-ridden, and to have a mad relative was an unpleasant experience.

After several years of lobbying by J. C. Carothers, who had succeeded Gordon as medical superintendent, a new Lunacy Ordinance was approved in February 1949, replacing the existing Indian Lunacy Asylums Act.[15] It provided a legal framework to protect the rights of patients and brought the service, formally at least, into line with metropolitan practice. As elsewhere in Africa, the major problem at Mathari was the lack of resources, and throughout the 1950s psychiatric services in Kenya remained static. Overcrowding was chronic and there was only one specialist who was assisted by a junior medical officer. Ideally, Mathari had space for 500 beds but in 1958 it housed over 700 patients.[16] At the Blida asylum in Algeria and at Ingutsheni overcrowding was even worse.

[13] At Ingutsheni, ECT was used on virtually all inmates, sometimes with disastrous effects. See Jock McCulloch (1995), *Colonial Psychiatry and the 'African Mind'*, Cambridge: Cambridge University Press, pp. 12–20.

[14] Correspondence for Department of Public Health (1948), *Annual Reports*, KNA, p. 41.

[15] On the subcontinent, the Indian Lunacy Asylums Act had been superseded in 1912.

[16] E. L. Margetts (1958), 'Psychiatric Facilities in Kenya', in *Mental Health Disorders and Mental Health in Africa South of the Sahara*, CCTA/CSA-WFHM-WHO Meeting of Specialists on Mental Health, Bukava. CCTA Publication no. 35, p. 43.

However, Kenya, like Algeria and Southern Rhodesia, did at least have the rudiments of a mental health system. Most colonies did not.

In Senegal, the first psychiatric clinic was established in September 1956, while in the Cameroon, a small centre with thirty-five beds was opened at Douala in 1957. In the following year, a similar centre was opened in the Belgian Congo.[17] In Angola, a neuropsychiatric section was opened at the main hospital in Luanda in 1946 but it was a further seven years before ECT was available in the Portuguese colony. In Sudan, the first mental hospital was opened in 1950 and before that date there were no specialist services. The situation was little better in Ethiopia, where facilities for the mentally ill were made available by 1940. By 1958, there was one psychiatrist at the Ammannel Hospital, near Addis Ababa, which had 150 beds.[18] In Mozambique, the first asylum for the criminally insane was opened in 1930 at a short distance from the capital, Lourenzo Marques. The institution dealt specifically with dangerous African patients and mentally ill Europeans were often sent to South Africa for treatment. In 1943, the first psychiatrist was appointed and he worked at the Miguel Bombarda Central Hospital.[19] While there was a sizeable European community in Mozambique, the poverty of metropolitan Portugal was reflected in the lack of health services. As in Belgian Congo, little attempt was made to provide funds for infectious diseases, let alone care and treatment for the mentally ill.

PATIENTS

In the Kenyan National Archive there is an abundance of material documenting the history of Mathari. The files stretch back into the first decade of the asylum's existence and it is possible to recount that history with some precision. There is little evidence, however,

[17] See *Mental Health Disorders and Mental Health in Africa South of the Sahara*, Bukava, 1958, pp. 20, 28, 31.

[18] See F. B. Hylander (1958), 'Summary Information on Mental Diseases in Ethiopia' in *Mental Health Disorders and Mental Health in Africa South of the Sahara*, Bukava, pp. 35–6.

[19] See 'Mental Hygiene and Mental Health in Mozambique', author uncited in *Mental Health Disorders and Mental Health in Africa South of the Sahara*, Bukava, 1958, pp. 45–9.

of the lives of the men and women who comprised the majority of its inmates and who, in some cases, spent years in confinement. Although eight out of ten patients were Africans, their stories have simply disappeared. There are no case histories, (in most instances none were taken) and there is no correspondence from relatives or friends or from government officials inquiring about their welfare. In contrast, the Kenyan archives are filled with the stories of insane Europeans and their relatives who were ruined by the loss of a husband or wife. Those files reveal the fragility of settler families and the intensity of the stigma which was attached to mental illness throughout the colonial era. It was the fate of those people which led to Mathari's reputation as a dirty, overcrowded and unpleasant place. That judgment was made, however, from the perspective of the White minority, and there is no evidence as to what Africans thought of Mathari. All that we do know is that African families were willing to place their sick members in the asylum.

In the colonial world, psychiatric practice preceded psychiatric theory and there was no discrete philosophy about mental illness in African men or women before the establishment of the asylums. There was an oral tradition to which writers such as Galton had contributed but there was no system of therapeutics justifying medical intervention. Ethnopsychiatry was the product rather than the cause for the building of those institutions.

There are a number of explanations as to why so much money was spent in maintaining colonial asylums. One of the major reasons was the problem of what to do with mentally ill Europeans. Such people caused financial and emotional distress to their families and posed a financial problem for the state. It was the reduction in the considerable cost of keeping such patients in South African institutions which was used to justify every major infusion of funds to Mathari and Ingutsheni. The problems posed by mad Africans were rather different. The insane, both civil and criminal, were difficult to manage within the walls of a gaol and the vagabond or violent lunatics were sent to the provincial gaols. The asylums allowed for some segregation of prison populations and the establishment of Mathari enabled, in principle, a distinction to be made between criminals and the mad, even though in practice, psychotics continued to be kept in prisons. No doubt this was some comfort to prison directors and attorneys-general who were determined to conform with Colonial Office directives. There were, however, other factors which were important.

From the work of contemporary historians we know that in Europe the building of asylums led to an increase in the numbers of psychiatric patients, and that to an extent those numbers were an artefact of the institutions themselves.[20] Foucault and Scull have argued that the asylums were intended to inculcate obedience to established authority and the great confinement of the mad was designed to control and regulate Europe's working classes. Such intentions were merely hidden beneath liberal rhetoric. Whatever the merits of that interpretation of European experience, such an argument has little relevance to Africa.

Colonial states were never so influential nor so developed as their metropolitan counterparts, and they were incapable of providing the kinds of surveillance of which Foucault has written with such imaginative force. In none of the colonial states was there an attempt at a great confinement, and the methods for identifying and then incarcerating the mad were haphazard. Those procedures always relied upon some dramatic event such as a crime or the decision by a family that a relative was unmanageable. Even with the new legislation and the expansion of services carried out in the 1930s and 1940s, the majority of mentally ill Africans did not come to the notice of district commissioners or mental health authorities.

The asylums in colonial Africa did, however, serve the interests of the medical profession by giving psychiatrists exclusive competence in treating mental illness. The asylums also served the interests of White settlers by affording them a haven for their mad relatives and by providing a means for disposing of dangerous African employees. Perhaps most important aspect was that the building of asylums was evidence of the civic virtue of settler societies, symbolising their ability to construct a state which mimicked the grand configurations of the metropolis.

Throughout colonial Africa, patients were recruited from urban areas and there was a correlation between urbanization and the size of asylum populations. The physicians who worked in the

[20] See, for example, David Rothman (1970), *The Discovery of the Asylum*, Boston: Little, Brown; Andrew Scull (1979), *Museums of Madness*, London: Allen Lane; Michel Foucault (1979), *Discipline and Punish*, New York: Random House.

asylums were in an unusual position to view the social changes which wage labour and land alienation were bringing to indigenous communities. While social anthropologists were intent upon documenting the vanishing world of primitives, the ethnopsychiatrists were watching a world being born.

THE KENYAN SCHOOL

Once mental health services were established, a scholarly literature dealing with the Africans soon emerged. Most of the literature was produced in Algeria, South Africa, and Kenya, thus following the centres of White settlement.

When J. C. Carothers arrived in Kenya in 1929, he was introduced to psychological medicine by H. L. Gordon. In 1934, Gordon published an account of European psychiatry in Kenya and offered a number of observations about the mentality and culture of the Africans.[21] Like the other ethnopsychiatrists, Gordon used the generic term 'the African' to the more discrete entities such as 'the Luo' or 'Kikuyu'. According to Gordon, the most serious problem confronting European physicians was in distinguishing between normal and abnormal behaviour. The African had no regard for the sanctity of life and no sense of decency. As a consequence, the forms of mental illness found in Kenyans were at best a poor imitation of European disorders. Schizophrenia was limited to the Europeanized tribes, and in all his years in the colony Gordon had never seen a case of paranoid insanity or manic-depressive psychosis. The majority of patients at Mathari came from urban areas and Gordon believed that Africans often broke down when they came in contact with civilization. Gordon further developed this idea of a 'clash of cultures' in a paper presented to the British Medical Association (BMA) in Nairobi in December 1935.[22]

During his period at Mathari, Gordon conducted a survey of the inmates, noting the frequency of some disorders and the dearth

[21] H. L. Gordon (1934), 'Psychiatry in Kenya Colony', *Journal of Mental Science*, 80, pp. 167–70.

[22] 'An Inquiry into the Correlation of Civilisation and Mental Disorder in the Kenyan Native', presented to a meeting of the Kenya Branch of the BMA, Nairobi, 18 December 1935, subsequently published in *East African Medical Journal*, 12 (1935–6): pp. 327–35.

of others. He found particular significance in the absence of affective and paranoid psychosis and the high incidence of illness among adolescents. According to Gordon, under ordinary circumstances only those with the weakest frontal brain suffer from mental breakdown, and yet in Kenya a disturbing number of adolescents were becoming ill. Gordon believed the reasons were obvious: 'The evidence today is against our natives being as well equipped in the frontal brain as the average European. Under a traditional environment, their adolescent breakdowns may be few. Under the stresses and strains of the foreign environment that we are introducing, who will say they may not be many? A specimen of these stresses and strains should be found within what is vaguely called the impact of civilization'.[23] He was particularly concerned about the effects of European schools on young minds incapable of assimilating complex forms of knowledge. From a study of nineteen of Mathari's younger inmates, all of them educated, he concluded that exposure to Western schooling was the reason for their illness. Gordon was unsure what policy the colonial government should follow, but he was confident that science would eventually provide an answer.

Like many of his contemporaries, including many socialists, Gordon was an enthusiastic supporter of eugenics. He also believed that the imprint of race could be found in the structure of the brain. Gordon gave a number of lectures in Nairobi about the brain of the East African, and over a two-year period, he carried out thousands of measurements and physiological tests of Kenyan subjects.[24] He also encouraged F. W. Vint of the Pathological Research Laboratory in researching cranial capacity and brain weight. Using material obtained from autopsies carried out at

[23] Gordon, 'An Inquiry', p. 333.

[24] An abstract of Gordon's findings was published by a colleague, James Sequeria, who concluded: 'If it is proven that the physical basis of mind in the East African differs from that of the European, it seems quite possible that efforts to educate these backward races on European lines will prove ineffective and possibly disastrous. It has long been recognised among highly civilised races that the educational methods applied to the normal child cannot be applied to the backward defective.' Sequeria hoped that further research into this subject could be funded by either the League of Nations or the Carnegie or Rockefeller Trusts. See James H. Sequeria (1932), 'The Brain of the East African', *British Medical Journal*, 7, p. 581.

Nairobi hospitals, Vint conducted a study of 351 brains and at Gordon's invitation, in March 1932, he presented his findings to a meeting of the BMA in Nairobi. Although Vint had no evidence of *ante mortem* mental capacity, he was confident that since most of the subjects had been in the employment of Europeans his material was representative of the best Africans.[25] He weighed the brains immediately after removal and found the average weight to be 1276 grams. This compared unfavourably with the results from five major studies of the European brain in which the average weight was 1428 grams.

Research into brain volume or weight had been popular for more than a hundred years but by the 1920s it had begun to fall into disfavour. Vint's research, however, was concerned particularly with evaluating the cortex, which he believed gave a better guide to intellectual capacity. He studied the five layers of the cortex of his Nairobi sample and discovered, what he believed, were significant variations, especially in the pyramidal cell layer. Vint concluded that in terms of cortical development, the brain of the adult African corresponded to that of a European child of 7 or 8 years of age. He was uncertain, however, whether under different cultural and educational circumstances, the African could develop to maturity. In the lively discussion which followed his paper, Gordon and another physician commented upon the widespread incidence of mental retardation among the native population. Gordon claimed that almost half the inmates at Mathari were mentally deficient while a physician named Anderson remarked that in his 32 years in East Africa he had never met a native who had achieved the intelligence of a normal European.[26] Both expressed concern that the African was in danger of being forced to live in an environment unsuited to his intellectual capacity.[27]

While today the concept of intelligence covers a wonderfully complex set of attributes, in the past clinical psychologists were more concerned with the ranking of individuals and groups in

[25] See F. W. Vint (1932–3), 'A Preliminary Note on the Cell Content of the Prefrontal Cortex of the East African Native', *East African Medical Journal*, 9, pp. 30–1.

[26] Cited in Vint, 'A Preliminary Note', pp. 52, 54.

[27] Two years later Vint published a second paper on the brain of the African in which he repeated most of his previous findings. See F. W. Vint, 'The Brain of the Kenya Native', *Journal of Anatomy*, 68, (1934), pp. 216–23.

terms of abstract markers of proficiency. Practitioners such as Binet, Goddard, Terman, and Yerkes used various methods to define what Francis Galton had referred to as 'the serviceable citizen'—the type of person believed to be socially the most useful.[28] The qualities associated with such a person may have been a type of conscience, the ability to plan, to defer gratification, or particular attitudes toward the body. The absence of particular qualities in women, the poor, or criminals were taken as proof of the social danger they posed. In that way, the study of intelligence and temperament justified the social subordination of women, ethnic minorities, and lower-class Whites.[29]

Although intelligence testing was not intended primarily to order racial groupings, it proved useful to colonial science providing a career for the Australian psychologist Stanley Porteus who worked briefly in Southern Rhodesia.[30] In claiming that Africans were intellectually inferior, emotionally unstable, and immoral, Gordon and Vint were echoing the findings of scientists working on the under classes of Europe and North America. In that sense their work was conventional. It was distinctive in that it focused upon brain structure rather than brain function and disregarded the significance of culture.[31] Those who came after them adopted rather different approaches.

[28] See Francis Galton (1869), *Hereditary Genius: An Inquiry into its Laws and Consequences*, London: J. M. Dent, p. 36.

[29] See Daniel. J. Kevlis (1985), *In the Name of Eugenics: Genetics and the Uses of Human Heredity*, New York: Alfred A. Knopf.

[30] For a history of clinical psychology in South Africa, see Saul Dubow (1995); *Scientific Racism in Modern South Africa*, Cambridge: Cambridge University Press. See also Stanley Porteus, (1969), *A Psychologist of Sorts*, Palo Alto: Pacific Books; (1931), Stanley Porteus *The Psychology of Primitive People*, New York: Books for Libraries Press; (1937), *Primitive Intelligence and Environment*, New York: Macmillan.

[31] Attempts at aptitude testing were also few. One exception was the work of R. A. C. Oliver. Oliver carried out a series of tests on the intelligence of Kikuyu and White adolescents using White boys from the Prince of Wales School, Kabete and Kikuyu from the Alliance School, an academically selective Protestant college. The test used by Oliver was prepared by Oliver and presented in English. The Europeans had an advantage in terms of language by attending a superior school while the Africans were older. The average score for the Europeans was 312.34 while that for the Africans was 266.40. Oliver argues that the reason for this variation is race, as tests on American

J. C. CAROTHERS

Gordon's colleague J. C. Carothers was the most prominent psychiatrist of his generation. He was the best travelled, the most widely published, and leaving aside Frantz Fanon the only one to enter directly into political debate. Carothers wrote reports on the mental health systems of Northern Rhodesia, Uganda and Nigeria; he authored a survey of mental health for the WHO and in 1954, he was commissioned by the British government to produce a study of Mau-Mau. His career best represents the achievements of ethnopsychiatry.

John Colin Carothers was born in Simonstown in the Cape in 1903.[32] His father was a civil engineer who worked for the admiralty at various ports throughout the British Empire. Carothers was educated in England and in October 1921 he was admitted as a student to St Thomas' Hospital, University of London. Upon graduating, Carothers toyed with the idea of a career in public health when in March 1929 he saw an advertisement for employment in the Kenyan medical service. On his arrival in Nairobi in 1929, he was posted to a rural station and for the next 10 years Carothers enjoyed the life of a district medical officer. In August 1938, he received a telegram ordering him to report to Mathari. Carothers was to replace the medical superintendent, Dr Cobb, who had been forced to resign. The appointment was temporary and at first Carothers did not consider himself qualified to supervise a mental hospital. To his surprise he enjoyed the work, and as no replacement could be found he remained at Mathari. Carothers attempted to educate himself by reading the standard psychiatric texts, but the symptoms exhibited by many of the inmates failed to correspond to the expected clinical profiles.[33]

Negro adolescents, also of Bantu stock, having produced similar results. See R. A. C. Oliver, 'The Comparison of the Abilities of Races: With Special Reference to East (1932) Africa', *East African Medical Journal*, 9, pp. 160–78.

[32] This account of the life of Carothers was provided to me during a series of interviews at his home in Havant, England in November 1986.

[33] Carothers used as his text Henderson and Gillespie's, *Text-Book of Psychiatry*, a manual which went through eight editions between its original date of publication and 1956. Even in the editions published after World War II, it contains a long section expounding the merits of both positive and negative eugenics programmes. See D. Henderson and R. D. Gillespie (1956),

Carothers felt initially that his lack of formal training was to blame.

In 1946, Carothers spent six months at The Maudsley Hospital, London, completing his diploma of psychiatric medicine. Before his studies at The Maudsley, Carothers had written little, feeling unqualified to participate in scientific debate. On returning to Mathari he found that writing helped to clarify his clinical practice and so he began to publish widely. Carothers took early retirement in May 1951 and accepted a post as a psychiatric specialist at St James's Hospital, Portsmouth.[34] It was the work he published after his return to England which allowed him to dominate the science during the last two decades of colonial rule.

Carothers's first article published in the *East African Medical Journal* in 1940 was a review of Mathari's inmates in which he made some reflections on the distinctive features of mental illness in the Africans.[35] Noting the predominance of male patients, Carothers rejected the obvious explanation that women were less violent than men and, therefore, less likely to be certified; on the contrary African women at Mathari were, he claimed, aggressive and more troublesome than the men.[36] Carothers explained that the behaviour of women on the reserves was stereotyped and, therefore, even psychotics were able to maintain their place within the community. Significantly, women were also less exposed than men to an alien European culture.

According to Carothers, by European standards Africans lived in a world of fantasy. Rather that observing their environment in a detached or scientific way, they projected their own qualities and emotions onto the world about them. When things went wrong

---

A Text-Book of Psychiatry, 8th edition, London: Oxford University Press, pp. 45–59.

[34] Carothers retired at the age of forty-seven in order to be eligible for employment in the British Health Service. At that time, employment was restricted to physicians under the age of fifty.

[35] J. C. Carothers (1940), 'Some Speculations on Insanity in Africans in General', *East African Medical Journal*, 17, pp. 90–105.

[36] A similar pattern was found in the asylum in Southern Rhodesia, for it was among African women at Ingutsheni that the first lobotomies were performed. Presumably as at Mathari, these women were perceived as the most difficult patients to manage. See Carothers, 'Some Speculations', p. 92.

the cause was always found in some external agency, be it gods, enemies or ancestors. The African, Carothers wrote, 'seldom blames himself, but projects his guilt. He sees no sharply defined aspects of reality: wish and truth, possible and impossible, dreams and waking thoughts, phantasy and reality are one to him'.[37] The African family furnished the individual with specific rules for every situation, to such an extent that '...initiative, personal responsibility, self-reliance are foreign to [the] system, and are even suspect'.[38] In situations in which no rule was prescribed, Africans felt lost for they had no experience of accepting responsibility for their own actions. According to Carothers, the common element linking schizophrenia and the African mind was the denial of responsibility: 'The normal African is not schizophrenic, but the step from the primitive attitude to schizophrenia is but a short and easy one'.[39] In traditional society few individuals would have gone mad. Those who became psychotic under European rule did so because they were forced to choose between alternative modes of action or accept responsibility.

The relationship between culture and psychosis was further explored by Carothers in his next article which was titled 'A Study of Mental Derangement in Africans'.[40] It was a review of his seven years at Mathari and contained a discussion of the effects upon mental health of the transition from traditional rural to urban life. Many of the subjects of the study were members of Kenya's nascent proletariat.

Carothers limited himself to the 558 patients admitted in the period from January 1939 until December 1943.[41] That number was, he pointed out, no indication of the actual incidence of mental illness. African communities rarely expelled a member and the sick were cared for within the family; on an average, new arrivals to Mathari had already been nursed at home for a period of six months. Although nine in ten Africans lived on reserves, only half

[37] Carothers, 'Some Speculations', p. 99.

[38] Carothers, 'Some Speculations', p. 100.

[39] Carothers, 'Some Speculations', p. 99.

[40] J. C. Carothers (1948), 'A Study of Mental Derangement in Africans and an Attempt to Explain its Peculiarities, More Especially in Relation to the African Attitude to Life', *Psychiatry*, 11, pp. 47–86.

[41] He excluded military personnel treated at the Military Hospital during the war and patients of Arab descent. Carothers, 'A Study', p. 47.

of Mathari's patients came from that source and it was clear to Carothers that once an African joined the migrant labour force, he became prone to mental illness. Significantly, Carothers did not distinguish between the incidence of mental illness and the reasons for admission to the asylum. He made no attempt to analyse urbanization or the complex process which drew individuals into contact with the Christian churches, secular education, government officials, wage labour and White employers. In his view, the susceptibility of migrant workers to (nervous) breakdown was attributable solely to the structure of the African mind.

Among Mathari's patients mania was common but depressive illness was rare.[42] Of the inmates exhibiting mania, Carothers found that prior to becoming ill most had held positions of responsibility under a European employer, and he was convinced that in attempting to develop self-reliance and initiative they had become deranged. Carothers saw a constant stream of male patients who had committed senseless violent acts such as arson or murder. In such cases, a high level of anxiety was diffused throughout the mind and the individual felt impelled to act. According to Carothers, such behaviour, which he termed frenzied anxiety, '...tended to replace in Africans many of the types of anxiety neurosis, and perhaps some of the depressions, that are seen in Europeans'.[43] Unknown to Carothers, in Algeria Antoine Porot had reached the same conclusion about the Maghrebian Muslim.[44] In circumstances in which a European would develop depressive illness or commit suicide, the African turned instead to arbitrary violence or murder and Carothers's essay, like the work of Porot, carried a clear warning to White employers.

But how accurate were Carothers's findings? Was it common for Black workers to kill White employers? Such crimes were in fact rare but we do know that in British Africa the casual killing of Black workers by White farmers and mine managers for some

[42] During my interviews with Carothers in Portsmouth in October 1986, he also referred to the typical cases of depressive illness he encountered at Mathari. However, in his published work his position on the absence of such illness among the African is consistent with that of his contemporaries.

[43] Carothers, 'A Study', p. 71.

[44] See Antoine Porot and D. C. Arrii (1932), 'L'impulsivite criminelle chez l'indigene algerien: ses facteurs' *Annales Medico Psychologiques*, vol. 90, pp. 588–611.

trivial offence was common. In Southern Rhodesia, for example, there were many cases in which White employers were tried for such murders. The Battlefields and Laidlaw cases of 1908 were justly famous because despite having beaten African employees to death, the White defendants were acquitted by all White male juries thus precipitating a crisis with imperial authorities. What is less well known is how common such cases were. For example, in a period of six months, in 1910, the Salisbury High Court heard seven cases of White on Black homicide. The prevalence of such killings suggests that the ability to control violent impulses was a problem of colonial labour relations, but of a rather different kind to the one envisaged by Carothers and Porot.

Both Carothers's post-war training at The Maudsley and the work of Gordon and Vint concentrated on the brain and its structure rather than on the influence of culture upon behaviour. It is not surprising, therefore, that in his next publication, 'Frontal Lobe Function and the African', Carothers should have turned to physiology.[45] The study arose from a request by the director of laboratory services in Nairobi for a 'test of character' to help in the selection of reliable Africans for employment. Carothers began by reflecting upon the forms of mental derangement which he related, in turn, to personality structure. He also solicited the comments of a number of Europeans who had experience with African workers. Surprisingly, he did not list the qualities required in an efficient employee—indeed, one can best identify such qualities by their absence in his African subjects.

It was conventional wisdom among Whites in Kenya, as elsewhere, that Africans made poor employees and Carothers cited thirty-three examples illustrating their failings in that capacity. The examples, he claimed, revealed an inability to see an event within a context and a tendency to follow blindly routine procedures. They also revealed supposedly a lack of interest unless a situation happened to appeal in a direct or personal fashion.[46] Many of the cases were drawn from the domestic setting where an African was employed as a servant. What is most significant about the case studies is that they can be seen as examples of passive resistance

[45] J. C. Carothers (1951), 'Frontal Lobe Function and the African', *Journal of Mental Science*, 97, pp. 12–48.

[46] Carothers 'Frontal Lobe Function', pp. 31–2.

by a powerless employee. A house boy was instructed never to place black shoes on top of white shoes. He followed that instruction for several days and then reverted back to his old habits which damaged the shoes and infuriated his employer. A house boy would dust certain items in a room but he would fail to keep the rest of the room clean or tidy. House boys could not be taught to put furniture back against a wall or to hang pictures correctly. Carothers assumed that such anecdotes demonstrated a literalism on the part of the servant. More likely, the anecdotes suggest passive resistance against capricious employers rather than stupidity.

According to Carothers, African education precluded the understanding of general rules. Consequently, servants would absorb explicit instructions but fail to comprehend an abstract idea such as tidiness or cleanliness. Africans had no respect for the truth, and their understanding of what was true would vary from one moment to the next.[47] Carothers concluded that the divergence from European notions of normality was so great that the African was hardly an individual.

How, then, were these differences to be explained and what were the prospects for training Africans? In answering these questions Carothers turned once again to psychopathology. As a student at The Maudsley, he had learned of the technique that its originator Egas Moniz called 'prefrontal leucotomy', a procedure which involved destroying part of the patient's brain. The technique was introduced into the United States by Walter Freeman, who during a career spanning three decades carried out hundreds of operations. For a time, he performed the procedure at his New York office using ECT for an anaesthetic and an ice pick for an instrument.[48] The operation was performed on a number of Mathari's inmates and Carothers had access to the patients before and after surgery. He had also read some of the literature on the subject. In general, patients who had undergone surgery displayed

[47] 'If one asks any African a question, he is very apt to give the answer that he thinks you want'. Another way to interpret such behaviour is to locate it within the context of relations between master and servant. See Carothers 'Frontal Lobe Function', p. 31.

[48] See Elliot S. Valenstein (1986), *Great and Desperate Cures: The Rise and Decline of Psychosurgery and Other Radical Treatments for Mental Illness*, (New York: Basic Books, 1986), pp. 84ff.

an emotional shallowness, a loss of creative activity, and a tendency to live in the present. Freeman, patients exhibited a cheerful self-satisfaction and had little desire to learn anything new. Where there was any personality change it usually consisted of an inability to see an event as an element in a total situation; patients could perceive details but not concepts. The portrait struck Carothers as familiar and he observed that except for the ability to verbalize and conjure up fantasies, the resemblance between Africans and leucotomized Europeans was complete. 'It seems not without significance that at least one of the few Europeans leucotomized in Kenya has, since his operation, consorted much more happily with Africans than with Europeans, in marked distinction from his previous behaviour, and to the great embarrassment of his relations'.[49]

It is easy from the vantage point of hindsight to dismiss Carothers's work as reflexive ideology and to accuse him of bad faith or at the least, bad science. However, such an explanation is only adequate if Carothers's views were heterodox, which they were not, and the supposed resemblance between brain-damaged Europeans and Africans was endorsed by other practitioners. In an article published in 1956, C. G. Smartt observed that Africans were unreliable and irresponsible and had little ability to tolerate mental or physical stress. Like leucotomized patients, they lacked initiative; 'There is no doubt that [Carothers's] summary of the changes which may follow leucotomy presents a graphic picture of the East African native; one with which most people who have had experience with Africans would agree'.[50]

By 1948, Carothers had become the most prominent psychiatrist in the field. His work was widely read and well received, and in the immediate post-war era, represented the mainstream of ethnopsychiatric science. During the late colonial period, the standard medical text on illness among the African was Michael Gelfand's *The Sick African.* The monograph, which is over eight hundred pages in length, went through three editions between 1943 and 1957. Gelfand worked at Salisbury Native Hospital and he produced a number of books on the Shona of Zimbabwe. From its second edition, *The Sick African* contained a chapter on

[49] Carothers 'Frontal Lobe Function', p. 38.

[50] C. G. F. Smartt (1956), 'Mental Maladjustment in the East African', *Journal of Mental Science*, 102, p. 444.

mental illness in which Gelfand relied almost entirely upon Carothers.[51]

Conclusion

The portrait of the African presented by Carothers was original in the sense that there was no reference to the African in the psychiatric texts of the day. Even so, in using those texts it is possible to discover its origins. In Henderson and Gillespie's *A Text-Book of Psychiatry*, a reference used by Carothers, there is a clinical profile of the psychopathic type which in various ways resembles Carothers's African.[52] The category dates back to 1835 when a Bristol physician J. C. Pritchard coined the terms 'moral insanity' and 'moral imbecile'. Psychological immaturity prevents the psychopath from adapting to reality or in profiting from experience. He lacks judgment, foresight, and prudence and often behaves like a spoilt child. He is also prone to violence. The disorder was believed to have no specific cause but was attributed to a combination of hereditary and environmental influences. Like many of their contemporaries, Henderson and Gillespie assumed that poverty, divorce, and illegitimacy were major contributing factors. Those factors were important elements in the culture of the British working class whose divergence from middle-class mores was almost axiomatic to the definition of the psychopath. In the case of the African, that divergence was even greater and so the concept could be applied readily to the inhabitants of Britain's African empire. In Carothers's hands, the barely repressed class status of the concept was absorbed into his theory of African inferiority.

Among the ethnopsychiatrists, only Octave Mannoni and Frantz Fanon acknowledged the existence of colonialism and the term appears so rarely in the literature that it is possible to survey the science without being aware of the context in which it was written. The ethnopsychiatrists supposed that their work had nothing to do with politics or wider social processes. They had no formal interest in relations between Black and White communities

[51] See Michael Gelfand (1957), *The Sick African: A Clinical Study*, 3rd edition, Cape Town: Juta.

[52] See D. Henderson and R. D. Gillespie (1956), 'Psychopathic States' in *A Text Book of Psychiatry*, London: Oxford University Press, pp. 389–402.

and they presumed to ignore the ways in which colonial contact had reshaped African societies.

The ethnopsychiatrists did not write about mental illness among settlers, and they rarely discussed White society. It was always present, however, in their language where it appeared as order, reason, standards, discipline, sexual continence, self-control, altruism, and prestige. Its antithesis was savagery, violence, laziness, and sexual promiscuity. Like the concept of race in earlier literatures, the emphasis on the virtues (belonging to Whites) and vices (belonging to Blacks) was so strong that it erased all gradations from representations of both societies. In the place of social complexity it produced a smooth, mythical homogeneity.

By 1945, the colonial system had lost considerable prestige. That loss was reflected in the psychiatric literature and the surviving texts convey something of the nostalgia, resentment, and fear which were the dominant characteristics of settler culture. Settlers were anxious about the potential violence of Africans (Carothers/Porot), they were alarmed by the threat of sexual assault upon White women (Laubscher) and they feared sharing political power (Mannoni, Ritchie). The ethnopsychiatrists idealized European society and refused to recognise the instability of the world in which they lived. While all expatriates tend to view their former homes as static, in the work of Carothers and his contemporaries, the image created of Europe was immutable.

The ethnopsychiatrists acknowledged no distinctions between town and countryside. Even so their texts, like the populations of the asylums, were structured around distinct classes of urban wage labourers and peasants. That distinction was evident in discussions of intellectual work and mental illness. Carothers often wrote of the intellectual failings of Africans and in the work of Gordon, Mannoni, Laubscher and Ritchie there were references to the ill effects of Western education on the African mind. The intellectuals about whom the ethnopsychiatrists wrote were the men and women contesting for political power, and included the leaders of the nationalist generation. The Africans were perceived as deficient in those qualities regarded as essential to citizenship, namely self-governance and the ability to sublimate aggressive impulses.

Most psychiatric texts are fabricated from the case histories of individual patients. In schools as dissimilar as British eclecticism and psychoanalysis, the case study both explicates and justifies the theory. By contrast, within ethnopsychiatry there were few case studies and little reference to the kinds of particularities found in texts about Europeans. With the exception of Wulf Sach's *Black Anger*, there were no biographies and in general, ethnopsychiatry produced a literature without anecdotes. It was also a literature without individuals. Carothers's charges at Mathari were simply Africans, Fanon's patients in Algeria and Tunisia became Muslims, and Mannoni's Malagasy were colonial subjects.

In evaluating their African patients, the ethnopsychiatrists employed a particular category of the person drawn from western European culture. In their hands, however, personhood had less to do with the possession of life plans or consciousness than with self-control, especially in regard to sexual behaviour and the sublimation of aggression. Carothers, for example, deplored the lack of individuality and the rigid conformity to rule, which he believed typified African societies. He felt that native Kenyans should develop the kind of self-control characteristic of the British working class. According to Mannoni, among Africans there was no disharmony between the social being and the inner personality and the individual was held together by the collective shell. Mannoni believed the Malagasy were not individuals.[53] Each of those judgments suggested that Africans were unfit for citizenship or for the right to political equality.

Black wage labourers and urban dwellers formed the majority of the inmates at colonial asylums, and in the lives of their patients the ethnopsychiatrists saw vividly the impact of the new economic relations upon indigenous society. Carothers and his colleagues were the only scientists to study urbanized Africans. Consequently, their position was one from which they could look backwards to the hegemony of White ruling minorities and forwards to the rise of the class which would replace them.

Because the judgments of Carothers were presented as science, they have more to tell us about the colonial relationship than does the self-conscious rhetoric characteristic of political debate. In the science there is a lack of the self-consciousness found in other forums where discourses about race and class were contested. Viewed from the vantage point of almost half a century, the work

[53] See Octave Mannoni (1964), *Prospero and Caliban*, New York: Frederick A. Praeger, p. 41.

of Carothers and his contemporaries appears at best idiosyncratic, but it is only so because of the historical changes which separates the society in which they lived from our own. Their writings are valuable, however, for the testimony they provide into the kinds of perceptions which governed that world.

REFERENCES

Banton Michael (1987). *Racial Theories.* Cambridge: Cambridge University Press.

Beechey Veronica and Donald James (eds) (1985). *Subjectivity and Social Relations.* Milton Keynes: Open University Press.

Biesheuvel S. (1943). *African Intelligence.* Johannesburg: South African Institute of Race Relations.

Burton-Bradly B. G. (1973). *Long-Long: Transcultural Psychiatry in Papua and New Guinea.* Port Moresby: Public Health Department.

Carothers J. C. (1953). *The African Mind in Health and Disease.* Geneva: WHO.

——— (1952). 'Frontal Lobe Function and the African', *The Journal of Mental Science*, 97: 12–48.

——— (1972). *The Mind of Man in Africa.* London: Tom Stacey.

——— (1954). *The Psychology of Mau Mau.* Nairobi: Government Printer.

Corfield F. W. (1960). *Historical Survey of the Origins and Growth of Mau Mau.* London: Her Majesty's Stationary Office.

Cox John L. (1986) (ed.). *Transcultural Psychiatry.* London: Croom Helm.

Devereux George (1980). *Basic Problems of Ethnopsychiatry.* Chicago: University of Chicago Press.

Dubow Saul (1995). *Scientific Racism in Modern South Africa.* Cambridge: Cambridge University Press.

Fanon Frantz (1955). 'Reflections sur l'ethnopsychiatrie'. *Conscience Maghrebine*, 3: 1.

——— (1967). *The Wretched of the Earth.* London: Penguin Books.

Fernando Suman (1988). *Race and Culture in Psychiatry.* London: Croom Helm.

Field Margaret (1960). *Search for Security: An Ethno-Psychiatric Study of Rural Ghana.* New York: Norton & Co.

Galton Francis (1869). *Hereditary Genius: An Inquiry into its Laws and Consequences.* London: J. M. Dent.

——— (1908). *Inquiries into Human Faculty and Its Development.* London: J. M. Dent.

——— (1889). *Narrative of an Explorer in Tropical South Africa.* London: Ward, Lock.

Gelfand M. (1957). *The Sick African*. Cape Town: Juta & Company Ltd.

Heller, Thomas *et al.* (eds) (1986). *Reconstructing Individualism: Autonomy, Individuality, and the Self in Western Thought*. Stanford: Stanford University Press.

Henderson David and R. D. Gillespie (1956). *A Text-Book of Psychiatry*. London: Oxford University Press.

Hirsh S. R. and M. Shepherd (eds) (1974). *Themes and Variations in European Psychiatry*. Bristol: John Wright & Sons.

Howells John (ed.) (1975). *World History of Psychiatry*. London: Bailliere/Tindall.

Kevlis Daniel J. (1985). *In the Name of Eugenics: Genetics and the Uses of Human Heredity*. New York: Alfred A. Knopf.

Kiev Ari (1972). *Transcultural Psychiatry*. New York: The Free Press.

Kleinman Arthur (1988). *Rethinking Psychiatry: From Cultural Category to Personal Experience*. New York: The Free Press.

Kuklick Henrika (1993). *The Savage Within: The Social History of British Social Anthropology 1885–1945*. Cambridge: Cambridge University Press.

Lambo T. Adeoye (ed.) (1962). *First Pan-African Psychiatric Conference Report*. Abeokuta.

Laubscher B. J. F. (1937). *Sex, Custom and Psychopathology: A Study of South African Pagan Natives*. London: George Routledge.

Lebra W. (ed.) (1976). *Culture Bound Syndromes, Ethnopsychiatry and Alternate Therapies*. Honolulu: University of Hawaii Press.

Leighton J., H. Alexander *et al.* (1963). *Psychiatric Disorders among the Yoruba*. Ithaca: Cornell University Press.

Littlewood Roland and M. Lipsedge (1982). *Aliens and Alienists*. London: Penguin Books.

Mannoni Octave (1964). *Prospero and Caliban*. New York: Frederick A. Praeger.

McCulloch Jock (1983). *Black Soul, White Artefact: Fanon's Clinical Psychology and Social Theory*. New York: Cambridge University Press.

——— (1995). *Colonial Psychiatry and the 'African Mind'*. Cambridge: Cambridge University Press.

Manganyi N. Chabani (1991). *Treachery and Innocence: Psychology and Racial Difference in South Africa*. London: Hans Zell.

Mead Margaret (1954). 'Review of "The African Mind in Health and Disease"'. *Psychiatry*, 17: 303–6.

Mental Health Disorders and Mental Health in Africa South of the Sahara (1958). CCTA/CSA-WFHM-WHO Meeting of Specialists on Mental Health, Bukava. CCTA Publication No. 35.

Mundy-Castle A. *et al.* (1953). 'A comparative Study of Electroencephalograms of Normal Africans and Europeans of Southern Africa',

Electroencephalography and Clinical Neurophysiology Journal, 5: 533–43.

Orley John (1970). *Culture and Mental Illness*. Makerere: East African Publishing House.

Porot A. and D. C. Arrii (1932). 'L'impulsivite criminelle chez l'indigene algerienses facteurs'. *Annales Medico Psychologiques*, 90: 588–611.

Porot A. and C. Sutter (1939). 'Le primitivisme des indigenes Nord-Africains. Ses incidences en pathologie mentale'. *Sud Medical et Chirurgical*, 226–41.

Porteus Stanley (1969). *A Psychologist of Sorts*. Palo Alto: Pacific Books.

——— (1931). *The Psychology of Primitive People*. New York: Books for Libraries Press.

——— (1937). *Primitive Intelligence and Environment*. New York: MacMillan.

Ritchie J. F. (1968). *The African as Suckling and as Adult: A Psychological Study*. Manchester: Manchester University Press.

Rivers W. H. R. (1926). *Psychology and Ethnopsychology*. London: International Library of Psychology.

Roheim Geza (1925). *Australian Totemism: A Psycho-Analytic Study in Anthropology*. London: George Allen & Unwin.

——— (1950). *Psychoanalysis and Anthropology*. New York: International Universities Press.

Sachs W. (1947). *Black Anger*. New York: Grove Press.

Smith Edwin (1946). *Knowing the African*. London: Lutterworth Press.

Torgovnick Marianna (1990). *Gone Primitive: Savage Intellects, Modern Lives*. Chicago: University of Chicago.

Tooth G. (1950). *Studies in Mental Health in the Gold Coast*. London: Colonial Research Publication no. 6, Colonial Office.

Vaughan Megan (1991). *Curing Their Ills: Colonial Power and African Illness*. London: Polity Press.

Westley David (1993). *Mental Health and Psychiatry in Africa: An Annotated Bibliography*. London: Hans Zell.

WFMH (1987). *Africa Social Change and Mental Health*. New York: World Federation of Mental Health.

5

From Colonial Dependence to Independent Centre: Australian Psychiatry, 1788–1980

Milton J. Lewis

INTRODUCTION

The continuing ties with the empire meant that Australian psychiatry was heavily influenced by British psychiatry for a century and a half from the beginning of European settlement in 1788. Until well into the twentieth century, virtually all teachers and a great many practitioners were recruited from Britain, and the 'organic' bias of British psychiatry was reproduced in the Antipodes. Yet, ideas and practice originating in continental Europe and the United States affected Australian psychiatry from the middle decades of the nineteenth century. The American social and cultural experience—an expanding frontier of settlement, an egalitarian, ethos and a continuing influx of immigrants—seemed at times more relevant than that of the mother country. Moreover, from 1856, when colonial medical journals began to be continuously published, they carried reports on psychiatry, as they did on other branches of medicine, in the United States and Western Europe. British reports may have predominated but colonial practitioners at the periphery were eager for information on the latest developments, wherever they occurred in European and American centres of medical innovation and best practice.

Local social, cultural and political factors also shaped psychiatry in Australia. Criminality and insanity were associated from the beginning of the penal colony, and the association continued after the demise of the convict system. In rural areas, gaols were used to hold lunatics. Even in the 1880s, in New South Wales, 60–70 per cent of lunatics had been arrested by police and then committed by magistrates. From quite early, and until quite recently, psychiatry was almost wholly practised within highly bureaucratic public systems in which large, often overcrowded and understaffed, hospitals had environments suited to physical rather than psychological treatments. These poorly resourced hospitals were closed institutions, far removed from community awareness and, therefore, low in the priorities of the democratically elected colonial and State governments which financed them: they were 'out of sight, out of mind'. Neglect by the state continued because citizens themselves were largely indifferent to the welfare of the mentally incapacitated. Social attitudes and values, derived from the mother country but accentuated in a colonial setting, shaped the institutional environment and official policies. A significant tradition of self-help in health and welfare matters, a tradition rooted in nineteenth-century British middle-class values and reinforced by a difficult pioneering experience in a natural environment often inhospitable to European settlement, limited the growth of collective responses even to morally neutral physical health problems. Governments from the outset had been ready to make some public provision for the mentally disordered in the interests of social order and safety. But they continued to be parsimonious in the provision of resources because community attitudes and values were at one with a policy of minimum support for public psychiatric facilities.

THE SOCIAL, ECONOMIC AND POLITICAL DEVELOPMENT OF COLONIAL AUSTRALIA

There has been a long-standing debate about the reasons for settling in Australia. Modern historians have suggested that in addition to providing a new dumping ground for criminals after the loss of the American colonies in 1775, the Botany Bay colony was founded to promote trade with China and to provide supplies for the Navy in the Indian Ocean (Martin, 1978). When embarking with the First Fleet, Governor Arthur Phillip (1738–1814) was instructed to take possession of all territory from Cape York to Tasmania, west to 135° and east to the adjacent islands, and to develop the land with convict labour on government farms and through private lots given to freed prisoners. In the mid-1820s, Britain extended its control to the whole continent. Phillip arrived in January 1788 with 1024 male and female convicts and their civil and military keepers. The immediate environment of the new colony was healthy and unspoilt by permanent human settlement. The aborigines who had occupied the country for 40,000 years were hunter-gatherers and were widely scattered in small 'tribal' groups, free of serious epidemic or endemic diseases as far as is known. They represented no health threat to the Europeans, although the converse was unhappily not the case. Estimates of the total Aboriginal population in 1788 have varied from a figure between 250,000 and 500,000 to claims that numbers in Victoria and New South Wales alone were five times as great. Enormous population decline from infectious disease and social and econogical dislocation followed quickly on European settlement, but by about 1880, a stable state had been attained, with high birth and death rates of about 35 per 1000. With the death rate down to about 16 per 1000 by the 1970s, the aboriginal population was expanding vigorously by 2–2.5 per cent per annum, and at the 1971 Census there were just over 106,000 full and part Aborigines (or fewer than 1 per cent of the total Australian population).

In 1802, the first free settlers arrived. However, European population growth was slow in the convict era, reaching a total of 10,262 in 1809 in New South Wales and 44,588 in 1830; plus in the latter year a minuscule 1172 in the newly founded colony of Swan River (Western Australia), and 24, 279 in Van Diemen's Land (Tasmania). In the 20 years from 1830, the population grew dramatically from 75,981 to 405,356, swelled by free as well as convict immigration. The character of the population changed from one with an excess of males and comparatively few children to one more like a normal European community. The first million of population was reached in 1858, the second million in 1877, the third in 1889, and the fourth in 1905 (Cumpston, 1989). By the 1830s, British opinion had become increasingly critical of the practice of assigning convicts to private employers, seeing it as a form of slavery, and the practice was abolished in 1840. Transportation of convicts to the eastern Australian colonies was ended by

1852, but it was re-started at the request of colonists eager for labour in Western Australia in 1850 and continued until 1868.

The constitutional structure of the early colony was autocratic and power was vested exclusively in the Governor. Judicature Acts of 1823 and 1828 created executive and legislative councils made up of senior officials and private individuals, the latter being nominated. A supreme court was established in New South Wales in 1814 and in Tasmania in 1824. Between 1830 and 1860, constitutional and economic change was rapid and all the colonies except Western Australia achieved responsible self-government by the end of this period. In 1842, an imperial act established in New South Wales a legislature with a two-thirds elected membership. The Australian Colonies Government Act extended this privilege to Victoria, South Australia and Tasmania. By the 1860s, all (including Queensland, which separated from New South Wales in 1859) possessed bicameral legislatures with ministers responsible to the Lower House. Wool and minerals powerfully promoted economic growth in the second half of the century. Sheep farming quickly occupied a vast area of the eastern mainland from Adelaide in the south-west to Brisbane in the north-east. Gold was discovered in New South Wales in 1851 and soon after in much greater quantities in Victoria. It was discovered in southern Queensland in the 1860s, then in the Northern Territory and tropical Queensland in the 1870s, and in very large quantities in Western Australia in the 1890s. Silver, copper and tin discoveries added to the wealth generated by gold. Large capital inflows, private and public, accompanied this great economic expansion. Railway construction assisted the development of rural areas, and during 1875–91, miles laid increased from 1600 to more than 10,000. While not contributing to exports, secondary industry (mainly food, furniture and clothing) developed to meet the quickly growing needs of urban areas. Manufacturing and building construction predominantly taking place in the capital cities accounted for 25 per cent of national product by the end of the 1880s and the larger cities accounted for a considerable portion of population growth. Australia was becoming one of the most highly urbanized counties in the world. The two largest cities, Sydney and Melbourne (each having about a half a million people), were, by the turn of the century, large even by international standards. However, the total population remained small in relation to the physical size of the country: in 1901, when the six colonies federated to form the Australian nation, only 3.8 million, occupying a continent as large as mainland United States (without Alaska). The scattered nature of the population and the small numbers outside the few large cities meant that local government was comparatively weak. Weakness at the local level was combined with a legacy of autocratic government from the convict era so that a tradition of highly centralized administration was established in each colony. Since mental health care was overwhelmingly provided by government, it too had a centrally controlled structure. Private practice of psychiatry developed to any large degree only quite late.

British Psychiatry in the Nineteenth Century

The legal, administrative and institutional models followed by Australian psychiatry were created in England in the first 50 years of the nineteenth century. By the later eighteenth century, pauper lunatics were being accommodated in workhouses and lunatics whose families had sufficient means were lodged in private madhouses. The new urban hospitals established by voluntary effort—St Luke's, London (1751), Manchester Lunatic Hospital (1763), and the York Retreat (1792)—were meant to provide the quality of care which neither the workhouse nor madhouse offered. In the first decades of the nineteenth century, county asylums were established, some on a large scale like the Middlesex Asylum at Hanwell which had 1000 patients. A legislation was progressively enacted which sought to put down abuses (especially the wrongful detention of patients in private establishments) and which provided for inspection, licensing, and regular reporting on institutional conditions. The Lunatics Act of 1845 created a national system of supervision operated by a commission with five lay, three medical and three legal members. The Act also required more detailed forms of certification, the keeping of records of admission, removal, and treatment, and regular notification of admissions, discharges, deaths and escapes or transfers (Jones, 1972).

There were significant innovations in treatment. An eighteenth-century authority, William Cullen, had written that madness was sought to be brought under control by intimidation of the patient as well as by restraint and isolation. The superintendent of

St Luke's, Mr Dunstan, claimed in 1812 that fear was the great key to orderly conduct and employed punishment extensively (Bostock, 1968). But a more humane approach, pioneered in France by Philippe Pinel and his pupil, J. E. D. Esquirol, was beginning to influence British practice. At the York Retreat, Samuel Tuke pioneered moral management. Under the new dispensation, mechanical restraint was minimized. The doctor tried to encourage the development of the 'moral capacities' of the patient: habit, will, character, and perseverance were forces in the patient to be used against insanity. Patients were to learn self-control and so to moderate those feelings, which, out of control, produced insanity. The threat to rational behaviour and order was thus overcome by internal rather than external mechanisms of restraint. Like the poor and the child, the lunatic could be educated in self-help and taught to employ inner resources against his condition (Skultans, 1975). Employment, recreation, classification of patients, and individualized treatment were the main measures used within asylums by the exponents of moral therapy to promote their aim of helping the patient gain control of his or her socially unacceptable behaviour. British doctors like John Conolly, Robert Hall, and W. A. F. Browne applied moral management in the county asylums. Conolly's great achievement at Hanwell was to show that it could be applied successfully in a large institution. But his use of seclusion as an alternative to mechanical restraint for refractory patients—he believed that the successful practice of moral therapy was not possible unless seclusion could be employed—was controversial. Some psychiatrists, especially in the United States, claimed that the use of seclusion effectively stood in the way of the objective of self-control, the primary aim of moral therapy, and reduced it to a mockery (Swomowitz, 1990).

In nineteenth-century British psychiatry, both moral and physical causes were recognized: 'moral' for Victorian psychiatrists had a psychological as well as an ethical dimension. Where moral causes were stressed earlier in the century, the emphasis was placed on the physical basis of insanity—heredity and insanity as a brain disease—in the later decades. Both the internal development of psychiatry itself and its cultural, social, and economic context influenced this change in emphasis. The work of Henry Maudsley and its reception illustrate this shift in emphasis.

With figures like John Charles Bucknill, Daniel Hack Tuke, and

Thomas Clouston, Maudsley came to enjoy an international reputation in the later nineteenth century. His *Physiology and Pathology of Mind* (1867) was translated into Japanese as well as various European languages, and Charles Darwin quoted him in the *Descent of Man* and the *Expression of Emotions*. Maudsley clearly discounted the possibility of encouraging the self-development considered central to moral management. It would be quite useless to inculcate rules for self-formation when character itself developed only slowly and this development followed an immutable path.

Although somewhat isolated from medicine itself, psychiatry could not ignore the deepening knowledge of physical processes and systems being established by medical researchers. Bichat's tissue theory of disease was followed by German research in the later nineteenth century which localized the source of disease in the cells. Rudolf Virchow postulated that diseases resulted when severe stimuli disturbed the life processes of the cells. Moreover, the overgrowing success of bacteriology in establishing that the causes of major diseases were specific microbic pathogens challenged psychiatry to find the physical substrates of madness. Pervasive medical concern with syphilis as a protean cause of illness and death and the linkage established between syphilis and general paresis (a very common contemporary cause of insanity) more specifically encouraged a physicalist bias within psychiatry. This emphasis on the physical causes of insanity, incidentally, supported the doctor's claim to leadership in the care of the lunatic because only he had the expertise to deal with illness arising from brain disease. The pervasive ideological influence of Darwinian evolutionary theory, in stressing the concept of the survival of the fittest, encouraged the idea that the lunatic and the idiot were unfit stock destined to be eliminated in the evolution of the race. Not only was treatment unlikely to be successful, it worked against the longer-term health of the race by allowing defectives to reproduce. Growth in the size of institutions made moral management increasingly difficult to pursue because it required personalized care of the patient. Public institutions, already large, became larger as the insane poor were removed from the workhouse to asylum. Further, the sheer accumulation of chronic cases encouraged custodialism and therapeutic pessimism.

Ideas about treatment were related to more general ideas about the nature of society, which, in turn, related to the social and economic order. The powerful belief in progress, which sustained philosophical individualism and the doctrine of self-help in earlier Victorian Britain, faltered in the later nineteenth century in the face of vigorous international challenges to British economic and political power and internal threats to the middle-class sense of security from the rise of organized labour and from revelation of the extent of poverty by social investigators like Booth in London and Rowntree in York. The appeal of the physicalist notion of defective heredity as the cause of poverty, crime, insanity, and other social ills became irresistible (Skultans, 1975, 1979).

PSYCHIATRY IN AUSTRALIA IN THE NINETEENTH CENTURY

COMMITTAL

In the early colony, the Governor's authority was almost absolute. Phillip's commission gave him the right to exercise the Crown's powers to confine lunatics and idiots in order to protect the community and to preserve their personal estates: 'Wee (sic) have thought fit to entrust you with the care and commitment (sic) of the said ideots (sic) and lunaticks (sic) and their estates and Wee (sic) do by these presents give and grant unto you full power and authority to give order and warrant for the preparing of grants of the custodies of such ideots (sic) and lunaticks (sic)... as are... found by inquisitions thereof to be taken by the Judges of our Court of Civil Jurisdiction and thereupon to make grants... and commitments (sic)... to such person or persons... as according to the rules of law... you shall judge meet for that trust...' (Bostock, 1968).

Committal procedure developed along two lines. Where a person of some means was involved, a jury decided whether incapacity existed. Where it did, the court appointed trustees to manage his affairs and private individuals (after creation of an asylum, the superintendent) to take care of his person. The writ, *de lunatico inquirendo*, under which the process was carried out, was first employed in Sydney in 1828. Blackstone, the great authority on English law, had said of this legal process: 'By the old common law there is a writ *de idioto inquirendo*, to inquire whether a man be an idiot or not; which must be tried by a jury of twelve men... it seldom happens that a jury finds a man idiot *a navitate*, but only *non compos mentis* for some particular time... if he be found *non compos*, he usually commits the care of his person, with a suitable allowance for his maintenance, to some friend who is then called his committee' (Cummins, 1973). After the Lunacy Act of 1878 created the position of Master in Lunacy, he took over responsibility for administration of estates of those declared insane. In the early colony, where a pauper or convict was concerned, the common law procedure by writ was not followed. The committal process was launched by a magistrate's order or surgeon's opinion, and the lunatic was kept in gaol or hospital at the Governor's pleasure.

INSTITUTIONAL DEVELOPMENT

Governor Lachlan Macquarie (1762–1824) established the first asylum at Castle Hill to the west of the main settlement at Sydney Cove, in 1811. He cautioned the superintendent to ensure that the keepers, most of whom were convicts, did not 'exercise any unnecessary severity towards the lunatics, but see they are at all times treated with mildness, kindness, and humanity' (Dax, 1975). As was to happen so often with later institutions, the asylum quickly became overcrowded, and Governor Ralph Darling (1775–1858) removed the inmates to the renovated but inadequate courthouse building at Liverpool, where overcrowding again soon developed. By the late 1830s, the Liverpool Asylum housed fifty males and thirty females (half of whom were convicts) for whom twelve handcuffs, one leg iron and six straight waistcoats were available when restraint was needed. The lay superintendent, Thomas Plunkett, had earlier been superintendent of the convict barracks at Parramatta. In 1838, Tarban Creek Asylum was opened because Liverpool had become too overcrowded. The new institution (which was absorbed into the larger Gladesville Asylum later in the century) was built specifically as an asylum and was to house sixty patients. It received patients by sea from Port Phillip (Melbourne), 600 miles to the south until the opening of a local asylum, Yarra Bend, in 1848, and Yarra Bend remained officially a ward of Tarban Creek until the colony of Victoria separated from New South Wales in 1850. A layman, Joseph Thomas Digby, was brought out from England to run the new institution at Tarban Creek. He was the steward and his wife was the matron. They had been employed for some years at St Luke's Hospital, London, under the supervision of Dr Alexander Sutherland, a well-known psychiatrist of the time. During 1838–46, 311 males and 178 females came to the institution, suffering variously from 'acute mania', 'ordinary insanity', 'monomania', 'melancholia', 'dementia', 'idiocy', 'paralysis', 'epilepsy', 'homicidal insanity', 'imbecility', and 'puerperal insanity'. From the late 1840s, convicts were not admitted and were housed in a convict institution at Parramatta, west of Sydney (Bostock, 1968; Dax, 1975). Digby was responsible to the Governor and not the Principal Surgeon (the head of the colonial medical service). The lunacy establishment remained administrtively separate from the government medical services thereafter. Sir George Gipps (1791–1847), who was Governor from 1837, had stated the position clearly: 'The lunatic asylum is not a hospital; it therefore is not under the charge of the Deputy Inspector General of Hospitals, though in the management of it, it will often be necessary to have the benefit of his advice' (Dax, 1975).

Like reformers in England, Joseph Digby tried to minimize physical restraint at Tarban Creek, even in the face of lack of resources and administrative problems. In the 1840s, Digby was replaced by a doctor, Francis Campbell, and so the modern era of medical control of psychiatric institutions was inaugurated in Australia at about the same time as in England. Campbell, who was superintendent from 1846 to 1867, also favoured a policy of non-restraint and employed moral therapy: 'Restraints and their application not only retard the cure, but frequently drive the insane to despair for while they subdue the man, they exasperate and degrade the mind' (Swomowitz, 1990).

As the other Australian colonies were created, asylum facilities were established. Too often these became overcrowded and too often patients were neglected and ill-treated. The convict heritage meant that a penal mentality dominated the behaviour of the attendant staff, who in any case lacked nursing training. The commissioners in charge of Tasmania's New Norfolk Asylum (originally a convict hospital) complained in 1855: 'The internal accommodations...were small, badly constructed, ill ventilated, dark and dismal.... The principle of the treatment of the patients generally was one of coercion, which in the case of the excited or refractory, was carried out by the familiar resort to the strait waistcoat' (Brown, 1972). Queensland's Woogaroo Lunatic Asylum was opened in 1865 after an imperial inquiry into colonial hospitals and asylums criticized the use of gaols to accommodate lunatics and after the Brisbane gaol itself had become very overcrowded. In the same year, Western Australia opened its carefully planned asylum but within a few years overcrowding was such that patients could not be properly classified. Yerra Bend, Victoria's first asylum, opened in 1848, and five years later, it too was overcrowded. A medical superintendent, Robert Bowie, replaced the layman in charge, who had quarrelled with the resident medical officer. In this way Victoria, like New South Wales, and the mother country, accepted medical control of asylums from about mid-century. Victoria's population grew spectacularly with the gold rushes of the 1850s and the government decided to construct a new institution on the model of the progressive Colney Hatch Asylum in England. About a decade after its establishment as colony, South Australia opened its first permanent asylum in 1852. Yet, even in 1855, twenty-eight patients were still lodged in Adelaide gaol. The poor conditions of Australian asylums were paralleled in the public asylums of the mother country. Overcrowding and poor standards quickly came to dominate the county asylums in England, as their historian has noted: 'Even as the new county asylums were built... the system was becoming the System.... Perhaps the causes lay elsewhere—in the pressure of the relentlessly growing population which kept the asylums constantly overcrowded; in the local parsimony and unimaginativeness which dragged down standards and turned good new ideas into bad old ones' (Jones, 1972). In Australia, attempts were made to reform facilities, most notably by Frederic Norton Manning in New South Wales following the 1878 Lunacy Act, but the general tendency was for institutions to revert to type, and inadequate accommodation remained the norm. A Victorian board of inquiry reported in the early 1880s that in Sunbury Asylum: 'The exercise yards are so muddy in winter that they are quite unfit to be used... They (the patients) never know what it is to have a hot dinner...' (Brothers, 1962). At the same time, a report on New Norfolk Asylum stated, 'A large part of the accommodation...is dark, comfortless, and quite unfit for the curative treatment of insane persons...an unwise parsimony has for some time been exercised in the control of the institution' (Brown, 1972). An 1877 Queensland Royal Commission concluded that 'Woogaroo suffered from mistaken...economy on the part of the government', and a major inquiry of 1915 found that conditions were to a large extent as bad as they had been forty years earlier (Evans, 1969, Report of Royal Commission, 1915).

LEADING CONCEPTS IN AUSTRALIAN PSYCHIATRY

English-born and trained Frederic Norton Manning, New South Wales Inspector General of the Insane, was the leading figure in colonial psychiatry. President of the Psychological Medicine Section at the Intercolonial Medical Congress of 1887 and the Congress of 1889—the Congress was the only national forum for medicine in this period—Manning espoused the prevailing British view that insanity was a 'disease of the brain', not a 'disorder of the intellect' to be cured by moral therapeutic intervention. One historian of late nineteenth-century British psychiatry has written recently: 'As Victorian asylums silted up with the chronically crazy...so Victorian psychiatry moved steadily towards a grim determinism, a view of madness as the irreversible produce of mental degeneration and decay.... The profession's rigid and pessimistic somaticism, while it appeared to leave but little scope for expert intervention, had the compensating advantage of explaining away psychiatry's dismal therapeutic performance' (Scull, 1993). Manning publicly urged his colleagues to become more concerned with neurology and to view insanity as a condition basically like a physical disorder: '...we have gravitated...round psychology, and it is only of comparatively late years that we have recognized that diseases of the cerebrum are only a part of the great subject of diseases of the nervours system' (Manning, 1989). He was impressed by the idea of hereditary degeneracy, which, originating with the French psychiatrist, A. B. Morel, came to enjoy a wide influence in medicine and psychiatry across Europe. For Manning, mental illness was progressive over successive generations, with idiocy and imbecility being the final stages of this terrible legacy of degeneration.

Now that psychiatry was focused on the physical causes of insanity, much effort went into the search for brain lesions as the somatic substrates of 'madness'. In England and Scotland, pathologists were appointed to the larger asylums and the postmortem search for lesions was systematically pursued. The pathological work of men like Frederick Mott, a student of Henry Maudsley, was seen as being at the frontier of knowledge. Inevitably, the number of postmortems expanded. In 1870, autopsies were performed on 42 per cent of inmates who died in English asylums, but in 1890 they were carried out in just under 77 per cent of cases. Neuropathology became popular, too, in the Australian colonies. New South Wales and Victoria, which possessed the largest populations and so had the largest asylum systems, appointed specialist pathologists at the turn of the century.

Even in the nineteenth century, Australian colonial psychiatry and medicine could look beyond the mother country for new ideas and approaches. One important example was the treatment of alcoholism. In Australia, as in other parts of the Western world, inebriety in the later nineteenth century came to be viewed by the medical profession and the state as a disease to be cured rather than a crime to be punished. Some colonies adopted inebriate legislation permitting the committal and compulsory treatment of alcoholics akin to the procedures followed with the insane under the lunacy statutes. Prior to this legislation, inebriates were commonly admitted to lunatic asylums, and even after its enactment, psychiatric institutions were often designated reception centres for alcoholics under compulsory treatment orders. Inebriate asylums in the United States were the inspiration for the leaders of the treatment reform movements in the Australian colonies and, indeed, in the United Kingdom itself. As early as 1830, the Connecticut State Medical Society had wanted a specialist inebriate asylum to be established, and Samuel Woodward, patriarch of institutional psychiatry in America, had published *Essays on Asylums for Inebriates* in 1838. The impressive cure rates reported by the pioneers of the inebriate retreat movement in the United States were never achieved in Australia, and this had much to do with the much less select and more recidivist nature of the population usually treated in the very custodial environments of the few public facilities in this country. For this and other reasons (like the notable decline in per capita consumption of alcoholic beverages here), the treatment movement had virtually disappeared by the 1930s, only to revive with the upswing in consumption of alcohol in the 1950s and 1960s (Lewis, 1992).

Psychiatry in the Twentieth Century

In Britain, psychiatry continued largely to pursue a physicalist model of mental illness despite the fact that psychotherapeutic techniques were shown to be effective in the treatment of battle neuroses in World War I. The term, 'shell-shock', itself indicates a desire to establish a physical cause of neurotic breakdown. But with large numbers of 'shell-shock' patients cured by psychotherapy, British Army medical services finally accepted officially the psychogenic nature of 'shell-shock'. The Maudsley Hospital in London became a centre for treatment of such neuroses and psychodynamic ideas won a small foothold in British psychiatry when Hugh Crichton-Miller, who had worked with shell-shock patients, established the Tavistock Clinic in 1920 (Dicks, 1970). Australian Army medical services shared the physicalist outlook of the British. However, a few psychiatrists, notably Major A. W. Campbell of Sydney, supported a psychogenic approach. Special facilities were created for military patients so that they could avoid the stigma of certification. Indeed, for some years senior psychiatrists had been pressing governments for establishment of early treatment facilities in public hospitals for all psychiatric patients, and the first voluntary civilian patients were admitted to New South Wales asylums in 1915. 'Neurasthenic' military patients were treated at the new Broughton Hall facility in Sydney and by June 1918, the following military psychiatric hospitals were in operation: Broughton Hall, New South Wales, 71 beds; Mont Park, Victoria, 42 beds; and Cottesloe, Western Australia, 30 beds. From 1921, Broughton Hall, under the first superintendent, S. E. Jones, one of the few Australian psychiatrists to espouse Freudian ideas, became a centre for treatment of civilian neurosis cases.

The dominance of the somaticists both in Britain and in Australia limited the interwar impact of psychotherapy, despite its achievements in the First World War. In Australia in the early 1930s, the great importance of heredity in the aetiology of mental disorder could still be strongly claimed, even if the moderating effects of 'good environment' and 'appropriate education' could be equally asserted. W. A. Lind of the Victorian Lunacy Department could argue in the 1926 Beattie Smith lectures—these lectures, named after a prominent Victorian psychiatrist of the late nineteenth century, were the main public forum for discussion of psychiatry in the interwar period—that vulnerability of the neurones was the royal road to understanding of mental disorder. He vehemently rejected depth psychology's emphasis on unconscious motivation, dismissing analysis as no more than suggestion (Lind, 1926). The very organization of psychiatric practice limited the expan-sion of psychological treatments. The state psychiatric services remained the centre of practice; private practice was little developed; and psychiatry was largely divorced from general medicine. The bulk of patients remained incarcerated in large, isolated asylum-hospitals.

Psychoanalytic ideas reached Australia quite quickly, even if most psychiatrists were sceptical of their usefulness. Enthusiasts David Fraser and Andrew Davidson arranged in 1909 for Freud to be invited to the Australasian Medical Congress. While Freud did not attend, he, C. G. Jung, and sexologist Havelock Ellis sent papers to be read at the 1911 Australasian Medical Congress. Frued told a colleague: 'Then two days ago a new continent announced itself. The Secretary of the Neurological Section of the Austrlian Congress... asks for a short account of my theories which is to be printed in the reports of the Congress since they are still quite unknown in Australia' (Gold, 1982). In 1913, the *Australian Medical Journal* found merit in psychoanalysis as a treatment for neurosis, even if assumptions about sexual symbolism in dreams were often preposterous (Anon, 1913). Many senior psychiatrists assigned at best small place to Freudian ideas. In 1923, the University of Sydney had established the first Chair of Psychiatry in Australia and appointed Sir John Macpherson, a traditionalist from Britain, to the post. He told the 1924 Australasian Medical Congress that he was unable to accept 'this one speculative conception of the fixation of the libido' as the cause of mental illness (Macpherson, 1926). Sydney psychiatrist, John McGeorge asserted that the theory of infantile sexuality was quite misguided: 'When an enthusiastic Freudian explains a child's natural timidity... as the expression of a repressed sadistic impulse, it gives one cause to wonder to what absurd... ends this pseudo-science will eventually go in an attempt to explain natural tendencies and instincts' (McGeorge, 1936). But some influential psychiatrists were ready to reconcile depth psychology with neuropathology. W. S. Dawson replaced Macpherson in the chair at Sydney in 1927. British-trained Dawson had done postgraduate work with Adolf Meyer in the United States and he introduced into the Sydney curriculum many aspects of Meyer's approach, thus helping to move Australian students away from a colonial dependence upon Britain and into the international mainstream. Dawson said soon after his arrival in Australia: 'Present day psychiatry appears chaotic unless it is recognized that the theories advanced by Freud,

Jung, Janet, Morton Prince, and Kretschner... are not so much antagonistic as complementary...' (Dawson, 1928). Drawing on Hughlings Jackson's conception of malfunctioning of the nervous system being responsible for two types of symptoms—negative ones due to suspension of function and positive ones due to the activity of levels normally under the control of the higher damaged level—Dawson proposed that this approach was reconcilable with that of the psychological school: Freud's concept of the ego could be viewed as the highest level of integration functioning in the physiological state of attention, the psychological counterpart of which is consciousness; impairment of the highest level by organic lesion or fatigue produced variable degrees of disintegration and phenomena recognized as evidence of mental illness.

In Britain and the United States, psychological treatments were widely employed with military patients during World War II. Group therapy, which had the practical benefit of getting limited professional expertise to a much larger number of patients, was commonly employed, and the idea of a therapeutic community, as developed by Maxwell Jones and D. H. Clarke, involved patients as well as staff in the management of treatment. These new approaches were quickly taken up in Australia. In the late 1940s, Paul Dane introduced analytically oriented group therapy into civilian practice. New types of briefer individual psychotherapy began to be applied here. Non-Freudian psychotherapy such as the client-centred approach of American psychologist Carl Rogers also appeared, although this was probably more influential in counselling circles outside the realm of psychiatry itself. Psychodynamic concepts and ideas became more widely established after the Second World War, even if psychoanalysis itself continued to enjoy only a minor place in psychiatric practice in this country.

Freudians established a permanent presence by setting up training facilities in Melbourne in 1940, only a decade after the first American training institute was opened in New York. A handful of Melbourne psychiatrists, supported by R. C. Winn of Sydney and Ernest Jones of London, brought into being the Melbourne Institute for Psychoanalysis, and Clara Lazar-Geroe, who had trained in the school of Ferenczi in Budapest, was appointed training analyst. The British Medical Association (in Australia) was disturbed at the idea that this foreign analyst should direct training but was reassured by the argument put forward by a leading neurologist that it was preferable to have the institute under medical direction than see analysts functioning independently as osteopaths were, regrettably, doing. The institute operated at first under the auspices of the British Psychoanalytical Society but once enough local analysts were practicising, an Australian society was formed. A bequest from R. C. Winn allowed the Sydney Institute to open in 1951 and Andrew Peto, former Secretary of the Hungarian Psychoanalytical Society, became training analyst there. By the early 1960s, two Australian practitioners had been accredited as training analysts. But there were only eight trained analysts in practice in the whole country—four in Melbourne, three in Sydney, and one in Adelaide—although an unknown number of psychiatrists had undergone a personal analysis. By 1980, there were only twenty-eight full and associate members of the Australian Psychoanalytical Society. These figures may be compared with the following: at the end of the 1970s, the Royal Australian and New Zealand College of Psychiatrists had in New South Wales 72 psychiatrists, and in Victoria, 60 psychiatrists training for membership (Opit and Donnan, 1979) and there was a total of 1123 Fellows and Members of the College (Cramond, 1981). The number of psychiatrists in Australia had grown dramatically during the 1960s and 1970s. Between 1970 and 1976, New South Wales recorded an increase of 64 per cent, while the other States experienced growth of between 35 and 50 per cent. Moreover, where, hitherto, most psychiatrists had worked in the public sector, in the state psychiatric services, from 1970, growth in the population of psychiatrists occurred mainly outside the state facilities. The significant expansion of private practice was underpinned by a fee-for-service national health care system financed by private insurance and heavily subsidized by the federal government. This system had been established by post-war Conservative administrations.

Entry of Australian Psychiatry into the International Mainstream

In the interwar period, movement away from a colonial dependence of British psychiatry is clearly discernible and by the end of the 1930s entry into the international mainstream of psychiatric ideas, practice, and policy has been achieved. Complete location in the mainstream comes after the Second World War, even if elements of the special historical connection with the United Kingdom remain visible. In the interwar years, the new physical treatments developed overseas were quickly applied here. Such treatments were appealing not only because they seemed to have some effectiveness but because they were compatible with the prevailing institutional environments where large numbers of patients were under the care of a small number of doctors, most of whom favoured a somaticist approach. In 1927, Wagner von Jauregg received the Nobel prize for medicine for his successful treatment of general paralysis of the insane (GPI) by induction of malaria. From the late 1920s, induced malaria therapy was used in Australian psychiatric hospitals, with reasonable results, on patients with GPI. Thus, Dawson (1928) reported that over a two-year period, 191 patients had received malaria therapy and 33.5 per cent were discharged as improved, while 20 per cent had died from GPI. In the late 1930s, patients with schizophrenia and with depressive psychosis were treated with insulin and cardiazol 'shock' therapy at first, and, during the next decade, with electro-convulsive therapy (ECT). A controversial therapy, medically and ethically, ECT did, nevertheless, allow some chronic patients to leave hospital, and it reduced the incidence of suicide in psychiatric hospitals. Psychosurgery, like ECT, a treatment around which much controversy developed, was introduced in the 1940s to relieve severe and continuing depression and, later, to control aggressive behaviour. If the speedy application of the physical treatments developed overseas was one instance of movement into the international mainstream of psychiatry, another was the taking root of psychoanalytic training here, as discussed above. Yet another was the growth of branches of the international mental hygiene movement in the 1930s.

Prevention came to assume much greater significance in the interwar period and psychiatrists not only sought to educate the medical profession and the general community about the need for early treatment and prevention, but worked with interested lay people in mental hygiene councils to further the cause of mental health by trying to remove the stigma of mental disorder and by providing information on such matters as normal child development in public lectures, in radio talks and in the print media.

Child guidance clinics, hospital clinics for 'nervous' children and adolescents, and centres for psychometric testing and other work with the intellectually handicapped were established. Influenced strongly by eugenist ideas, progressive psychiatrists were keen to identify and segregate the hereditarily unfit from those who might benefit from treatment. Indeed, the mental hygiene movement concerned itself with a growing range of socially deviant behaviours and the concept of mental disorder was expanded to 'psychiatrise' all forms of social maladjustment: as Clifford Beers (1932), a former psychiatric patient from America and founder of what became an international mental hygiene movement (of which the Australian movement was one branch), affirmed: '...psychiatric studies of crime, delinquency, dependency, suicide, and other social problems have thrown considerable light upon the relationship of abnormal behaviour to states of mental health. In consequence, mental hygiene now deals with all forms of human behaviour, including those not formally considered as matters of health'.

Australian delegates attended the first International Mental Health Hygiene Congress in Washington in 1930. Soon after, the *Medical Journal of Australia* noted approvingly that the aim of the movement had broadened from better treatment of the mentally disabled to conservation of the mental well-being of the entire community (Clifford Beers,1932). In 1932, one of the pioneers of the movement here and a delegate to the 1930 Congress, psychiatrist Ralph Noble, became Clinical Professor of Mental Hygiene at Yale University in the United States. The considerable growth of treatment facilities outside the public psychiatric hospitals, the wider medical and community acceptance of the mental hygiene movement's message about prevention, and psychiatry's emphasis on differentiating curable and incurable patients contributed to a fundamental change in the nature of the patient popu-lation. In addition, underlying these psychiatric factors was a basic demographic shift, as the very masculine composition of colonial population gave way with natural growth and immigration to a more normal distribution of the sexes. The typical late nineteenth-century patient in New South Wales was a single, male unskilled worker apprehended by police for drunken or violent behaviour, considered dangerous or a public nuisance, and commonly diagnosed as manic. But the typical patient of the 1930s was a single, female domestic servant or a married woman, diagnosed as severely depressed or suffering from anxiety neurosis. She was not considered dangerous except to herself (Garton, 1988). In its treatments, in its emphasis on prevention and in the changing nature of its patient population, Australian psychiatry was fast merging with the international mainstream by the outbreak of World War II.

This process of merging was completed in the postwar decades. New treatments and treatment facilities developed overseas were applied here almost as soon as in the Atlantic heartland of modern psychiatry, the United States and Western Europe. The self-confidence of international psychiatry, growing stronger with its claims to expertise in many new areas of deviance in the interwar years, peaked in the 1950s and 1960s. With the arrival of the psychotropic drugs, for the first time, the socially debilitating symptoms of the major psychiatric afflictions could be alleviated to the point where many more patients could be allowed to leave institutions and return to the community. Here, the new community-based facilities offered them further support. Chronic wards were transformed, and although enthusiasts overestimated the wonder-working powers of the new drugs, they did contribute to a major reorientation of psychiatry in Australia and in other parts of the Western world, as one senior Queensland psychiatrist recognized: '...the treatment of chronic schizophrenia by phenothiazine drugs alone has proved far more effective than psychotherapy, ECT, or combinations of either of these three methods of management' (Whitlock, 1979).

'Deinstitutionalization' gathered momentum. In the 1950s and 1960s, open-door policies had been introduced into Australian psychiatric hospitals as they had been in the United Kingdom and elsewhere. Voluntary admissions had increased—in South Australia, for example, from twenty-nine in 1955–6 to 1022 ten years later. But discharges also increased—from the main Western Australian hospital, for example, from ninety to 100 a year in the mid-1950s to almost 190 in 1960. Pioneers of community psychiatry in the United States in the 1960s hailed it as the third psychiatric revolution. Through crisis intervention and early treatment, and, at one step further removed, through mental health education, community psychiatry would prevent unnecessary hospitalization. In addition, it would help maintain patients discharged from institutions in the community. Supporters of community psychiatry in Australia likewise had great expectations of the new approach. The Director of Psychiatric Services in New South Wales confidently reported in 1969: 'There has been a considerable growth of community services during the past year... reduction of resident patients in psychiatric hospitals in the face of a substantial increase in the number of patients... can only be... effected with humanity and safety if there is a corresponding growth in community mental health services...' (Report of Director Psychiatric Services, 1969).

The outlook for community-based services became clouded in the course of the 1970s. One problem was reduced Federal (or Central Government) funding. In the early 1970s, the socially progressive Whitlam Labour Government introduced comparatively generous funding for community mental health services, but the advent of harsher economic conditions and the election of the conservative Fraser Liberal-Country Party Administration meant that in the later 1970s, funds became restricted. Another problem was inherent in the development of community services: their objectives were too often left general and little emphasis was placed on identification of specific goals. From the outset there had been dispute about whether patients in the community were gaining self-reliance from deinstitutionalization or just being neglected. Reviewing community psychiatry in 1975, the *Medical Journal of Australia* cited the troubling findings of a recent study of patients discharged from New South Wales institutions. The study concluded that while patients claimed they were happier out of the hospital, placement in the community amounted to no more than the substitution of one type of institution for another (Whitlock, 1975). In Australia, as earlier in the United States and Britain, the effectiveness of community psychiatry (whether in the narrower sense of treating psychiatric disorders in the community or in the broader sense of preventing disorders by influencing social conditions) was increasingly questioned.

Just as in the United States, the United Kingdom and Europe, in the 1960s and 1970s, psychiatry here was subjected to a growing volume of criticism from a broad alliance of new social groups, protesting about the oppression of 'minorities'—women, students, Blacks, gays and lesbians, and psychiatric patients—and seeking fundamental cultural change rather than the narrower political and economic goals of traditional Left-wing reformers. Inspired by libertarian, anarchist and humanist notions, looking for guidance to individual experience and feeling, and pursuing immediate action in a co-operative mode, and personal as well as political civil liberties, these liberationists saw all existing authority as oppressive. They saw psychiatry not as a benevolent means of rehabilitation of the mentally suffering but as a major form of social control upholding the norms of male-dominated, heterosexual, White society. The anti-psychiatry movement drew powerfully on the views of critics within the psychiatric profession itself. American psychiatrist Thomas Szasz and British psychiatrist Ronald Laing shared the position that psychiatry is an inherently political activity devoted to the defence of established power structures by pacifying those social 'rebels' labelled the mentally ill. Szasz rejected the reality of mental (as opposed to physical) illness, and argued that psychiatry, as much as law itself, is concerned with the upholding of dominant norms of conduct. Laing proposed that the psychiatrist, in conspiracy with the family whose deviant member is conveniently labelled a patient, abrogates the rights of the patient. Women's and gay liberation groups pursued their own critiques of psychiatry. They asserted that women and homosexuals were labelled mentally ill when they were in fact expressing the pain an anger produced by an inescapably oppressive society. Psychiatrists, misguidedly seeing individual problems and illnesses when the basic problem was social and cultural, worked to get patients to conform in attitude and behaviour to prevailing social norms and roles. Feminists complained that their analysis was seen by orthodox psychiatry not as a serious critique but a collective expression of neuroses widespread among liberationists. Gay critics complained that the history of psychiatric therapies for male homosexuality was one of unpleasant experiments ending in abject failure. One of the more abhorrent experiments, they said, was psychosurgery. It was employed much more widely in the United States and Europe than in Australia and was employed to change the sexual preference of gay men. Indeed, only one team, is known to have used the technique for this purpose here (Bates, 1977), (Bates and Wilson, 1979). While the anti-psychiatry movement in this country got under way somewhat later, and it was never as visible as in the United States, Australian psychiatrists had an early taste of the militancy of the movement when protesters disrupted an American–Australasian Psychiatric Congress in San Francisco in 1969 (Edward, 1978).

Criticism of psychiatry was not confined to the liberationist movement. During the 1970s, law reformers and those concerned about civil liberties, became increasingly vocal about what they saw as the excessive discretion permitted to psychiatrists in the management of patients. They called for recognition in law of the patient's right to freedom, to maintenance of reputation, and to adequate representation. The more radical wanted recognition of the patient's right to refuse treatment and abandonment of controversial physical therapies like psychosurgery and ECT. A number of states began to inquire into procedures affecting the rights of patients, and in particular, gave consideration to introduction of quasi-judicial reviews of the mental health status and treatment of patients. These review bodies would reduce the independent decision-making power of psychiatrists. In New South Wales, the Letts Committee on Patient Care proposed in 1976 that a mental health tribunal should regularly examine the health status of all psychiatric patients. In Queensland, a new mental health legislation in 1974 was intended to balance compulsory treatment (where the person was incapable of rational decision-making) and minimization of loss of freedom. Compulsory admission had to be supported by a doctor's opinion and a second medical opinion was required within three days of submission. The case could be taken to an appeals tribunal, even against a psychiatrist's report, after 21 days of detention. In South Australia, the new Mental Health Act of 1977 recognized the patient's right to adequate treatment but it also recognized the patient's right to the least loss of freedom consistent with his or her proper protection and that of the community. The Act established a mental health tribunal which was to carry our regular reviews of the status of patients and hear appeals against continuing detention orders (Bates and Wilson, 1979; Kirby, 1981; Clarke, 1988).

CONCLUSION

The development of psychiatry in Australia since the Second World War reflects in its significant features the development of psychiatry in the United States and in the United Kingdom and other parts of Western Europe. The same broad features mark the postwar history here and in the more important countries of the Western world. Whether in psychiatric policy, in treatment approaches and facilities, or in patient populations, Australian psychiatry had become, by the 1980s, an integral part of an international psychiatric culture.

It is true that certain aspects of the legacy of the old imperial connection with Britain continued to operate in postwar decades. In the 1950s, when the Victorian Government had sought an eminent person to supervise a major and, for the time, innovative re-organization of public psychiatric services, they had chosen a distinguished British psychiatrist, E. Cunningham Dax, for the task. As late as 1980, British graduates filled a good many of the most senior academic positions in psychiatry: in Melbourne University, the professor had trained at the Maudsley Hospital, London; at Adelaide University, the two professors who had been head of department were from overseas; at Queensland University, the occupant of the chair was a Cambridge graduate who had been at Newcastle-upon-Tyne; at the University of Western Australia, the three appointees to the chair had come from Britain, as had the professor at Monash University, Melbourne, and both occupants of the chair at the University of Tasmania. However, the fourth occupant of the chair at the University of Sydney (the oldest chair in Australia) was an Australian graduate, as were the holders of the new chairs at the University of Newcastle, New South Wales, and Flinders University, Adelaide (Cramond, 1981). The continuing dependence on Britain for recruitment of senior academic psychiatrists reflects the general lack of a research tradition in Australian universities and the smallness of the academic establishment until after the Second World War. Ph.D. degrees were not available until the later 1940s and able postgraduate students in science and medicine went to Britain, and, in the 1950s, also to the United States. Moreover, career opportunities in universities were very limited until State funding following the Murray report on the condition of Australian universities in the late 1950s created a rapid and unprecen-dentedly large expansion of university positions (Fleming, 1964). Unlike the granting of formal constitutional and political independence, the process of gaining independence in science and medicine, as in other areas of intellectual and professional life, can be an untidy and prolonged affair, marked by fits and start of activity (Fleming, 1964). Progress may not be uniform on all fronts. The progress of Australian psychiatry to independence is no exception. But by the fourth decade after the end of the Second World War, it indisputably functioned as an independent centre of activity contributing to, and receiving contributions from, the mainstream of international psychiatric culture.

REFERENCES

Anon (1913). 'Psychoanalysis'. *Australian Medical Journal*, August, 1161.

Bates E. M. (1977). *Models of Madness*. St Lucia (Q): Queensland University Press.

Bates E. M. and P. R. Wilson (eds) (1979). *Mental Disorder or Madness? Alternative Theories*, St Lucia. (Q): Queensland University Press.

Beers C. W. (1932). 'Mental hygiene', *Med. J. Aust.*, 2: 235–6.

——— (1952). *A mind that found itself: An autobiography*. New York: Doubleday.

Bostock J. (1968). *The dawn of Australian psychiatry: An account of the measures taken for the care of mental invalids from the time of the First Fleet, 1788 to the year 1850*. Sydney: Australian Medical Association.

Brothers G. R. (1962). *Early Victorian Psychiatry, 1835–1905*. Melbourne: Mental Hygiene Authority.

Brown J. C. (1972). *Poverty is not a crime. The development of social services in Tasmania, 1803–1900*. Hobart: Tasmanian Historical Research Association.

Clarke J. (1988). 'Scientists as intellectuals' in B. Head and J. Walter (eds). *Intellectual movements and Australian society*. Melbourne: Oxford University Press.

Cramond W. A. (1981). 'The overseas contribution to Australia 1950–80'. *Australian and New Zealand Journal of Psychiatry*, 15: 199–204.

Cummins C. J. (1979). *A History of Medical Administration in New South Wales, 1788–1973*. Sydney: Health Commission of NSW.

Cumpston J. H. L. (1989). *Health and Disease in Australia: A history* (Introd. and ed. M. J. Lewis). Canberra: AGPS Press.

Dawson W. S. (1928). 'The integration concept applied to psychiatry'. *Med. J. Aust.*, 1: 265–70.

——— (1928). 'The treatment of general paralysis by malaria'. *Med. J. Aust.*, 1: 10–13.

Dax E. C. (1975). 'Australia and New Zealand' in J. G. Howells (ed.). *World History of Psychiatry*. New York: Brunner Mazel.

Dicks H. V. (1970). *Fifty years of the Tavistock Clinic*. London: Routledge and Kegan Paul.

Edwards G. A. (1978). *Mental illness and civil legislation in New South Wales* [dissertation]. Sydney (NSW): University of Sydney.

Evans R. (1969). *Charitable Institutions of the Queensland Government to 1919* [dissertation]. Brisbane (Q): University of Queensland.

Fleming D. (1964). 'Science in Australia, Canada, and the United States: some comparative remarks'. *Proceedings of International Congress of History of Science*, 1: 179–96.

Garton S. (1988). *Medicine and Madness: A social history of insanity in New South Wales, 1880–1940*, Kensington. NSW: New South Wales University Press.

Garton S. (in press). 'Mental health in Australia', in M. Bradbury and M. Lewis (eds). *From medical periphery to medical centres: Essays in the history of American and Australian medicine.*

Gold S. (1982). 'The early history'. *Meanjin*, 3: 342–57.

Jones K. (1972). *A history of mental health services*. London: Routledge and Kegan Paul.

Kirby M. D. (1981). 'Mental health law reform', *Mental Health in Australia*, 1: 6–20.

Lewis M. J. (1992). *A rum state: Alcohol and state policy in Australia*, 1788–1988. Canberra: AGPS Press.

Lind W. A. (1926). 'On insanity', *Med. J. Aust.*, 1: 315–24.

Macpherson J. (1926). 'The psychiatric clinic', *Med. J. Aust.*, 2: 174–8.

Manning E. N. (1889). 'President's address: Section of psychology', *Transactions of Intercolonial Medical Congress*, 816–33.

Martin G. (ed.) (1978). *The founding of Australia: The argument about Australia's Origins*. Sydney: Hale and Iremonger.

McGeorge J. (1936). 'Psychoanalysis'. *Med. J. Aust.*, 1: 383.

Opit L. J. and A. E. Donnan (1979). *Psychiatrists in Australia 1978: The existing manpower pool and its future*. Prahan. Vic.: Department of Social and Preventive Medicine, Monash University.

Report of royal commission on management of hospital for insane, Goodna, Queensland, Brisbane, 1915.

Scull A. (1993). 'Museums of Madness revisited'. *Social History of Medicine*, April, 6(1): 3–23.

Shlomowitz E. A. (1990). *The treatment of mental illness in South Australia, 1852–84: From care to custody* [dissertation]. Adelaide (SA): Flinders University of South Australia.

Skultans V. (1975). *Madness and morals: Ideas on insanity in the nineteenth century*. London: Routledge and Kegan Paul.

——— (1979). *English madness. Ideas on insanity, 1580–1890*. London: Routledge and Kegan Paul.

Whitlock F. A. (1969). *Report of Director of Psychiatric Services*, New South Wales.

——— (1975). 'The psychiatric patient in the community'. *Med. J. Aust.*, 1: 797.

——— (1979). 'The traditional psychiatric view' in E. M. Bates and P. R. Wilson (eds). *Mental disorder or madness? Alternative theories*. St Lucia (Q): Queensland University Press.

6

Remnants of the Colonial Past: The Difference in Outcome of Mental Disorders in High- and Low-income Countries

Joop de Jong

INTRODUCTION

This chapter deals with the uneasy relations between official mental health care systems and folk therapy practices. Folk therapy or 'traditional' or local healing is defined as being based on oral traditions, whereas official mental health systems are regarded as the product of academic psychiatry and psychology. Folk healers existed long before the advent of colonialism. They were often restricted, prohibited or persecuted by European colonial authorities, which instead introduced psychiatric asylums, which later formed the core of the emerging mental health care systems in low-income countries.

This chapter is partially built on my own ten-year experience as a doctor, public health professional, psychotherapist, transcultural psychiatrist and researcher in Africa and Asia. In addition, each year over the last seven years I visited a number of Third-World or low-income countries either to supervise one of our Transcultural Psychosocial Organization (TPO) projects aimed at refugees or victims of human right violations, or as a consultant to international or local mental health care organisations. Some reflections in this chapter are the result of a review of the existing literature, while others are based on observations during my visits or work in low-income countries. Instead of using words such as 'the West' or The Third-World it would be more correct to use the terms 'centre' and 'periphery' in the sense of Galtung or the dependencia theories, for it is obvious that many cities in the Third-World are 'westernized' and 'modern', whereas rural areas in the West are often 'traditional' or 'developing'. In this chapter I prefer to use the terms high- and low-income countries.

The structure of this chapter is as follows. I shall describe a few aspects of the introduction of psychiatry during colonial and post-colonial times. For an extensive description of the role of psychiatry in the colonial era, see chapter 1 of this volume. I shall then argue that a person with a psychiatric disturbance, especially a psychosis, is better off regarding treatment possibilities in a high-income country than in a low-income country. But with regard to resocialization and giving a meaning to the predicament the West has less to offer than the South or the East. When it comes to psychosocial problems a person in a low-income country may be better off. The arguments used here have both a quantitative and a qualitative character. Quantitative arguments focus on epidemiological data and on mental health care outcomes of state mental health care versus the reported results of local healing. Qualitative arguments focus, among other aspects, on the differences in attribution styles across cultures. I shall conclude my chapter with some recommendations regarding the development of psychiatry and psychology in low- and high-income countries.

THE GREAT WHITE FATHER

Throughout history, mankind has been striving after vertical social mobility, which in many cultures is balanced by a tendency towards egalitarianism. This universal tendency towards social mobility is in part guided by what sociologists call the 'law of anticipatory socialization', that is, the tendency of individuals to identify with the values of the dominant class to which they want to belong. The law of 'anticipatory socialization' applies, for example, to the butler who identifies with the values of his lord, or the slave who dreams of becoming equal to his master. But the law also applies to the Third-World psychiatrist who wants recognition from his Western colleagues. These Western colleagues dominated—and often still do so today—the agendas and the priorities of 'world psychiatry', as crystallized in journals which are printed in the West and mostly reviewed by Western peer reviewers. As a result, throughout colonial and post-colonial history there has been a long tradition of accepting Western norms. These norms reflect the ductile ethics of Christianity, justifying suppression, colonization, and neo-colonization. These norms also determine in part what is considered as normal and deviant behaviour and what should be undertaken to correct the perceived abnormality.

When medicine was exported to the colonies, initially for the colonizer and, after the abolition of slavery, as a means to increase the survival rate of the indigenous population, nobody ever questioned the universal applicability of Western medicine. Psychiatry was introduced in a later stage of colonial history and, like somatic medicine, initially embraced a universal stance. In the initial decades of the twentieth century, after the decline of the evolutionary anthropology of, for example, Morgan and Tylor and the emergence of the relativistic anthropological school of Boas and others, some psychiatrists started to question the universality of Western psychiatry and focused instead on exotic syndromes such as *amok, kuru,* and *koro*. However, as in the West, mainstream psychiatry in low-income countries maintained its universal stance from colonial times until today.

Even though in the universalism-particularism debate most psychiatrists probably embrace the current 'rule of thumb' that disorders which better fit within a biomedical paradigm show more universal features, whereas deviant behaviour that fits within a social-psychological paradigm shows more particularistic and culture-specific features. In other words, the cultural varnish is thinner when there is more disturbance of biophysiological processes of the brain and thicker when there is less disturbance of biophysiological processes. But many psychiatrists seem reluctant to draw conclusions from these insights in their daily work, be it as a clinician or as a researcher.

As a fairly young specialization within medicine, it took time for psychiatry to find its place in the colonial medical system. The advent of academic medicine and psychiatry was, and still is, confronted by three particular problems.

THE ABROGATION OF CULTURE

The indigenous population was educated in a school system which mostly bartered Christian values and the abrogation of one culture against the possibility of access to formal education and employment within the colonial administration. This can be illustrated by a remarkable statement of the President of the Catholic Missionary Order of the Oblates some years ago. He apologised for the role of his order in destroying native American language and culture and for the sexual and physical abuses of priests and brothers (McGraw, 1991). In exchange for possible social mobility, the future indigenous elite had to renounce its own religion and customs, burn its statues and shrines, and abstain from its 'pagan' rituals and ceremonies, including the healing rituals. After being alienated from its cultural roots, the local elite gradually gained access to the professions that had been reserved for the Whites. Indigenous doctors, including psychiatrists, appropriated the medical colonial model much as in recent decades psychiatrists have appropriated the biological psychiatric model that became predominant in the West.

I shall give a few examples of the concomitant process of alienation. In 1980, I did the last half year of my residency training as a psychiatrist in the famous Dakar School of Psychiatry. I was embarrassed by the way its anti-psychiatric ideology resulted in anti-anti-psychiatric practice (Sarr, 1980; de Jong, 1987). The mixture of philosophy, religion, Lacanian thinking and nosology of the French-dominated staff and the weekly 'Senegalese' ritual of the *penc* could hardly compensate the neuroleptic rigidity and the mainly ancilliary function of the *Hôpital de Fann*. In the southern part of Senegal, there was a psychiatric village called Kénia, inspired by Aro village in Nigeria, which in turn was inspired by similar initiatives in Sudan and in the Belgian village of Gheel. Although the residents in Dakar, coming from all over West Africa, were supposed to do part of their specialization in this psychiatric village, most of them considered the situation too primitive and preferred to stay in the metropolitan capital. As a result, the village was left to the care of one psychiatric nurse who, despite the large number of admitted patients, had no support in manpower and little support in funding and drugs in comparison to the psychiatric clinic in Dakar.

A similar preference for the Western symbol of the 'White House' hospital has been noted in the psychiatric villages in Tanzania and in the villages near Aro Mental Hospital (Erinosho, 1979). Lambo once formulated the acceptance of Western values with a deprecatory statement on the 'indigenization' of the professional health care sector. He wondered why Africans would have to make do with a coral while a newly built modern hospital could be afforded. Later on, I was became confronted with a variant of this way of thinking when I had to build a psychiatric hospital in Guinea-Bissau. The Guinean government just wanted to copy the psychiatric model of the previous colonizer, Portugal, without accounting for the fact that at that time Portugal lagged behind in the development of modern mental health care services. Although I could convince the Guinean government that the hospital should not be built far away from the capital, as the Europeans used to do until some decades before, that a wall was not needed, that one isolation chamber would do, and that sixty beds were more than enough for one million inhabitants, the government insisted that it should be a 'decent' clinic instead of a psychiatric village; it is now regarded as the most beautiful hotel in town (de Jong, 1987). But, like in many other low-income countries, foreign funding is required for the maintenance of the hospital, making the country dependent on donors, who in general regard mental health as one of their last priorities. Although a WHO study showed that worldwide 33 per cent of primary care attenders suffer from a psychological disorder (Üstün and Sartorius, 1995), Western donors are still reluctant to fund mental health activities. This reluctance is the other side of accepting Western norms: in my view one of the last prejudices of Westerners towards Africans or Asians is the feeling that their psyche is less sophisticated and that they suffer less when confronted with psychological problems, death, or traumatic events. The issue of the psychiatric villages is interesting because it illustrates the ambivalence of African psychiatry towards its cultural heritage. In an overview article, Ilechukwu (1991) suggests that the villages are one of the assets Africa has to offer to world psychiatry. The advantages of the villages are well known (de Jong ,1987): they are cheap to build, to maintain, and to accommodate patients. They have a low admission threshold for the patient and facilitate contacts with the neighbouring population. Contacts with the social environment resembling the patients' norm is a crucial therapeutic tool, helping patients to build a bridge between their own explanatory models and those of the mental health staff. Since treatment is more in line with the daily life of patients, they become less alienated, especially when one or several family members participate in the therapeutic programme. This contributes to resocialization. The villages create fewer hazards for staff and patients regarding institutionalization in Gofman's sense. In view of all these advantages, it is remarkable that the hospital as the whitewashed symbol of medical power always seems to win when it comes to allocating manpower and funding.

THE ABROGATION OF THE POPULAR AND FOLK HEALTH CARE SECTOR

The abrogation of their own culture not only applies to the choice of a psychiatric model, but also to religion and the congenial healing sector. Apart from the struggle of psychiatry to conquer its place in the colonial and post-colonial health care system, it also had to define itself vis-à-vis the so-called obscurantism of the 'witch-doctors' or the local healers. The identification of the ruled with the ruler and the subsequent rejection of traditionalism created an ambivalence towards folk practices that is still vividly present in most low-income countries. For example, during international meetings of the WHO, government officials endorse the discourse on the advantages of local healing systems and their complementary function within the health care sector. Back in their own countries, they often tacitly accept the undeniable health care consumption within the folk sector. Since many officials were themselves socialized in a family that practised healing rituals, and since like all human beings they tend to regress to earlier developmental stages during illness, they themselves or one of their family members engage in the rituals that often meet disdain in the official discourse. The origin of this ambivalence is rooted in colonial times when healing practices were either stigmatized as pagan or simply repressed. This ambivalence was often reinforced during academic studies in the home country or abroad. But the ambivalence can also be influenced by the strain caused by the obligation to leap, within one or two generations, from a predominantly 'magico-religious' way of thinking towards modern scientific thinking. As a result of these factors, in many cultures the local healing system went 'underground'.

In a first encounter, both patients and health professionals often deny the use of the local healing sector. There is a great difference in the extent and intensity of denial in several countries. It is, for example, more pronounced in former British colonies than in Portuguese colonies for reasons such as the predominance of Protestantism among the British and the presence of magico-religious thinking within Portuguese Catholicism. The denial is also related to the imposition and the penetration of the colonizer's culture in the local culture and the destruction of the latter; for example, the presence of the British in the Asian subcontinent hardly influenced Ayurveda and Unani medicine nor other locally developed healing methods. The same applies to the French in Cambodia, Laos or Vietnam.

The denial of the use of local healing methods can still be felt today in the form of social desirability. Time and again, I am surprised by local health workers or public health trainees in international courses who mention that, for example, east Africans do not visit local healers, whereas the opposite has been recorded (Orley, 1970; Peltzer, 1987). This social desirability even manifests itself in current studies about help-seeking behaviour. In the WHO 'Pathway to Care Study', the results of all the sites except Sulawesi showed that patients use state health care facilities as their first resort (Gater *et al.*, 1991). (As we shall see further on, previous studies on help-seeking behaviour found that in South-East Asia there was a slight preference first to visit the state health care sector.) In my view, the data in the WHO study are biased because patients were given a retrospective interview in a state health care facility. In such a setting patients need to be facilitated in order to resist the social desirability to deny visits to the healer which is regarded as the first resort for the illiterate and the poor. If half of the patient sample were interviewed at a healer's site, a completely different picture would emerge regarding the complementary use of folk and state health care sector.

I shall conclude this section with an example of 'de-alienation', that is, an attempt to change the colonial and post-colonial attitude towards healers, in Mozambique. After the struggle for independence in 1975, the Marxist Frelimo accused healers and their associations of collaboration with the Portuguese regime. The healers' associations were dismantled and many healers were persecuted and some even killed. The attack on the healers was part of a policy to undo the *obscurantismo* of traditional authorities. Renamo cleverly persuaded the children of the traditional authorities to rebel against the elder family members who had betrayed their rights, which of course would be restored if they sided with Renamo (Geffray, 1990). As a result, many Mozambicans were confronted with a serious problem. Most of them believed in the rituals marking, for example, liminal stages in their life and visited healers as well as health workers, as we found out during a study. For the Frelimo cadre this dilemma was particularly difficult because going to a healer meant disobeying the party. Moreover, Renamo's policy was aimed at destabilising the country, for example, by destroying 80 per cent of the primary health care structure, which made it even more difficult to use the state health care sector. This situation greatly improved when in 1991, the Minister of Health made the wise decision to study the possibility of the use of healers, repealing the law prohibiting their use, by allowing the re-establishment of the healers' association, and by studying the possibility of training them for some basic priorities in primary health care.

THE COMPETITION BETWEEN PSYCHIATRY AND FOLK PRACTICE

Psychiatrists in many low-income countries had and still have to find a place within the folk and popular health care sectors. There are several obstacles that academic psychiatry has to overcome. First, both healers and psychiatrists are better at dealing with illness than at curing disease. Although psychiatrists, in contrast to healers, are able to treat major psychiatric disorders, their patients need maintenance treatment. This distinguishes psychiatry from the somatic specialities, especially in low-income countries where Western medicine is able to treat previously fatal disorders such as tuberculosis and malaria. In contrast to these remedies for physical diseases, both psychiatrists and healers have to convince their patients that there is no quick fix solution for their problem.

Secondly, there is a scarcity of psychiatrists in comparison with healers. As a result, the psychiatrist has to see many patients with psychiatric symptoms that cannot be treated by the healer. This obliges the psychiatrist to use psychotropic drugs as the predominant treatment. Since the notion of a long-term treatment does not exist in all cultures—in which case healers interpret a relapse as a new predicament or disorder—psychiatrists are often confronted with poor compliance on the part of their patients. This is one factor in a vicious circle of low status of psychiatry in low-income countries. The somewhat stereotypical picture that emerges is that psychiatrists have little time for each consultation, limit themselves to pills, and spend little time on psychoeducation or psychotherapy. Subsequently, psychiatrists draw the self-fulfilling conclusion that their patients prefer pills and are not fit for psychotherapy. This results in a kind of psychiatry where a differential diagnosis between psychosis and neurosis leads to the selective application of a few essential drugs. But this type of psychiatry makes a poor impression on medical colleagues and on students who have to choose a speciality, further contributing to the low status of psychiatry. Consequently, the number of psychiatrists remains limited. Therefore, they have to see large number of patients per day thus continuing the vicious circle.

On a number of occasions I witnessed colleagues in Asia giving large amounts of drugs and Electro-convulsive Therapy (ECT) for a variety of diagnoses to low-income patients, while reserving (psychoanalytic) psychotherapy for a small elite in a private practice. Although this practice is not much different from some areas in the West, I met only a few colleagues in low-income countries who were both equipped and willing to make the painstaking and time-consuming efforts to develop eclectic psychotherapy for their low-income patients. And those who did try had to cope with many suitable patients insisting on medication. Another way to get out of the vicious circle is to delegate a larger part of drug treatment to auxiliary personnel such as psychiatric nurses. This could enable the psychiatrists to spend more time on changing the biological model towards a more complex, less tangible and somewhat threatening psychological model adapted to the local culture. It would also enable them to develop culturally responsive types of psychotherapy. A quick consultation again contrasts with the methods of the healer, who often has more time for patients and who is able to manipulate culturally validated symbols, working on the patient's affectivity to mobilise natural healing resources. More important is that many patients are of the opinion that the psychiatrist may be able to decrease the symptoms, but only the healer is able to diagnose the cause and deal with it. Many healers such as medicine men, shamans, cult leaders or religious healers use some sort of divination technique, communicating with supernatural beings such as ancestral or other spirits (theomancy); they may also use a revelation in a dream or vision (oneiromancy), or interpret an oracle using some of the hundreds of geomantic techniques. They then provide the deity's or their own explanation, that is, whether the disease is caused by irate supernatural causes, by human beings (witchcraft or sorcery), by the contravention of a social value or a taboo by an individual or a family, or by a natural agent (de Jong, 1987; Helman, 1993). The healer's treatment, depending on the diagnosis, is composed of a combination of techniques. For example, a thanks offering may propitiate the supernatural forces, a ceremony may neutralize the sorcery, witchcraft or the evil eye, or the balance of the elements or the humours may be restored.

Thirdly, in contrast with their colleagues in high-income countries and in contrast with the healer, psychiatrists in low-income countries have to struggle to establish a position of trust and respect. As Ellenberger (1970) described, over the last hundred years psychiatrists and psychotherapists gradually took over the work and the respect of priests and ministers. Although to some extent a similar process is going on in low-income countries, psychiatry had, and still has, to find its place among the healers who continue their work despite the influence of colonialism. The healer has the relative advantage of ascribed authority, often based on knowledge and intuition, that is carried over during generations of culture-congenial work within a given community. Psychiatrists have to acquire status, in part from their academic training and from the use of Western medicine. During my own experience in Africa I also acquired status by treating a number of healers with a psychiatric disorder who previously went in vain to healer colleagues. Because my treatment was successful, I had access to more powerful forces than they or their colleagues had.

Treatment Outcomes in High- and Low-Income Countries

Psychiatrists and healers do not only have an uneasy relation, but their work condemns each to the other. In the remaining part of this chapter I would like to pose the question whether patients with mental problems are better off in the 'West' than in the 'Third-World'.

My hypothesis is that if people suffer a neurotic or a psychosocial problem, they are better off in the Third-World than in the West. And conversely, that the West can be somewhat more advantageous for people with psychotic problems, at least if they find a health worker who takes care of their follow-up treatment. The arguments used to support this hypothesis have both a quantitative and a qualitative character.

QUANTITATIVE ARGUMENTS

Epidemiological studies in a number of cultures show that the prevalence of psychiatric disorders among the population does not differ significantly between high- and low-income countries. One-year period prevalence is estimated at 250—300 per 1000 at risk per year (Giel, 1972; Goldberg & Huxley, 1980; Giel, 1986; Westermeyer, 1989).

On the level of primary medical care, the number of mental cases seen in low-income countries is somewhat lower than in high-income countries. In twenty-seven studies carried out at the primary health care level, the recorded frequency of mental disorder in developing countries varies between 10 per cent and 36 per cent, and the differences in registered morbidity between low- and high-income countries varies from 2 per cent to 10 per cent (Kessel, 1960; Giel & van Luijk, 1969; Goldberg & Blackwell, 1970; WHO, 1973; Dormaar *et al.*, 1974; Goldberg, 1974; Dilling *et al.*, 1978; Hankin & Oktay, 1979; Hoeper *et al.*, 1979; Marks *et al.*, 1979; Ndetei & Muhangi, 1979; Climent *et al.*, 1980; Harding *et al.*, 1980; Cooper, 1981; Hough *et al.*, 1983; Dhadphale, 1984; Hoeper *et al.*, 1984; Schulberg *et al.*, 1985; de Jong *et al.*, 1986; de Jong, 1987; Bellantuono *et al.*, 1987; Burvill, 1988). The international WHO study on Mental Illness in General Health Care (Üstün and Sartorius, 1995) in urban areas in fifteen countries found that, over all the centres, 24 per cent of consecutive attenders had current mental disorders (depression, dysthymia, generalised anxiety disorder, agoraphobia, panic, somatization disorder, neurasthenia, hypochondriasis, alcohol dependence and harmful use; psychosis and drug abuse were excluded), another 9 per cent had subthreshold disorders, while 31 per cent had two or more symptoms of mental disorder. In the USA and western Europe, prevalence rates for common mental disorders are typically twice as high in primary care attenders as in the general population. The differential selection of distressed community residents into primary care clinics (the 'first filter', according to Goldberg and Huxley, 1992) may vary across different cultures and different health care systems.

The three- to four-fold differences of psychological disorder in primary care may have several causes (Üstün and Sartorius, 1995, p. 364). First, they may reflect true variations in population prevalence rates. Second, differences in prevalence may reflect differences in the selection of patients into primary care because in some cultures specific complaints may prompt a distressed person to visit a healer. Third, different rates of psychological disorder may reflect differences in the 'retention' of distressed patients in the primary care clinics.

Based on these studies, it is possible to make a few statements about the differences between high- and low-income countries on the frequency and character of morbidity. Of the above mentioned morbidity of 10 per cent to 36 per cent in primary care, 90 per cent consists of neurotic and psychosocial disorders, and about 1.5 per cent to 8 per cent of psychotic disturbances (Ndetei & Muhangi, 1979; Orley & Wing, 1979; Harding *et al.*, 1980; Shepherd *et al.*, 1981; Lamberts & Hartman, 1982).

In developing countries a slightly higher percentage of psychoses is found on the primary care level for the following reasons. The health worker may not recognize the psychosis, so the patient does not pass the filter to the next health care level. This 'under-diagnosing' may be caused by the somatized presentation of the psychosis. Or it may be caused by the fact that the local cosmology, that is, the health concept of health worker and patient, does not distinguish a psychosis from a possession state, therefore, turning to the healer for treatment (Eliade, 1964; de Jong, 1987). A third reason for the under-reporting may be that health workers recognize the disorder as a deviation from culturally accepted norms, but they do not refer the patient because they doubt that the state health care system can offer relief in such a case, or because the patient expects little from the referral.

The higher percentage of psychoses contrasts with a somewhat lower percentage of neuroses found on the primary care level in developing countries. The reason for this under-representation of neuroses is that patients tend to end up in the treatment setting of a healer. In developing countries, a great number of patients pass the filter to the state health care system, if necessary, only in a later stage of illness (Buschkens, 1977; Ademawugun *et al.*, 1979; Kleinman, 1980; de Jong, 1987). Exceptions to this rule have been described in South-East Asia but patients soon follow a consultation with a 'modern doctor' with a consultation with a traditional healer if medicine does not take effect immediately (Carstairs and Kapur, 1976).

What about the West? Do patients with a psychiatric disorder get access to health workers and are these able to help them?

Health workers or primary care physicians in the West diagnose slightly more cases of mental disorders as such than their colleagues elsewhere. In the UK and the Netherlands, the diagnostic sensitivity of GPs was 65 per cent, whereas several American studies found a sensitivity of 24 per cent on average (Ormel & Giel, 1983; Goldberg & Blackwell, 1970; Goldberg & Huxley, 1980; Hoeper *et al.*, 1980; Kessler *et al.*, 1985; Jones *et al.*, 1987). A WHO study in Asia, Africa and Latin America, which aimed at the extension of mental health into primary health care, showed that diagnostic sensitivity of the health workers was 37 per cent (WHO, 1975, 1981, 1984; Harding *et al.* 1980). Üstün and Sartorius (1995) mention that physicians' diagnosis of psychological disorders in their usual practice varies between 4.8 per cent and 58.8 per cent. The concordance of physicians' diagnosis with the research diagnosis ranged from 18.3 per cent to 75 per cent. They also found that recognition of mental disorders was about twice as high in what they called type A centres as compared with type B centres. (Type A meant that a patient knew the physician, made an appointment, the physician kept a record and remained responsible for coordinating the patient's care; in type B, the patient came to a clinic without an appointment, and the time given to a consultation depended on the total number of patients.) Although primary care physicians in the West recognize a number of neurotic patients, they seldom refer them, either because they think that the treatment of these disorders is their own task, or because patients do not want a referral because expectations concerning the treatment of non-psychotic disorders by a specialist are low (Goldberg & Huxley, 1980). This results in a limited referral of 5 per cent of neurotic patients to the mental health care system, although some studies report figures up to 15 per cent

(Hollingshead & Redlich, 1958; Swaen & Ten Horn, 1980; Shepherd *et al.*, 1981; Giel & Ten Horn, 1982; Ormel & Giel, 1983).

What happens to the 80–90 per cent of the neurotic patients who are not referred for proper treatment? About one-third to two-thirds of these receive some form of treatment from the family doctor (Regier *et al.*, 1978, 1982, 1984). In the recent WHO study (Üstün and Sartorius, 1995), primary care physicians reported that they provided treatment for 77.8 per cent of the patients whom they identified as having a psychological disorder. The most common treatments provided were: counselling (52 per cent), sedative medications (23 per cent), and anti-depressant medications (12 per cent). An important finding in the WHO study was that the type of treatment did not necessarily relate to the diagnostic status or the research diagnosis of the patient. This random application of treatment is of course extremely questionable and not efficacious. The patients who are not referred are often compared with patients who had minimal treatment but not extensive psychotherapy as well as subjects who were, for the most part, untreated. The median spontaneous remission rate varied widely, with a range from 0 per cent to 90 per cent at follow-up. According to other authors, the non-referred patients have a similar outcome to 'waiting-list patients', that is, about one-third recover within a year, a few less than half improve somewhat, and a quarter do not get better or get worse (Huxley *et al.*, 1979; Lambert & Bergin, 1980; Ormel & Giel, 1983; Mann *et al.*, 1981). But some of the non-referred neurotic patients find their way to a therapist without consulting a primary care physician. In the Netherlands, about 45 per cent of these patients reached a psychiatric service without being referred by their GP (Swaen & Ten Horn, 1980). In addition, an increasing number of people in the West go to alternative therapists (Van Dijk, 1993).

Referral and self-referral figures for other countries are hard to find, but if they exist they probably show little consistency because the figures depend on such factors as the organization of the mental health care system, access to psychotherapy through health insurance, information about the referral institutions, or the presence of a consultation relation with primary care.

And what about the results of the 5–15 per cent neurotic patients who are referred to a psychiatrist or a psychotherapist?

Although, according to Luborski *et al.* (1980), research on the outcome of psychotherapy is in its methodological infancy, one can say that one-third of these patients do not change and some of them even get a bit worse. Another third improve a little. And one-third improve considerably without necessarily being cured completely—they are simply no longer bothered by their phobia, their depression, anxiety or their alcohol abuse (Strupp, 1980; Garfield, 1983). Comparing these results with the figures for patients on waiting-lists mentioned above, one can say that the natural positive outcome is somewhat accelerated under the influence of psychotherapy, and that life is more endurable for two-thirds of neurotic patients (Schagen, 1983).

While more than 1000 quantitative studies on the outcome of psychotherapy have been carried out, few studies have attempted to evaluate the treatment effects of healing. In comparison with accepted minimum standards of psychotherapy evaluation (Sloane *et al.*, 1975; Strupp *et al.*, 1977; Schagen, 1983), one can be very critical about the methodology of these studies. This criticism concerns the (non-)use of psychodiagnostic and psychometric instruments, the estimates of change, assignment to healing and psychiatric treatment modalities, the sample size, and the generalizations drawn from these samples.

For example, Jilek (1974) provided treatment results on twenty-four members of an initiation cult of the Salish Indians. Only two candidates did not improve and one deteriorated. The remainder showed varying degrees of symptomatic and behavioural improvement. Jilek considered the cult to be effective for depression, anxiety, psychosomatic complaints, and for anti-social behaviour. However, the sample encompassed between 50 per cent and 80 per cent of the initiated spirit dancers in his study area. Jilek did not estimate the prevalence of spirit dancers before joining the cult, he did not use psychometric or psychodiagnostic instruments to asses the treatment effect, nor did he specify the duration of the follow-up period. Crapanzano's study (1973)—often cited as an empirical study although the author qualifies it as descriptive—declared that the greatest success of a Moroccan possession cult was in psychosomatic and hysterical cases. Except for a few case descriptions, he did not provide quantitative data. Finkler (1985), in her study in Mexico, concluded that healing attenuates symptoms associated with generalized anxiety or (pain associated with) depression in about 25 per cent of the patients. Kleinman's (1980) figures from Taiwan suggest a maximum positive treatment outcome for half of the neurotic patients. Neither Finkler nor Kleinman provide clear figures about treatment effects for specific categories of patients, while their methodology suggests that they should be able to provide such figures. Garrison's (1973, 1977) study among *spiritistas* and their clientele in New York seems to be a promising approach to the evaluation of the treatment effect of healers, but so far data on this aspect of her study have not been published. In a later study on Taiwan, Kleinman and Gale (1982) compared a group of patients treated by shamans with patients treated by physicians. More than three-quarters of all patients across five sickness groups improved. A higher proportion of patients were dissatisfied with shamanistic treatment than with medical care, even with regard to somatization. The authors frankly admitted the limitations of their research design.

Regarding the effect of healing in the prevention and treatment of alcohol and drug abuse, it has been reported that post-therapy abstinence rates among opiate addicts ranging from 8 per cent to 35 per cent in the total clientele of five different healers. A one-year follow-up study on Naikan therapy among alcohol addicts in Japan found that 53 per cent were totally abstinent six months after discharge and 49 per cent were abstinent after one year (Takemoto *et al.*, 1979). Among *curanderos* in Peru, 77 per cent of chronic alcoholics had post-therapy abstinence periods of over one year, and 44 per cent over six years. A study conducted in Malawi indicated that the average time of alcohol abstinence after joining a healing church was 2.8 years (Peltzer, 1987).

Although other aspects of these studies are very interesting with a view to the methodology used for the evaluation of treatment effects, they all await confirmation in future research. Scientific evaluation of the effectiveness of traditional healing is limited by the inherent constraints of scientific research in this field. Jilek (1994) mentions a number of constraints such as interference with the ceremonies, the healer's reluctance to divulge information, and the practical difficulties of conducting outcome studies when there are no reliable records, or the problem of finding former clients to verify their statements. For the purpose of this chapter, the lowest average estimates of treatment results from these studies on healers will be used: according to these authors at least 40 per cent of the neurotic cases treated by healers show some or considerable improvement.

Psychotic patients are confronted with different problems. From a curative point of view, both healers and doctors have little to offer (Finkler, 1985; de Jong, 1987).

When measuring the element of support given to their patients, doctors in high- or low-income countries can prescribe neuroleptics and facilitate the integration of psychotic patients into society. The maintenance of psychotic patients in their environment is easier in developing countries. Marsella and Westermeyer (1993) noted a number of cultural factors that may have impact on the course and outcome of mental disorders: conceptions of illness that limit responsibility and causation (as I shall discuss below, along with other factors, by handling a different attribution style), less social rejection of the ill member, continuous family care and involvement of the ill member (i.e., low personal burden), greater emphasis on role performance, reduced stress, lower competency requirements, greater social and religious involvement, lower emphasis on institutionalization and custodial care, reduced substance abuse and alcoholism, and sensitivity to class and ethnic differences between patient and professional. In other words, in low-income countries the course and outcome of the disorder may be improved because a number of cultural factors may mediate the disorder. However, some authors would consider this a romanticization of the Third-World, for persons with certain psychiatric disorders simply do not survive in some low-income countries (Westermeyer, 1979; Devereux, 1979). Moreover, as mentioned above, many severely mentally ill persons do not come to psychiatric attention in low-income countries. Even today, a country such as Angola has one mental health institution, that is, a collection of shacks run by a 'healer' chaining his patients. In Laos, only eight out of thirty psychotic people studied had been seen by a psychiatrist as outpatients (Westermeyer, 1983). Another factor undoing the potential benefit of local culture in developing countries is the fragmentary aftercare offered by the state health care system (Assen, 1988). And although Rauwolfia-induced sleep therapy in Nigeria has been set as an example of the healers' potential (Prince, 1960), it did not seem to have a positive effect on the outcome of psychosis (Asuni, 1979).

In the West, the treatment of psychotic patients is only slightly better. Almost all such patients are recognized and are referred for professional help (Ödegaard, 1962; de Jong *et al.*, 1983). But only some of these patients get adequate aftercare. In a Dutch study, it was found that almost half of a group of hospitalized psychotic patients got aftercare, and that about one-third of the discharged patients were hospitalized again within one year (Ten Horn, 1982; de Jong *et al.*, 1983). In a follow-up study, the percentage of patients who got aftercare within three months of their discharge from hospital rose to 73 per cent, but nevertheless 25 per cent of the discharged patients were again admitted to a psychiatric service within one year (Ommen *et al.*, 1986). An American study found a relapse rate of 31 per cent at six months, and of 59 per cent at twenty-four months. This was the same for a group of in-patients who were discharged in a routine way, and a group of patients who participated in a rehabilitation-oriented case management programme.

A British study showed that the time spent on aftercare is a factor contributing to the high recidivism rate. The mean time in therapeutic contact of community psychiatric nurses with psychotic patients was considerably lower (9 minutes) than with neurotic patients (twenty-five minutes) and was almost entirely devoted to the administration of an injection (Wooff *et al.*, 1986). With the exception of some experiments with small patient populations, other studies do not seem to be more positive.

Another quantitative argument may turn the scale in favour of 'therapists' or 'healers'. That is the number and distribution, as well as the accessibility of both groups of helpers.

In the USA, 156,139 professionals work in the mental health care sector, that is, one professional for 1561 inhabitants (MHSSR 1984). According to government statistics, there is one professional for 14,704 inhabitants in the UK and one for 2154 inhabitants in the Netherlands (HPSSS 1987, NCGV 1987).

The numbers of healers in developing countries are much higher. In Ghana, 1 per cent of the population is engaged as a priest(ess), a healer, a herbalist or a shrine-holder. Among the Yoruba, medicine men form 10 per cent of the adult population in rural areas, and about 4 per cent in urban areas (Ademawugun, 1979). In Guinea-Bissau, we found one healer for 475 inhabitants; in the Philippines, this number is about one healer for 200 inhabitants (de Jong, 1987; Tan, 1985). Although these figures are higher than the numbers of mental health workers in the West, the differences are levelled out if one includes family doctors and unregulated lay therapists, who have been estimated at one million for the USA (Kleinman, 1988). Another reason to wonder whether a comparison of numbers makes sense is that the healers, often are peasants who are part-time engaged in healing. Moreover, healers not only cater for somatic and mental problems, but for any other predicament as well.

With regard to accessibility, the Third-World is better off than the West. In contrast with health care facilities (both in urban areas in the West and in the Third-World), healers are well distributed among the rural population (Van der Geest, 1985; Pillsbury, 1979; de Jong, 1987). Governments will not be able to solve the problem of unequal distribution of health professionals in the foreseeable future by building more decentralized facilities or by training more staff and posting them in the countryside (Health, 1980). Moreover, as became clear in my work in Senegal, trained professionals are often reluctant to work in the periphery. In addition to the better geographic accessibility, it is above all, the cultural and economic accessibility of healers in comparison with mental health workers in the West which turns the scale in favour of low-income countries (Crapanzano, 1973; Fuller Torrey, 1986).

QUALITATIVE ARGUMENTS

To begin with, some elements will be mentioned which constitute the core of most therapies, be it by psychotherapists or by healers. When people have a problem and decide to seek help, they look for somebody with prestige and authority. A psychiatrist in the West derives this prestige from medical successes (Frank & Frank, 1993), whereas a healer enjoys a socially sanctioned prestige, often by descent. Hence, the asymmetric relation between healer and patient mostly is straightforward, whereas in the West the acceptance of this asymmetry often is achieved during the first phase of the therapy. A century ago, the relation between the Western healer and the client was quite similar to the somewhat authoritarian relation between the healer and the patient nowadays. At that time, the Western healer had an attitude of unshakable conviction (Ellenberger, 1970). In the meantime, the

Western society shifted from a society of command to a society of negotiation (de Swaan, 1979).

A second element of the therapeutic relation stems from the first element and has been called 'expectant faith' (Frank & Frank, 1993). In traditional societies, healers and their patients share a holistic world view. This congruence between their expectations reduces the risk of attrition (Freedman *et al.*, 1958) and gives the healer some advantage in comparison with a Western colleague. The latter works in a health care system which is split along Cartesian dualistic lines. This split may create problems for somatizing patients or patients from other cultures (de Jong, 1989).

The two elements of authority and faith lead to a third element, that is, mutual comprehension or positive regard (Rogers, 1975), which is similar to 'good enough mothering' as described by Winnicott (Arnon, 1984; Chabot, 1989). Comprehension may increase by 'non-specific factors' such as empathy, warmth, acceptance, engagement, confidence, and genuineness of the therapist or the healer (Strupp, 1970; Kazdin, 1979). A combination of these elements may result in reciprocal affirmation and in a strong therapist-patient relationship. Both in classical psychoanalysis and in client-centred therapy, the therapeutic bond is considered one of the most important therapeutic variables of psychotherapy. Among behaviour therapists, there is a growing acknowledgement of the role of this relationship in the therapeutic learning process (Rice, 1983; Strupp *et al.*, 1977; Luborski *et al.*, 1980).

Most studies about healing confirm the importance of the therapeutic bond (Fuller Torrey, 1986; Kleinman, 1980; de Jong, 1987), whereas a minority of these studies explicitly (Crapanzano, 1973; Mullings, 1984; Finkler, 1985) or implicitly (Giel *et al.*, 1968) do not consider the healer-patient relationship to be particularly significant. The latter studies deal with healing processes where possession plays a central role.

These therapeutic elements prepare the ground for a subsequent searching process which may take place on an unconscious (Erickson, 1980) or a conscious level (Ellis, 1974). The therapist stimulates the patient to engage in this searching process, whereas healers, during their (divinatory) trance, often engage in the search on their own, thus enhancing the dependence of their patient. The search occurs only after the breakdown of old frames of reference, which may happen in many ways; such as through the therapeutic setting (e.g., the lying position in the analyst's room and in the ancient Aesclepeia [Ellenberger, 1970] or in Moroccan shrines [Crapanzano, 1980]), the possession trance of healer and/or patient, the concentration on (day)dreams, the focus on body parts in therapies such as bioenergetics or gestalt, or the shock or surprise as used in Ericksonian therapy or in healing (de Jong, 1987).

Then the actual search takes place. During this process of exploration a patient focuses on inner experiences (Freud, 1913; May, 1958; Rogers, 1957; Levi-Strauss, 1963) or on interactions with others which can both result in corrective experiences (Masamba ma Mpolo, 1976; Janzen, 1978). These experiences can have an emotional or cognitive character and result in relief, catharsis, insight, self-acceptance, learning of cognitive or interpersonal skills, or working through conflicts of oneself and one's environment. Consequently, therapeutic realizations should enable patients and their families to handle old situations in more effective ways.

This bird's eye view of the therapeutic process applies both to psychotherapy and to healing. Now I shall focus on two differences between psychiatrists and healers which in my view are important.

The first difference regards the dozens of therapeutic factors described in the literature on healing and psychotherapy. Most healers use an arsenal which is strikingly wider than that of many Western therapeutic schools (Crapanzano, 1973; de Jong, 1987). With the advent of new psychotherapies, Western psychotherapy became characterized by stereotype intake and treatment, often organized in separated and contesting 'schools' of psychotherapeutic methods (Dijkhuis, 1988).

Fortunately, there also exists a tendency towards synthesis and mutual influence between therapeutic schools and healing techniques. In the West, the emergence of eclecticism is a fruitful counter-tendency. Eclecticism not only means the elective use of strategies from different therapeutic schools, but is also characterized by the mingling of Western therapeutic schools with philosophies from other cultures, especially from the East.

A similar tendency exists among healers changing their healing practice under the influence of Western culture. Examples of the latter are the espiritistas in New York, the spiritualistic healers in Ghana, the Zebola rituals in Zaire, the Zionist churches in Southern Africa or Malawi, the Umbanda and Candomble in Brazil, the Santeria and Naniguismo in Cuba, or the Winti cult in the Netherlands (Atiwiya, 1971; Sundkler, 1976; Garrison in Crapanzano *et al.*, 1976; Corin, 1978; Bourguignon, 1980; Mullings, 1984; de Jong, 1986, 1997; Peltzer 1987).

A second and even more important difference between psychiatrists and healers is their divergence in attribution styles. Healers' attributions in general are more external, specific, and non-stable, whereas the mainstream in Western psychotherapy handles what Seligman (1995) called internal, global, and stable attributions. Healers' attributions focus on external forces (angry supernatural forces, witchcraft or sorcery), whereas the psychiatrist prefers to adopt internal attributions (organic causes, anxiety, hypersensitive personality or oedipal conflict).

Moreover, the attribution of a hypersensitive personality or an oedipal conflict is global, that is, the patient will have difficulties with other situations as well. In contrast, the healer's attribution of the deity's anger or human malevolence is specifically linked to that illness episode.

The attributions of the healer are non-stable, which means that the patient has a temporary problem which can be resolved with a thanks offering, an expiatory sacrifice, or the neutralization of evil intentions. Not only has every illness episode its specific cause but in general, the cause can be counteracted as well (Horton, 1967a, b; Shelton, 1968; Asuni, 1979; Horton, 1993). In contrast, the psychiatrists' attribution of an oedipal conflict or a panic disorder is a stable attribution, and is much harder to change.

As Seligman (1995, 1996) shown, Western-style attributions tend to continue or increase feelings of helplessness, self-deprecation and depression.

EAST VERSUS WEST

The majority of people suffering from a neurotic or a psychosocial problem seem to be better off in the Third-World than in the West. Healers are geographically better distributed and more easily accessible than their allopathic colleagues. Moreover, healers are culture-congenial, that is, they share or are familiar with the value system of their clients. Within a holistic approach they use a wide variety of therapeutic interventions which are part of the local culture. Healers' effective therapist variables are reinforced by the involvement of the patient's in-group and by their religious and secular position within their society.

However, the original hypothesis needs differentiation in the sense that the relative advantage of the Third-World population regarding neurotic and psychosocial problems mainly exists in rural areas. In urban areas, the positive role of healers is challenged by rapid sociocultural changes. The examples of Zaire, Ghana, Brazil and New York show that healers sometimes succeed in shifting to a syncretistic, more individualized, and psychologizing approach. In other cultures, healers are not able to adapt their idiom to the process of acculturation, which is one of the reasons why patients continue proceed to the state health care sector. In my view, this is one of the reasons why the WHO study on 'Pathways to Care', with its focus on urban areas only, detected a minor proportion of health care consumption in the traditional healing sector. The other part of the interesting WHO study on psychological disorders in primary health care found an overall picture of morbidity which is quite similar worldwide (Üstün & Sartorius, 1995). As was mentioned in the introduction, in the process of globalization, urban areas are increasingly becoming alike, thus blurring possible interesting transcultural differences. In future, this kind of study should sample both urban and rural patients. Moreover, patients should be interviewed both in the state health care sector and in the traditional health care sectors, and both local idioms of distress and Western psychological and psychiatric categories should be studied.

Those clients who do not feel understood by the healer's interpretation and treatment will proceed to the state health care sector, where their need for psychotherapy is rarely met. There are a number of reasons for the lack of coverage of psychotherapeutic needs in low-income countries, of which I shall mention a few. First, many low-income countries only have a couple or even no clinical psychologists being trained in psychotherapy. Second, there have been very few initiatives to develop psychotherapy which fits the local culture, and especially the rural and middle-class population. Third, the lack of 'indigenization' of Western therapeutic approaches and the lack of cultural appropriateness is in part caused by the acceptance of Western norms and the difficulty the local elite have in synthesizing their own cultural roots with their later academic teaching. Fourth, within the universalism-relativism debate it became clear that disorders or idioms of distress that can be better explained within a social-psychological paradigm are often more culture specific. Hence, their treatment also has to be more adapted to local culture. Fifth, in contrast with high-income countries, in general there still is less resistance to medicines and less demand for psychological interventions. As a result, psychologists and psychiatrists in low-income countries have an enormous task in the next decades to develop psychotherapeutic approaches that fit the cosmology and the expectations of their clients. In my view it will be very useful for them to study their non-academic colleagues—the healers—because they show what works in the local culture and because studying the healer explains much of the behaviour of the client in the psychologist's consulting room.

With regard to the treatment of psychotic disorders, a patient in a low-income country is handicapped in comparison with one in the West: first because the problem often is not recognized by the healer or the health worker; second, because the healer in fact has little to offer from a curative point of view; and third, because few patients reach the state health care sector, where aftercare in the form of maintenace therapy is often fragmentary (Assen, 1988; cf. Edgerton and Cohen, 1994). If psychotic patients in developing countries get access to psychiatric care and if they get drugs and especially depot medication, their prognosis can be better than in industrialized countries (Waxler, 1977; WHO, 1979; El-Islam, 1983; de Jong, 1987; de Jong, 1997). However, recent re-analysis of the data of the WHO, International Pilot Study of Schizophrenia (IPSS) and Determinants of Outcome of Severe Mental Disorders (DOSMD) studies make the better prognosis of schizophrenia in low-income countries questionable, as suggested by Jablensky *et al.* (1992). Manton *et al.* (1994) and Susser & Wanderling (1994) have shown that there was a subgroup of patients among the 'schizophrenic' patients in these WHO studies, suffering from what Susser *et al.* call a NARP (non-affective acute remitting psychosis). Since NARP has a 10-fold higher prevalence in low-income countries, it may explain the previously found better prognosis of schizophrenia in low-income countries. In a recent re-analysis of the DOSMD data, Craig *et al.* (1997) found that the course of illness was best predicted by the centre and two high-income country centres were compared with the low-income country centres in this respect. Their finding that the type of onset (insidious versus non-insidious) was the next strongest predictor is also relevant in relation to the discussion on the NARP. Their finding that those with non-insidious onset did very well in low-income countries may also be explained by the fact that the DOSMD cohort of 'schizophrenic' patients was indeed 'contaminated' by patients suffering from the relatively benign, acute and short-lived type of psychosis which they call the NARP.

However, the potential positive effect of the local culture is mostly undone by the aforementioned fact that an insignificant proportion of the patients with a chronic functional psychosis have access to psychiatric care. With the exception of a few countries such as Nigeria and Guinea-Bissau, and with the exception of a few areas such as the Fayoum government in Egypt, or the Bangalore, Bellary and Chandigarh areas in India, most state health care programmes in low-income countries only reach a few per cent of the psychiatric target population (WHO, 1976–89; WHO, 1988; ICMR, 1988, 1989; de Jong, 1989b; de Jong, 1996). Lack of resources plays an important role in the low coverage of the mentally ill population. Low-income countries often have economic difficulties in changing the colonial, centralized, curative and hospital-based approach into a decentralized and preventive one. On the other hand, governments are sometimes reluctant to reallocate funds for community services when psychiatrists do make serious efforts to de-institutionalize the custodial services, despite the finding that once an existing basic health care structure exists, one US $ may cover fifty-four people in a public mental health care programme (de Jong, 1996). And when a mental health department has succeeded in integrating psychiatric priorities into primary care, de-institutionalization becomes a serious option; in my opinion thirty to fifty beds per million inhabitants may be enough in most low-income countries. This is possible because of the social support from the family and the role of healers in explaining and giving a meaning to the psychiatric disorder, even though they are not able to treat the symptoms.

Attribution theory can be helpful in understanding the difference in outcome since attributions influence both the aetiological and the therapeutic level. Therefore, attributions have far-reaching consequences for the re-socialization of chronic patients.

In low-income countries, the local cosmology often does not differentiate an acute psychosis from a possession state. Both may be interpreted as an illness which should lead to an initiation as a healer. The strange behaviour is caused by an external force, that is, a deity, and this election is highly respected. This may be an important factor in studying the outcome of psychosis in different cultures since cognition psychologists regard self-esteem as one of the most important protective factors in dealing with hallucinations (Bentall, 1990). In addition to this positive 'reinterpretation', increasing social prestige, the deviant behaviour is regarded as a temporary problem which is not inherent in the personality of the person involved (although the election by the deity may be due to personal development). In other words, the deviant behaviour is attributed to an external, specific, and non-stable factor.

This approach is quite different from the Western view, for insanity in the West is more often associated with internal, global, and stable attributions. Madness is regarded as an inherent quality of the person and possibly the family, and once somebody is 'mad' it is not easy to get rid of that label. Although the systemic view takes an intermediate position between the Western and the non-Western view, it often delineates the system in such a way that the strange behaviour of the identified patient is the result of an imbalance for which all people involved are responsible. Systemic thinking is not yet very common in the West but it may become the bridge between mental health care philosophy in high- and low-income countries.

What happens if the person is not suffering from a self-limiting brief reactive psychosis? Of course, the initiation as a healer does not succeed if the person is suffering from what is called a schizophreniform or a schizophrenic disorder. In that case, the divination process continues and may attribute the problem to another specific external force such as sorcery, witchcraft, evil eye, or angry or malevolent supernatural forces. Again, the negative cause at first is interpreted as a temporary problem for it can be neutralized, for example, by a sacrifice, a ritual, or the reinstalment of the soul. Although the supernatural causes are immaterial, the consequences of the interaction between body and magic can correspond with a mechanistic representation. For example, witchcraft or sorcery may cause a swelling in the body and thus may be the representation of diseases which textbooks consider as filariasis, an abscess or a tumour; or it may result in the intrusion of objects in the body which may lead to sensations of heaviness or weight moving through the body ('somatizations'), and which may be superposed or juxtaposed to the same or another spell causing insanity. Therefore, a patient attributes magic power to the allopathic practitioner who is capable of treating such a somatic or a mental disease. But this does not erode the logic of the witchcraft and the desirability of consulting a healer to counteract the magic per se. The frequent diagnosis of sorcery is one of the reasons that the availability of modern health care does not necessarily imply a decrease of local health care consumption (de Jong, 1987). Healers know that they can neutralize witchcraft or sorcery. Therefore, healers are less afraid of their turf than doctors and they are often less hesitant to collaborate than their Western-style colleagues. On the somatic level, the mechanistic and reified representation of the interaction between the external forces (spirits, magic, etc.) and the victim again results in specific, circumscript anomalies which can be removed by sucking, cutting or sympathetic magic.

In general, the aforementioned external attributions are maintained when a person deteriorates, as in the case of a residual schizophrenic disorder. After consulting at a number of shrines or with healers, the family reaches consensus about the fact that this behaviour is caused by extremely strong evil forces or deities who just cannot be counteracted by somebody at hand.

The difference in outcome of psychotic patients in different societies is often attributed to—among other factors—a lower level of familial 'expressed emotions' (Karno *et al.*, 1987). In my view, the key to the comprehension of the differences in expressed emotions can again be found in the divergence of attribution styles between high- and low-income societies, for, in general, the non-Western cosmology provides an acceptable explanation for the bizarre behaviour of schizophrenic people, who, therefore, do not become the focus of emotional interactions. Within the highly rational logic of their culture, they can do little about their fate. They are not responsible and may work at their capacity level without losing the support of their social network. This availability of employment for disabled individuals is another factor that needs attention in further studies on outcome in high- and low-income countries. Within their cultures schizophrenic patients may be expected to perform at different levels. Moreover, reversal rituals or ventil mores may add to the relative tolerance of the mentally ill (de Jong, 1987).

In contrast to the therapist, the healer does not look for predisposing personality traits, contributing biological or genetic factors, schizophrenogenic mothers or double bind aetiological factors. A Westerner may consider the attitude of the healer and the patient to be fatalistic. This 'fatalism' may express itself in just performing a regular ceremony to prevent other predicaments, or in non-compliance with pharmacotherapy.

The difference in attribution styles does not mean that the local cosmology has no explanations at hand to justify marginalization or expulsion of a person who exhibits extremely disturbed or violent behaviour or who is not capable of contributing to the family's economy. And obviously, the attribution of a disorder to external factors may also have adverse effects when it is used by a patient to justify substance use or personality disorder.

The argument which I followed in this chapter has serious constraints and exposes a number of lacunae in our knowledge which will be interesting to study. A conspicuous shortcoming is the scarcity of epidemiological cross-cultural research using comparative and reliable methodologies. Whereas many authors as well as the WHO propagate the collaboration between doctors and healers or even the integration of healers in state health care systems, there are no reliable quantitative studies on the effects of healing. A similar shortcoming exists with regard to outcome studies on chronic functional psychoses and psychological disorders across cultures. The Epidemiological Catchment Area study (Regier *et al.*, 1984) confirmed the findings of Dohrenwend and Dohrenwend (1982) that only about 20 per cent of persons with psychiatric disorders had received treatment from any type of mental health practitioner. This article suggests that their findings may well be universally applicable. To conclude, one could say that a mental disorder is a burden for the patient and the family. And for the time being, the inadequate provision of mental health care is a great burden for the mentally ill.

References

Ademuwagun Z. A. *et al.* (eds) (1979). *African therapeutic systems.* Waltham: Crossroads Press.

Arnon J. (1984). 'Good enough mothering' bij D. W. Winnicott. Psychologiefaculteit: University of Amsterdam.

Assen (1988). *Personal communication about her research in Kenya.*

Asuni T. (1979). 'Modern medicine and traditional medicine' in

Z. A. Ademuwagun, J. A. A. Ayoade, and I. A. Harrison *et al.* (eds). *African Therapeutic Systems*. Massachusetts: Crossroads Press.

Atiwiya G. (1971). 'Le "Zebola" (Therapie traditionelle des maladies mentales dans un cadre urain)'. *Psychopathologie Africaine*, VII, 3: 389–417.

Bellantuono C., R. Fiorio, and P. Williams *et al.* (1987). 'Psychiatric morbidity in an Italian general practice'. *Psychol. Med.*, 17: 243–7.

Bentall R. P. (1990). 'The illusion of reality: A review and integration of psychological research on hallucinations'. *Psychological Bulletin*, 107, 1: 82–95.

Bourguignon E. (ed.) (1980). *A World of Women*. New York: Praeger.

Burvill P. W. (1988). Psychiatric Disorders in Primary Case in S. Henderson & G. Burrows (eds). *Handbook of Social Psychiatry*. Amsterdam: Elsevier Publishers, 221–32.

Buschkens W. F. L. (1977). *De houding van de bevolking van de Derde Wereld tegenover geneeswijzen*. Verslag symposion: R. U. Leiden.

Carstairs G. M., R. L. Kapur (1976). *The great universe of Kota: Stress, change and mental disorder in an Indian village*. Berkeley: University of California Press.

Chabot B. E. (1988). 'Gesprekshulp'. *Tijschrift voor Psychotherapie*, 14(6): 299–320.

Climent C. E., B. S. M. Diop, T. W. Harding, H. H. A. Ibrahim, L. LadridoIgnacio, and N. N. Wig (1980). 'Mental health in primary health care'. *WHO chronicle*, 34: 231–6.

Cooper B. (1981). 'Psychiatric illness in general medical practice. An investigation in Mannheim'. *Int. J. Rehab. Res.*, 4: 86–7.

Corin E. (1976). 'Zebola: une psychotherapie communeautaire en milieu urbain'. *Psychopathologie Africaine*, 12: 349.

Craig T. J., C. Siegel, K. Hopper, Shang Lin, and N. Sartorius (1997). 'Outcome in schizophrenia and related disorders compared between developing and developed countries'. *British Journal of Psychiatry*, 170: 229–33.

Crapanzano V. (1973). *The Hamadsha*. London: University of California Press.

Crapanzano V., V. Garrison (eds) (1976). *Case studies in spirit possession*. New York: John Wiley & Sons.

Crapanzano V. (1980). *Tuhami, Portrait of a Moroccan*. Chicago: University of Chicago Press.

Devereux G. (1979). 'Die Verunsicherung der Geisteskranken'. *Curare*, 2(4): 215–21.

Dhadphale M. (1984). Psychiatric morbidity among patients attending district hospital outpatient clinics in Kenya. *MD Thesis*. Kenya: University of Nairobi.

Dijk van Paul (1993). *Geneeswijzen in Nederland*. Ankh Hermes, Deventer.

Dijkhuis J. H. (1988). Psychotherapie: steeds weer ter discussie. *Tijdschrift voor Psychotherapie*, 14(4): 194–203.

Dilling H., S. Weyerer, and I. Enders (1978). 'Patienten mit psychischen Storungen in der Algemeinpraxis and ihre psychiatrische Uberbeweisungsbedurftigkeit'. *Monograph Gesamtgeb Psychiatrie*, 17: 135–60.

Dohrenwend B. P., Dohrenwend B. Snell (1981). Perspectives on the past and future of psychiatric epidemiology. *Am. J. Publ. Health*, 72(11): 1271–9.

Dormaar M., J. N. Luijk Van, and R. Giel (1974). 'Psychiatric illness in two contrasting outpatient populations'. *Soc. Psychiatry*, 9: 155–61.

Edelstein & Edelstein (1945). *Aesclepios*. Berkely: John Hopkins.

Edgerton R. B., A. Cohen (1994). 'Culture and schizophrenia: The DOSMD challenge'. British *Journal of Psychiatry*, 164: 222–30.

Eliade M. (1964), *Shamanism: Archaic techniques of ecstasy*. Pantheon: Princeton.

El-Islam M. F. (1983). 'Cultural change and intergenerational relationships in Arabian families'. *Int. J. of Family Pyschiat.*, 4(4): 321–9.

Ellenberger H. F. (1970). *The Discovery of the Unconsious*. New York: Basic Books.

Ellis A. (1974). *Humanistic Psychotherapy: The Rationalemotive Approach*. New York: McGraw Hill. (Ned vertaling 1979. Van Loghum Slaterus. Deventer).

Erickson M. H., E. L. Rossi (ed.) (1980). *The Nature of Hypnosis and Suggestion: Part I*. New York: Irvington Publishers.

Erinosho O. A. (1979). 'The evolution of modern psychiatric care in Nigaria'. *American Journal of Psychiatry*, 136(12).

Finkler K. (1985). *Spiritualist healers in Mexico*. New York: Praeger.

Frank, J. D. and J. B. Frank (1993). *Persuasion and Healing*. Baltimore and London: Johns Hopkins University Press.

Freedman N., D. M. Engelhardt, and L. D. Hankoff *et al.* (1958). Dropout from out-patient psychiatric treatment. *Arch. Neurol. Psych.*, 80: 657–6.

Freud S. (1913). 'Zur Einleitung der Behandlung'. *Gesammelte werke*, 8: 454–78.

Fuller Torrey E. (1986). *Witchdoctors and Psychiatrists*. New York: Harper & Row.

Garfield S. L. (1983). 'Effectiviness of psychotherapy: the perennial controversy'. *Professional Psychology: Research and Practice*, 14: 35–43.

Gater R., Sousa B. de Almeida, G. Barrientos *et al.* (1991). 'The pathways to psychiatric case a cross cultural study'. *Psychol. Med.* 21, 761–74.

Geest van der S. (1985). 'Integration or fatal embrace? The uneasy relationship between indigenous and western medicine'. *Curare*, 8: 914.

Geffray C. (1990). *La cause des armes au Mozambique*. Paris: Karthala.
Giel R., Y. Gezahegn, and J. N. Van Luijk (1968). 'Faith-healing and spirit possession in Ghion, Ethiopia'. *Soc. Sc. & Med.*, 2: 63–79.
Giel R. and J. N. Van Luijk (1969). 'Psychiatric morbidity in a small Ethiopian town'. *British Journal of Psychiatry*, 115: 149–62.
Giel R. (1972). 'Psychiatrie in de praktijk van de huisarts'. *Huisarts en Wetenschap*, 16: 203–9.
Giel R. Horn ten, G. H. M. M. (1982), 'Patterns of Mental Health Care in a Dutch Register Area'. *Social psychiatry*, 17: 117–23.
Giel R. (1986). Lecture at WHO conference Kopenhagen.
Goldberg D. P. (1974). 'Psychiatric disorders'. *Lancet*, II: 1245–7.
Goldberg D. P., B. Blackwell (1970). Psychiatric illness in general practice. A detailed study using a new method of case identification. *British Medical Journal*, II: 439–43.
Goldberg D. P., P. Huxley (1980). *Mental illness in the community: The pathway to psychiatric care*, 2nd edition 1992. London: Tavistock Publications.
Hankin J. R. and J. S. Oktay (1979). 'Mental disorder and primary care: An analytic review of the litterature'. *National Institute of Mental Health Series D*, no. 5, US Deptt. of Health, Education and Welfare Publication (ADM) 78–661.
Harding T. W., M. W. de Arango, J. Baltazar, Climent, C. E., Ibrahim, H. H. A., and L. LadridoIgnacio *et al.* (1980). Mental disorders in primary health care: A study of their frequency and diagnosis in four developing countries. *Psychological Medicine*, 10: 231–41.
Helman C. (1993). *Culture, health and illness*. Oxford: Butterworth-Heinemann.
Hoeper E. W. (1979). 'Observations on the impact of psychiatric disorders upon primary healthcare'. *Mental health services in general health care*. Washington, DC: National Academy of Sciences.
Hoeper E. W., G. R. Nycs, and P. Cleary (1979). 'The quality of mental health services in an organized primary health care setting'. Final report, NIMH contract number: DBE770071. Marshfield Medical Foundation. Wisconsin: Marhfield.
Hoeper E. W. and L. G. Kessler *et al.* (1984). 'The usefulness of screening for mental illness'. *Lancet*, 1: 33–5.
Hollingshead A. B. and F. C. Redlich (1958). *Social Class and Mental Illness*. New York: John Wiley & Sons.
Horn ten G. H. M. M. (1982). 'Nazorg geeft kopzorg'. *Maandblad voor Geestelijke Volksgezondheid*, 12: 12791294.
Horton R. (1967 a). 'African traditional thought and western science'. Part I: From tradition to science. *Africa*, 37(1): 5071.
——— (1967 b). 'African traditional thought and western science'. Part II: The 'closed' and 'open' predicaments. *Africa*, 37(2): 155–87.

——— (1993). *Patterns of thought in Africa and the West.* Cambridge: Cambridge University Press.

Hough R., J. Landsverk, and J. Stone *et al.* (1983). 'Comparison of psychiatric screening questionnaires for primary care patients'. Report on contract 278–81–0036. Rockville: NIMH.

HPSSS (1987). *Health and Personal Social Services Statistics for England.* London: Department of Health and Social Security.

Huxley, P. J., D. P. Goldberg, G. P. Maguire, and V. A. Kincey (1979). 'Prediction of the Course of Minor Psychiatric Disorders'. *British Journal of Psychiatry*, 135: 535–43.

ICMR (1988). *Community Mental Health News*, nos 11 & 12. Bangalore: NIMHANS.

——— (1988–9). *Community Mental Health News*, nos 13 & 14. Bangalore: NIMHANS.

Ilechukwu S. T. C. (1991). 'Psychiatry in Africa: Special problems and unique features'. *Transcultural Psychiatric Reseach Review*, 28: 169–218.

Jablensky A., N. Sartorius, and G. Ernberg *et al.* (1992). 'Schizophrenia: Manifestations, incidence and course in different cultures'. *Psychological Medicine.* A WHO ten-country study, monograph supplement, 20: 1–97.

Janzen J. M. (1978). *The Quest for Therapy in Lower Zaire.* Berkeley: University of California Press.

Jilek W. G. (1974). *Salish Indian mental health and culture change: Psychohygienic and Therapeutic Aspects of the Guardian Spirit Ceremonial.* Toronto: Holt, Rhinehart & Winston.

——— (1994). 'Traditional healing in the prevention and treatment of alcohol an drug abuse'. *Transcultural Psychiatric Research Review*, 31: 219–58.

Jones L., L. Badger, and R. Ficken *et al.* (1987). 'Inside the hidden mental health network'. Examining mental health care delivery of primary care physicians. *Gen. Hosp. Psychiat.*, 9: 287–93.

Jong de A., R. Giel, G. H. M. M. Horn ten, C. J. Slooff, and D. Wiersma (1983). 'Nazorg bij nietaffectieve psychosen: Ontwikkelingen in de samenwerking binnen de GGZ'. *Tijdschrift voor Psychiatrie*, 25(6): 422–39.

Jong de J. T. V. M., G. A. J. Klein, and G. H. M. M. Horn ten (1986). 'A base line study on mental disorders in Guinea Bissau'. *British Journal of Psychiatry*, 148: 27–32.

Jong de J. T. V. M. (1986 b). 'Palmwijn in nieuwe zakken, oftewel enkele gedachten naar aanleiding van een Ndoprituee'l'. *Nederlands Tijdschrift voor Psychiatrie*, 28(1): 15–29.

——— (1987). *A Descent into African Psychiatry.* Amsterdam: Royal Tropical Institute.

——— (1989 b). 'Sociale psychiatrie vanuit transcultureel perspectief'. *Tijdschrift voor Psychiatrie*, 31(4): 253–66.

——— (1989). 'Ambulatory mental health care for migrants in the Netherlands'. *Curare*, 17(1): 25–34.

——— (1996). 'A comprehenisve public mental health programme in Guinea-Bissau: A useful model for African. Asian and Latin-American countries'. *Psychological Medicine*, 26: 97–108.

——— (1997). 'Stemmen en visioenen: Een meta-culturele visie op het verschijnsel hallucineren'. *Maandblad Geestelijke Volksgezondheid*, 52(2): 142–56.

Jangde J. T. Komproe I (1997). 'A 14-year follow-up of a cohort of chronic psychotic patients in Guinea-Bissau', (unpublished data).

Kazdin A. E. (1979). 'Nonspecific treatment factors in psychotherapy outcome research'. *J. Cons. Clin. Psychol.*, 47: 846–51.

Kessel W. I .N. (1960). 'Psychiatric morbidity in a London general practice'. *British Journal of Preventive and Social Medicine*, 14: 1622.

Kessler L., P. Cleary, and J. Burke (1985). 'Psychiatric disorders in primary care'. *Arch. Gen. Psychiat*, 42: 583–7.

Kirk S. A. and M. E. Therrien (1975). 'Community mental health myths and the fate of former hospitalised patients'. *Psychiatry*, 209–17.

Kleinman A. M. (1980). *Patients and Healers in the Context of Culture.* Berkeley: University of California Press.

Kleinman A. M. and J. L. Gale (1982). 'Patients treated by physicians and folk healers: a comparative outcome study in Taiwan'. *Culture, Medicine and Psychiatry*, 6(4): 405–20.

Kleinman A. M. (1988). *Rethinking Psychiatry.* New York: The Free Press.

Karno M., J. H. Jenkins, A. de la Selva, F. Santana, C. Telles, S. Lopes, and J. Mintz (1987). 'Expressed emotion and schizophrenic outcome among Mexican-American families'. *J. Nerv. Ment. Disease*, 175: 143–51.

Lambert & Bergin in Garfield S. L. & A. E. Bergin (1980). *Handbook of Psychotherpy and Behavior Change: An Empirical Analysis.* New York: Second edition, Wiley.

Lamberts H., B. Hartman (1982). 'Psychische en sociale problemen in de huisartsenpraktijk'. *Huisarts en Wetenschap*, 25: 333–42 en 376–93.

Lévi-Strauss C. (1963). *The effectiveness of symbols: Structural anthropology.* New York: Basic Books.

Luborski L., J. Mintz, A. H. Auerbach, P. Cristoph, H. M. Bachrach, T. Todd, M. Johnson, M. Cohen, and C. P. O'Brien (1980). 'Predicting the outcome of psychotherapy: Findings of the Penn psychotherapy project'. *Archives of General Psychiatry*, 37: 471–81.

Mann A. H., R. Jenkins, and E. Belsley (1981). 'The twelve-month outcome of patients with neurotic illness in general practice'. *Psychological Medicine*, 11: 535–50.

Manton K. G., A. Korten, M. A. Woodbury, M. Anker, and A. Jablensky (1994). 'Symptom profiles of psychiatric disorders based on graded disease classes: An illustration using data from the WHO International Pilot Study of Schizophrenia'. *Psychological Medicine*, 24(1): 133–44.

Marks J. N., D. P. Goldberg, and V. H. Hillier (1979). 'Determinants of the ability of general practitioners to detect psychiatric illness'. *Psychol. Med.*, 9: 337–53.

Marsella A. J., J. Westermeyer (1993). 'Cultural aspects of treatment: Conceptual, methodological, and clinical issues and directions', in Sartorius *et al. The Treatment of Mental Disorders.* Washington/London: WHO/APA.

Masamba Ma Mpolo (1976). *La Liberation des Envoutes.* Yaounde: Edition CLE.

May R. (1958). *Man's Search for Himself.* New York: Dell Publishing.

McGraw B. (1991). 'Catholic missionary order issues an apology to Indians in Canada'. *Akron-Beacon Journal*, 7 August.

Mbiti J. S. (1969). 'African religions and philosophy'. London: Heinemann.

McDermott W. (1977). 'Evaluating the physician and his technology'. *Daedalus*, 106: 135–58.

Ministry of Health (1980). *Health for All: An alternative strategy.* Report of a study group set up by joint Indian Social Science Research Council and Indian Council of Medical Research, New Delhi.

Mullings L. (1984). 'Therapy, ideology, and social change: Mental healing in urban Ghana'. Berkeley: University of California Press.

MHSSR (1983–4). 'Specialty Mental Health Organisations USA'. National Institute of Mental Health, Division of Biometry and Applied Sciences, 5600 Fishers Lane, Rockville, Maryland 20857.

NCVG (1987). C. Jacobs, E. Ketting, GGZ in Getallen Amsterdam.

Ndetei D. M., J. Muhangi (1979). 'The prevalence and clinical presentation of psychiatric illness in a rural setting in Kenya'. *Brit. J. Psychiat*, 135: 269–72.

Ödegaard O. (1962). 'Psychiatric epidemiology'. *Proceedings of the Royal Society of Medicine*, 55: 831–7.

Orley J. (1970). *Culture and Mental Health.* Nairobi: East African Publising House.

Orley J. H., J. K. Wing (1979). 'Psychiatric disorders in two African villages'. *Arch. Gen. Psychiat.*, 36: 513–20.

Ormel J., R. Giel (1983). 'Omvang, beloop en behandeling van psychische stoornissen in de praktijk van de huisarts'. *Nederlands Tijdschr voor Psychiatrie*, 10: 688–710.

Peltzer K. (1987). 'Some contributions of traditional healing practices towards psychosocial health care in Malawi'. *Fachbuchhandlung fur Psychologie.* Eschborn near Frankfurt am Main.

Pillsbury B. (1979). *Reaching the rural poor: Indigenous health practitioners are there already*. Washington: USAID.

Prince R. H. (1960). 'The use of rauwolfia for the treatment of psychoses by Nigerian native doctors'. *American Journal of Psychiatry*, 118: 147–9.

Regier D. A., I. D. Goldberg, and C.A. Taube (1978). 'The de facto US mental health services system: A public health perspective'. *Arch. Gen. Psychiat.*, 35: 685–93.

Regier D. A., I. D. Goldberg, B. J. Burns, J. Hankins, E. W. Hoeper, and G. R. Nycs (1982). 'Specialist/generalist division of responsibility for patients with metal disorders'. *Arch. Gen. Psychiat*, 39: 219–24.

Regier D. A., J. K. Myers, M. Kramer, L.N. Robins, D. G. Blazer, R. L. Hough, W. W. Eaton, and B. Z. Locke (1984). 'The NIMH epidemiological catchment area program'. *Arch. Gen. Psychiat*, 41, 934–41.

Rice L. M. (1983). 'The relationship in client-centered therapy'. M. J. Lambert and Dow-Jones-Irwin (eds) in *A Guide to Psychotherapy and Patient Relationships*. Homewood Ill.

Rogers C. (1957). 'The necessary and sufficient conditions of therapeutic personality change'. *J. Cons. Psychol.*, 21: 95–103.

Sarr D. (1980). 'Problématique du village psychiatrique de Kénia en Casamance'. Thèse no. 21 Faculté de Médicine et de Pharmacie. Université de Dakar.

Schagen S. (1983). *Het Effect van Psychotherapie: Meetbaarheid en Resultaten*. Van Loghum Slaterus. Deventer.

Schulberg H., M. McClelland, and W. Gooding (1987). 'Six-months outcome for medical patients with major depressive disorders'. *J. Gen. Int. Med.*, 2: 312–17.

Seligman M. (1995). 'The effectiveness of Psychotherapy'. *American Psychologist*, 50, 905–14.

Seligman M. (1996). 'Science as an ally of practice. *American Psychologist*, 51, 1072–9.

Shepherd M., B. Cooper, A. C. Brown, and C. Kalton (1981). *Psychiatric Illness in General Practices* (2nd edition). Oxford: Oxford University Press.

Sloane R. B., F. R. Staples, A. H. Cristol, N. J. Yorkston, K. Whipple (1975). *Psychotherapy versus Behavior Therapy*. Harvard University Press.

Strupp H. H. (1970). 'Specific versus nonspecific factors in psychotherapy and the problem of control'. *Arch. Gen. Psychiatry*, 23: 393–401.

Strupp H. H., S. W. Hadley (1977). 'A tripartite model of mental health and therapeutic outcomes'. *American Psychologist*, 32: 187–96.

Strupp H. H., A. S. Gurman, and A. M. Razin (eds) (1977). *A Reformulation of the Dynamics of the Therapist's Contribution in Effective*

Psychotherapy: A Handbook of Research. New York: Pergamon Press.
——— (1980). 'Success and failure in time-limited psychotherapy'. *Archives of General Psychiatry*, 37: 595–603, 708–16, 813–41, 947–54.
Sundkler B. (1976). *Zulu Zion and some Swazi Zionists.* London: Oxford University Press.
Susser E., J. Wanderling (1994). 'Epidemiology of non-affective acute remitting psychosis versus schizophrenia: Sex and sociocultural setting'. *Archives of General Psychiatry*, 51(4), 294–301.
Swaan de A. (1979). 'Uitgaansbeperking of uitgangsangst. Over de verschuiving van bevelshuishouding naar onderhandelingshuishouding: De Gids'. Meulenhoff.
Swaen G., G. H. M. M. Horn ten (1980). 'Verwijzingen uit de huisartsenpraktijk naar de GGZ in de jaren 1973 tot en met 1978'. *Sociale Psychiatrie.* R. U. Groningen.
Takemoto T., K. Usukine, and M. Otsu (1979). 'A follow-up study of alcoholic patients treated by Naikan therapy'. *Communication to 2nd Annual Meeting on Naikan*, Kyoto (cit in Jilek 1994).
Tan M. L. (1985). 'Current state of research on traditional medicine in the Philippines'. *Research report no. 2.* AKAP research.
Waxler N. (1977). 'Is outcome for schizophrenia better in non-industrialized societies'. *J. of Nerv. and Ment. Disease*, 167: 144–58.
Westermeyer J. (1979). 'Mortality and psychosis in a peasant society'. *J. Nerv. Ment. Dis.*, 166: 769–74.
——— (1983). 'Treatment strategies for mental disorder in a society without psychiatric resources. *Med. Anthrop.* 7: 17–28.
——— (1989). Psychiatric epidemiology across cultures: current issues and trends'. *Transcult Psych. Res. Rev.*, 26: 5–25.
WHO Expert committee on mental health (1975). 'Organization of mental health services in developing countries'. *Technical Report Series 564.* Geneva: WHO.
WHO (1981). *Report from the WHO Collaborative Study on Strategies for Extending Mental Health Care.* Geneva: WHO.
——— (1984). 'Mental health care in developing countries: a critical appraisal of research findings'. *Technical Report Series 698.* Geneva: WHO.
WHO/MND/IND (1988). 'National mental health programme for India'. *Progress Report* 1982–88.
WHO (1976–1989). 'WHO special programme of technical cooperation in mental health'. *Reports of the Meetings of the African Mental Health Action Groups.* Geneva: WHO.
Wooff K., D. Goldberg, and T. Fryers (1986). 'Patients in receipt of community psychiatric nursing care in Salford, 1976–82'. *Psychol. Med.*, 16: 407–14.

7

Too Close for Comfort: Mental Illness and the Irish in Britain

Gerard Leavey

'The rage of Caliban at not seeing his face in a mirror......
–It is a symbol of Irish art. The cracked looking-glass of a servant'

JAMES JOYCE, *Ulysses*

INTRODUCTION

The Irish in Britain, and their second generation, have one of the worst health profiles of any ethnic or migrant group. While some of the excess morbidity of the Irish may be explained by class and poverty, there appears to the a gap of explanation for the rest (Haskey, 1996). Culture and environmental adversity may be influential factors. Unfortunately, there remains a general ignorance about the aetiology of ill health among the Irish in Britain. Despite being the largest migrant minority ethnic group, and an ethnic group in some distress, they have been largely excluded from academic medicine and psychiatry. Consequently, they do not feature prominently in health policy at local or national level (Bracken *et al.*, 1998; Leavey *et al.*, 1997).

The reasons for this exclusion are unclear but can, in part, be better understood in the way in which ethnicity and racial issues in Britain have been defined and contextualized. Discourse around ethnicity and race in Britain in the latter part of this century has focused mainly on Black people. The word 'immigrant', for example, is often taken as a reference to Black people despite the fact that the majority of immigrants to Britain are White (Skellington and Moss, 1992). Ethnic identities falling between the polarities of Black and White are generally eschewed from investigation. In addition, the Irish community, despite its size in Britain, has failed to effectively vocalize and register its concerns about issues affecting Irish people. Anti-Irish racism which has been a centuries-old feature of British culture was injected with increased meaning and force over the past 30 years. The social and political climate in Britain in this period pushed the Irish community into a nervous strategy of acquiescent invisibility. At a time when ethnic membership has been used a a bargaining counter for allocation of health and welfare resources, the Irish have been double-faulted by their invisibilty.

In this chapter, the issues of colonialism, migration and ethnicity in relation to the psychological ill health of the Irish in Britain will be covered. For consideration, too, is the question of class and the economic position of the Irish community. The first section will review the available evidence on the psychological ill health of the Irish in Britain, with particular regard to suicide and self-harm. The issue of Irish alcohol use and alcoholism, often avoided, containing as it does, a mixture of stereotyping and victim-blaming, requires exploration.

Irish migrants in Britain have faced difficulties which, at times, have strong similarity with those of other 'external' groups, regardless of colour. However, is this commonality of adversity in Britain a sufficient enough explanation of Irish vulnerability to mental distress or is there evidence of a genetic predisposition towards mental illness in the Irish? Are the Irish in Britain more at risk of psychological problems because of an inability to identify and support collectively? Do the Irish bring their psychological problems with them or do these problems arise following migration itself?

Social Class and Health

The Irish have a socio-economic profile similar to that of other disadvantaged minority ethnic groups in Britain. Owner occupation is a less common form of housing tenure for households with an Irish-born head than for all other Whites and many ethnic minority groups. More than a quarter of Irish-headed households were accommodated by the public sector in 1991, a percentage well above the average for White households and minority ethnic groups households. In addition, a disproportionate number of Irish people are found among the homeless and living in hostels. (O'Meachair *et al.*, 1988).

Men born in Ireland suffer an unemployment rate 50 per cent higher than the White average and men from the Republic of Ireland have an unemployment rate similar to those of other ethnic minority males. Despite a large percentage of the Irish-born being highly qualified, a third of Republic-born men work in the construction industry (Owen, 1995). Divorce is much more common than the average for White people as a whole.

All of the above would tend to suggest that the high level of psychological distress found among the Irish is related to their socio-economic position in British society. Recent studies, however, which examine morbidity and mortality data of Irish people, indicate strongly that poverty and class are unlikely to be the sole determinants of poor health in this community. Harding and Balarajan (1996) studied a 1 per cent sample of those people who were second generation Irish, aged fifteen or over, in England and Wales in 1971 and who died in the subsequent eighteen years. Earlier studies showed first generation Irish to have significantly poorer health than all other immigrant groups. A characteristic of immigrant groups is that their patterns of health and mortality tend to converge with those of the host population. Harding and Balarajan give evidence that the Irish do not conform to this pattern, in that the mortality of the second generation Irish is significantly higher than overall mortality for all causes and most major causes of death, including suicide and unexplained death. Clearly there is something about being Irish in Britain which provokes an increased vulnerability to poor health.

Irish Migrants and Mental Illness

The relationship between Jews and Tay-Sachs diseases, or sickle-cell anaemia and African Caribbeans, for instance, arouses little debate, and even less passion. Except, perhaps when the particular needs of these groups are not met. Studies of psychiatric morbidity, especially schizophrenia, and race and ethnicity seem predestined to fall into a bear-pit of fiercely contested views, within which it is often argued that the concepts of race and ethnicity are misapplied (Bhopal, 1997) or that, crucially, all such studies are prone to misdiagnosis (Littlewood and Lipsedge, 1981) and the pathologization of minority groups (Sashidharan, 1993). Much of the criticism suggests that this type of research, while focusing on ethnicity as an independent variable within which a genetic predisposition is often implicit, overlooks more salient adverse environmental factors and factors of class and racism. Whatever the criticisms surrounding psychiatric research and ethnicity, communities such as the Irish and the African-Caribbean, where high rates of mental illness are found, are locked in a 'no-win' dilemma. Rejection and denial of higher rates of mental illness may fragment a coherent and effective lobbying for increased health care resources. On the other hand, the acceptance of high rates of mental illness is often regarded by these communities as confirming ancient racial stereotypes. Thus, the natural concern follows that the issue of a community with problems can very easily manipulated into an issue of a 'problem community'. As will be examined later, those groups which have not been accorded full acceptance within British society may become further stigmatized and excluded.

Evidence of stress and psychological vulnerability among the Irish in Britain began to appear with the analysis of data on admissions to psychiatric hospitals where the Irish were found to have the highest rates for any groups (Cochrane, 1997 and Cochrane & Bal, 1989). They were found to have highest overall rates for all diagnoses (depression, alcohol abuse, neuroses, personality disorders, and other psychoses) with the exception of schizophrenia. Admission rates among Irish men were found to be excessively high for diagnoses of depression and alcohol abuse. Irish women and men had rates for alcohol related disorders between seven and nine times those of English-born people. Rates for diagnoses of depression among Irish women were particularly high: 410 per 100,000 compared to 166 per 100,000 for English-born women. Admissions-based data, however, may not provide a true indication of prevalence of psychiatric morbidity in the community. They are likely to be heavily influenced by socio-economic and service-utilization factors. Provoked by the results of the hospital admissions study, Cochrane and Stopes-Roe (1979) carried out community-based comparative research which perplexingly showed the Irish population to have lower levels of psychological distress than their English counterparts. In an effort to explain this contradiction, a 'twin selection' process has been suggested for Irish migration. Thus, there exists one group of unhealthy individuals, already vulnerable to mental distress and seeking escape from personal and social problems, contrasted with a second group positively selected, healthy and secure (Williams, 1992). In any case, the study was flawed by the unrepresentativeness of the Irish sample with a higher proportion of the Irish, as compared to the English respondents, being middle-class home owners. This is of course at variance with the true socio-economic picture. It may be argued that the issue of an excess of mental illness among Irish people is based upon stale data and may not be relevant today in the context of a changed pattern in Irish migration. However, other evidence of continuing stress and poor mental health in the Irish community is demonstrated by high rates of suicide, discussed below.

SUICIDE AND SELF-HARM IN BRITAIN

A number of small studies over three decades have shown high rates of suicide and attempted suicide among Irish migrants in Britain. Burke's studies in Birmingham showed that Irish people, particularly women, have about a 30 per cent higher rate for attempted suicide than UK-born people and that these rates were higher than those born of Belfast and Dublin. (Burke, 1976; Merril and Owens, 1985). Mortality data classified by country of birth (1988–92, Office of Population Censuses and Surveys (OPCS)) show the Irish to have a rate of 17.4 deaths from suicide and unexplained death per 100,000, an excess of 53 per cent (Balarajan, 1996). In a previous study, Raleigh and Balarajan examined suicide levels and trends among 17 immigrant groups in England and Wales for the years 1979–83. Many immigrant groups, especially Russians, Poles, Scots and Irish had considerably higher rates of suicide than the native population. Other migrant groups, such as people from the Caribbean, the Indian subcontinent and southern Europe, had lower rates than the national average. The research also indicated that suicide rates of most migrants tend to reflect the patterns in their country of origin and that migration in general does not increase the risk of suicide. To some extent the picture appears different for Irish migrants. Suicide levels in

England and Wales for Irish people, particularly women, were high compared to the level found in Ireland. Furthermore, immigrants from Ireland show an even greater excess at a younger age (20–9 years) compared to all other age groups. Trends in suicide over the periods 1970–72 to 1979–83 showed a national increase of 18 per cent among men in England and Wales. A marked and statistically significant increase was observed among men born in Russia (75 per cent) and Ireland (29 per cent). Research conducted in an area of inner London concluded that classification of suicide is biased with respect to ethnicity (Neeleman *et al.*, 1997). That is, suicide among minority ethnic groups, particularly the Irish and Scots, is under-reported. Neeleman *et al.* report a suicide rate for Irish people three times that of English-born Whites. The rate for Scottish-born migrants was also excessive, at twice the local rate.

The suicide rate in Ireland for the greater part of this century have remained low, indeed the lowest rate in Europe (Kelleher, 1996). The incidence of suicide remained low for Irish migrants to the USA and Australia, ranked twelth among thirteen ethnic groups in the USA (Sainsbury and Barraclough, 1968; Lester, 1972). It may be that these low rates in Ireland are explained by under-reporting in Ireland as shown by Clarke-Finnegan and Fahy (1983). However, under-reporting is not unique to Ireland as demonstrated by a recent study of London suicides by O'Donnell and Farmer (1995). Indeed, Kelleher (1996) suggests that suicide figures for Ireland are now more accurately recorded, as evidenced by a decrease in deaths recorded as undetermined. Furthermore, they may be more accurately recorded in Ireland than in England and Wales (An Roinn Slainte, 1996).

It has been suggested that stress associated with migration is unlikely to play a part in the high rates of mental illness, suicide and parasuicide found in Britain's Irish community (Bebbington *et al.*, 1981; Clare, 1974). In support of this belief is offered geographical propinquity, absence of language barriers and a cultural closeness. While seductive, this somewhat simplistic and reductionist arguments obscures a more complicated set of relationships and dynamics. It may be that this closeness in itself is a risk factor in the mental illness of Irish migrants to Britain. A parallel exists in Denmark where higher rates of mental illness are found in immigrants from bordering countries for whom immigration is easy and informal (Mortensen *et al.*, 1997). In a cross-cultural study of suicide and immigrant groups in Sweden, Ferrada-Noli (1997) found an over-representation among most immigrant groups, significantly for those migrants from neighbouring regions with comparatively close cultural affinity. Even allowing for the possibility that Irish migration could be considered a somewhat 'internal migration', there is sufficient evidence to suggest that this too is a risk factor for metal distress (Johannssen *et al.*, 1998).

While it is generally accepted that the act of migration in itself is not a predictor of mental disorder (Liebkind, 1992), Murphy (1977) points to data from countries such as Israel, Singapore and Canada which suggest that migrants often have lower rates of psychiatric hospitalization. In Britain, various studies report lower incidence of mental disorder among Asian immigrants (Cochrane, 1977; Cochrane, 1980). Raleigh and Balarajan (1992) show lower rates of suicide for some migrant groups such as African-Caribbeans. It is known, however, that certain factors associated with migration increase the risk of mental distress. These are: lowered socioeconomic status, language barriers, separation from family, antipathy of the host population, isolation from persons of a similar cultural background, traumatic experiences prior to migration, and unpreparedness for migration (Canadian Task Force Report 1988; Kunz, 1973).

For most intending migrants, excluding refugees, there is generally a long process of immigration interviews, health checks, financial preparation and arrangements for arrival. Migration to Britain from Ireland, however, is relatively inexpensive and free of restraint. This ease of flow will lead to a type of migration not found in other migrant groups. Many Irish people migrating to Britain see their migration as a temporary sojourn rather than a permanent laying down of roots. This in itself may establish problematic and poorly resolved conflicts that require further consideration.

A direct association has always existed between economic depression in Ireland and immigration. At times of high unemployment in Ireland, young Irish people appear to resign themselves, with somewhat sanguine fatalism, to migration (Carlsen and Nilsen, 1995). Their research shows significant differences between Irish men and women in attitudes and psychological effects of the prospect of migration. Men tended to be optimistic, while women were more likely to find it distressful. Women migrants were also likely to have lower self-esteem than those intending to remain. This may support the hypothesis, for women at least, of negative selection. The general pattern of migration to Britain has been that of individuals who arrive unprepared and without the intention of settling. In this case, the ease of migration works against them. It is likely that many would had felt that their whiteness, English language and cultural familiarity would afford them an advantage in the employment and housing markets. The socio-economic position of the Irish in Britain does not appear to support this optimism. It is also likely that, free of any family and social constraints placed upon them in the smaller, more close-knit communities of Ireland, they will adopt a lifestyle that places them at greater vulnerability to ill health.

Without any commitment to settle in Britain and aspiring to return to Ireland at some unspecified time, it seems that many young Irish people drift into an unsettled lifestyle of casual work, accommodation, and relationships. The higher rates of single people and divorce among the Irish in Britain may be supporting evidence. Irish people, regardless of length of stay in Britain, when speaking of 'home' are referring to Ireland. This may seem oddly sentimental but it underlines several points of significance about the Irish community in Britain. It underscores the point that while other ethnic groups, such as people of Caribbean or Asian descent, will argue ardently for inclusion within a British identity, the Irish will not, or at least, for reasons examined later, are not free to do so.

Rack (1982) considers the similarity between certain migrants in Britain and the Turkish Gastarbeiter in Germany. He does not include the Irish in this, but he should. He suggests that many Indian and Pakistani immigrants still hold to the notion of returning 'home' and adopt an isolationist attitude in Britain, maintaining a nostalgic view of the culture they have left but ignorant of the changes that have occurred in their absence. Only while visiting on holiday are they confronted with the reality that both they and the homeland have changed, the possibility of fitting in again a last hope. The Gastarbeiter, often later in life will experience 'marginality', a distressful state 'usually resolved by the adoption of one of the identity options and abandonment of the other' (Rack, 1982, p. 38). Similarly, Eisenbruch (1988) has coined the term cultural bereavement in describing the loss of familiar land

and culture and although the term generally refers to refugees or people traumatically uprooted by war or persecution, I would suggest that it has a wider applicability for many migrant groups.

Ethnic Identity and Social Organization

Associated with this sense of Irish temporariness in the British social landscape, there, too, has been a general lack of political galvanization constructed around a positive Irish ethnic identity, contrasted with the experience of the Irish in North America. This is all the more surprising, when one takes into account their comparative numerical strength and long-standing presence in Britain. It may be argued that this is evidence of the facility of the Irish to assimilate into British life, despite an unwillingness to do so. To some extent this is true. However, in contrast with the USA, we see that Irishness, and the substantial contribution that generations of Irish people have made to British economic, social and cultural life, remains largely disregarded and uncelebrated. In the USA, aspiring politicians will unearth scores of tombstones and search every family tree to uproot an Irish connection. In Britain, this is rarely the case. There is simply nothing to be gained and possibly, everything to be lost, in doing so. This is likely to have had a negative psychological effect on Irish migrants and their children growing up in Britain.

Colonialism and Anti-Irish Racism—The Missing Link

Ireland experienced a colonialism which, in most aspects, including starvation, slavery and expropiation of wealth, was as destructive as that experienced by other colonized peoples. Along with other colonized groups they share a long history of assigned racial difference and inferiority which lent permission for imperialist enterprise. Prior to domination of Africa and India by Western states, the experiment of colonialism in Ireland gave birth to a repertoire of self-serving philosophical, economic, and religious justifications that would be later employed in other colonial enterprises. Within this ideological framework, the Irish were variously characterized as indolent, simple-minded, savage, feminine and duplicitious (Kibberd, 1996). The overarching justification for English rule was that the Irish, an inferior race, were unfit to govern themselves and required the civilizing control of English power. The popularity of scientific racism in the nineteenth century witnessed the emergence of concepts such as 'negrescenece' by which the Irish were allocated a position in the racial hierarchy, halfway between the ape and the African—in short, the missing link (Curtis, 1978). This warrants scant attention except to say that racism of this kind was taken seriously within British academic milieu and quickly found expression within the broader social and cultural life. Thus the depiction of Irish people as simian-featured monsters became a staple feature of English cartoons in popular and informative magazines such as *Punch* (Curtis, 1978). The debasement of the Irish character and culture substituted for any rational debate concerning either the British presence in Ireland or indeed, the Irish presence in Britain. As Curtis (1978) has suggested, this negation of Irish grievance through the denigration of the Irish character has been a resonant feature of British social and political discourse. Latterly, the renewal of Irish nationalism in the 1970s contemporaneously witnessed an invigorated depiction in English popular culture of the Irish as neanderthal, stupid, and brutish. Long after jokes about African-Caribbeans and Jews ceased to be tolerated in the British media, the Irish as an ethnic group appear to remain exempt from this type of sensitivity (Leavey, 1998). Furthermore, throughout the past three decades the Irish in Britain have remained heavily scrutinized by the police and the secret services (Curtis, 1978). Others, such as the Birmingham six, the Maguire Family and the Guilford four were wrongfully convicted of terrorist crimes. Many in the Irish community in Britain have concluded that to be Irish is to be suspect. Thus, a strategy of invisibility and disengagement has evolved. In this context, the Irish have been disabled in creating a positive Irish identity in Britain. The notion of an internalization of racial hatred is well accepted. For many minority ethnic children who are Black and brought up in a dominant White culture, their blackness has been felt as an alien, unwanted characteristic. It is likely that the children of Irish parents, in the midst of a negative portrayal of Irish people, will have experienced a psychological splitting along the fault lines of identity, belonging and self-esteem.

Pilgrim and Rogers (1993) suggest that there is an alternative perspective on mental health and ethnicity which moves beyond attempts to identify the casual factors in the high incidence of mental illness among Irish and African-Caribbeans in Britain. This alternative perspective is provided by what they describe as the 'new racism' which is preoccupied by defining who rightly belongs within the national community. Thus:

...while the 'old racism', underpinned by eugenics, proposed sterlisation and extermination, the new racism suggests banishment and exclusion. In the context of the British historical legacy of colonialism, the debate on race and madness may be seen as central to the inner workings of the 'new racism'.

They suggest that the Mental Health Act and the Prevention of Terrorism Act may be viewed having the same purpose within the range of 'repressive state apparatus'. Coercive psychiatry provides the state with a useful post-colonial alternative to repatriation. It provides the repressive state with a legitimized interior banishment and control of people deemed as 'other'. As the authors indicate, the predominant aspect of this discourse is threat, not distress.

...conducting research along a dualistic notion of 'Black' and 'White', or (implicitly) ex-colonised and ex-coloniser, differences between these groups are accentuated and polarised, and the cause of the 'problem' is identified at the level of the pathology of the individuals. Thus we may find that the reason that Black and Irish people are 'madder' than Whites in the discourse and practices of academic and clinical psychiatry, not in epidemiological studies which try to measure the incidence of psychiatric morbidity among ethnic groups'. (Pilgrim and Rogers, p. 61).

Greenslade (1992) in his analysis of the high rates of mental illness in the Irish community in Britain finds the work of Frantz Fanon a useful theoretical template. This argues that the power relationship of servant–master firmly established in the colonial period have been internalized and remain entrenched by the actors well after the colonial stage has been exited. What remains, in other words, is a colonization of the mind. Survival strategies for the migrant in the homeland of the colonizer are inevitably impossible choices of failure and rejection. The migrant may opt for an obvious merging and identification with the 'host', or an attempted discreet disappearance. In this scenario, the migrant will, at every turn, pick up the 'go to jail' card. Any attempt at assimilation is treated with ridicule, while any endeavour at preservation of indigenous culture is variously interpreted as subversive, ungrateful, remote, and conspiratorial.

Every instance of contact with the colonist Other is potentially fraught with anxiety for the migrant. To be accepted, s/he must act in accordance with the stereotypes imposed on them (as long as they are the 'positive ones'), of the happy-go-lucky, easy-going and cheerful native. At the same time the migrant learns that s/he is an object of fear, an unpredictable and violent natural force.

Fanon's interpretation of the post-colonial migrant experience is bleak but persuasive. The landscape that the migrant inhabits is perpetually uncomfortable, inducing alienation, uncertainty, and neurosis. The Irish experience in Britain, as Greenslade argues, has a definite similarity with that of other migrant and post-colonial peoples. However, although the conceptual premise given here permits a much needed recognition of shared vulnerability to psychological disorder via a shared colonial and post-colonial experience, we are left to puzzle low rates of mental illness found among certain African and Asian communities. These communities, too, are not immune to racist adversity and arguably endure much greater racism than the Irish. In the context of the 'new racism' discourse outlined by Pilgrims and Rogers, it is highly unlikely that African and Asian groups have the benefits of inclusion within the circumscribed 'national identity'. What then are the protective factors operating for some minority ethnic groups and not others?

Rational objectivity in medicine, as a putative scientific discipline, maybe a laudable aim. However, clinicians, as social animals, are unlikely to view or treat patients in a value-free manner. Indeed, it would be surprising if attitudes and beliefs about gender, class, sexual preference, and ethnicity did not seep into the relationship between patient and doctor. In a pressured environment where there is little space for a comprehensive review of, let alone empathy with, a patient's history, a shorthand correlation between the illness type and some other characteristic of the individual, may often follow. Racial stereotyping can intrude on clinical assessment, producing misdiagnosis and inappropriate treatment. The diagnosis of cannabis-induced psychosis among African-Caribbeans in Britain, widely held in psychiatry, though largely discredited, is one example. Irish people and alcoholism is another.

ALCOHOL

There is an almost inevitable sense of foreboding when discussing the issue of Irish and alcohol use. The apprehension derives from a desire to avoid an implacable stereotype that has clung to Irish ethnicity over time throughout the diaspora, diligently maintained in the popular media (Leavey, 1998). Subsequently, the opposing danger is to reflexively remain silent or underplay the extent of drinking problems within the community (Grey and Kinane, 1990). Stereotypes often contain an element of truth. As Harrison and Carr-Hill (1992) point out in their report on Irish drinking behaviour and social disadvantage among the Irish in Britain:

> Clearly, it is important to come to a balanced view about drinking in the Irish community. Alarmist reports about the magnitude of Irish drinking problems are likely to reinforce unhelpful stereotypes, while attempts to minimise or deny the scale of the problems will in the end not be believed.

Heavy alcohol consumption and alcoholism among the Irish, at home and abroad, is well documented (Stivers, 1978; Walsh, 1987). This ethnic-behavioural relationship often reifies into an axiomatic and overarching explanation for their high rates of illness (Clare, 1974; Cook, 1990; Adelstein, 1986).

The relationship is not that clear-cut. Less commonly acknowledged is the high levels of life-time abstinence among the Irish, higher than most other European countries (Walsh, 1987). O'Connor's study of young drinkers in London and Dublin (O'Connor 1975) found a higher proportion of abstainers among the Irish group than in the English but found the heaviest drinkers among the second generation Irish. This was a similar finding to Stivers (1978) and Greeley *et al.* (1980) among Irish second generation in the USA. It has been suggested, however, that the Irish may be more inclined to drinking behaviour which provokes greater physical and mental morbidity. Harrison and Carr-Hill (1972) suggest that alcohol intake among Irish people increases following migration to Britain and the increase in alcohol consumption is related to social adversity.

Excessive alcohol use is universally a common feature of groups and individuals with lower social status and income but that the incidence of alcoholism and consumption of alcohol differs markedly between cultural groups, even within the same society

(Helman, 1994). Different cultural groups, according to O'Connor (1975), can be placed within four main typologies in relation to attitudes towards alcohol consumption, from the abstinent culture to the over-permissive culture with ambivalent and permissive in between. O'Connor places the Irish within the alcohol ambivalent culture. He argues that alcohol use has played an integral part of Irish economic and social life over centuries, yet, religion-inspired movements have vigorously promoted abstinence. This, O'Connor suggests, has denied the Irish a coherent attitude towards alcohol consumption, an ambivalence which may lead to problematic drinking and alcoholism. This may be true but O'Connor's cultural models of drinking attitudes lacks historical explanation. Alcohol consumption is reported as excessive in certain ethnic groups whose language and culture have been debased or fragmented or where certain ethnic groups have experienced geographical and cultural dislocation. Native Americans, Inuit peoples, native Australians, Maoris, and Irish may be included here. There is no historical evidence that these groups had a peculiar propensity towards heavy alcohol consumption and in many cases, the opposite. Moreover, he fails to acknowledge the heterogeneity of ethnic groups, whereby class, education and region are significantly influential. Importantly, drinking behaviour must be contextualized.

The experience of many Irish people, particularly working-class Irish men, mostly labourers, is similar to that of the Gastarbeiters described by Rack (1982, p. 37). At periods of high unemployment in Ireland and economic boom in England, many Irish migrated to find work on the building sites of the major conurbations. Generally this was considered a temporary measure, designed, for a single person to ease financial pressures on the family, or, for a 'breadwinner' to send remittances home. Arriving in England with little finance, they settled for cheap accommodation that offered no cooking facilities and little privacy. In this context, the personal and social life of the Irish migrant became highly visible. The importance that pubs play in the economic and social life of many Irish people has largely been disregarded or misunderstood. Pub life for many Irish people is a means to maintaining Irish identity and minimizing feelings of loss and alienation. Irish pubs also provide an informal networking system for jobs and accommodation, crucial in the very transient labour sectors that many Irish migrants are located in. In temporary jobs and housing, and unable to open bank accounts, many Irish people have been obliged to cash their cheques with willing landlords. Thus the pub provides a function beyond the merely social and as such, the dependence on this institution becomes clearer.

CONCLUSION

Undoubtedly, the Irish in Britain suffer high rates of mental distress, perhaps higher than any other minority ethnic group. There is some evidence also that poor mental health is a problem that continues into the second and third generation. To some extent, poverty and racism offer some explanation for the high incidence of mental illness and suicide among the Irish community but there are other factors, however, which remain unaccounted for. As suggested in this chapter, the nature of migration by Irish people to Britain is quite different to that of other migrant groups. The attitude of many Irish migrants towards settlement and return can be characterized as ambivalent and may ultimately be injurious to sound mental health in that they are left in limbo, without any sense of belonging, on either side of the Irish sea. It is hard to reject the possibility that existential crisis and psychological distress will follow.

It may be that future Irish migrants will find Britain a more comfortable place to be and that migration itself will be based upon meditated personal choice rather than economic imperative. In these circumstances, it is likely that the high levels of mental distress among the Irish in Britain will decline. Nevertheless, the present Irish community continues to be overlooked in academic medicine and psychiatry. It is desirable, though not altogether true, that health policy and provision should be influenced by research evidence. No doubt there are political considerations involved too, but it is likely that, in the absence of any attempt to understand the problems faced by the Irish in Britain, the provision of health care services to this community will remain inadequate.

REFERENCES

Adelstein A., M . Marmot, G. Dean, and J. Bradshaw (1986). 'Comparison of mortality of Irish immigrants in England and Wales with that of Irish and British nationals'. *Irish Medical Journal*, 79(7): 185–9.

An Roinn Slainte (Department of Health) (1996). *National Task Force on Suicide Report*. Dublin: Government Publications.

Balarajan R. (1996). 'Ethnicity and variations in the Nation's Health'. *Health Trends*, 27(4): 114–19.

Bebbington P. E., J. Hurry, and C. Tennant (1981). 'Psychiatric disorders in selected immigrant groups in Camberwell'. *Social Psychiatry*, 16: 43–51.

Bhopal R. (1997). 'Is researach into ethnicity and health racist, unsound or important science'. *British Med. Journal*, 314: 1751–6.

Burke A. W. (1976). 'Attempted suicide among the Irish-born population in Birmingham'. *British Journal of Psychiatry*, 128: 534–7.

Canadian Task Force on Mental health Issues Affecting Immigrants and Refugees (1988). Ontario: Ministry of Supply and Services in Canada.

Carlsen H. M. and E. L. Nilsen (1995). 'Ireland, Gender, psychological Health and attitudes towards Emigration'. *Psychological Reports*, 76: 179–86.

Clare A. (1974). 'Mental Illness in the Irish Emigrant'. *Journal of the Irish Medical Association*, 67(1): 20–4.

Clarke-Finnegan M. and T. J. Fahy (1983). 'Suicide rates in Ireland'. *Psychological Medicine*, 13: 385–91.

Cochrane R. and S. S. Bal (1989). 'Mental admission rates of immigrants to England: A comparison of 1971 land 1981'. *Social Psychiatry and Psychiatric Epidemiology*, 24: 2–11.

Cochrane R. and M. Stopes-Roe (1979). 'Psychological disturbance in Ireland, in England, and in Irish immigrants to England: A comparative study'. *Economic and Social Review*, 10: 301–20.

Cook G. (1990). 'Health and Social inequalities in Ireland'. *Social Science and Medicine*, 31(3): 285–90.

Curtis L. (1984). 'Nothing but the same old story: The roots of anti-Irish racism'. *Information on Ireland*. London.

Eisenbruch M. (1988). 'The mental health of refugee children and their cultural development'. *International Migrant Review*, 22: 282–300.

Ferrado-Noli M. (1997). 'A cross-cultural breakdown of Swedish suicide'. *Acta Psychiatrica Scandavica*, 96: 108–16.

Gray B. and K. Kinane (1990). 'Irish drinking: Breaking the silence'. *Alcohol concern*, 6(2): 6–7.

Greeley A. M and W. C. McCready (1978). 'A preliminary reconnaissance into the persistence and explanation of ethnic subcultural drinking patterns'. *Medical Anthropology*, 2: 31–51.

Greeley A. M., W. C. McCready, and G. Thiessen (1980). *Ethnic Drinking Subcultures*. New York: Praeger.

Greenslade L. (1991). 'White skins, White Masks: Psychological distress among the Irish in Britain' in P .O. Sullivan (ed.). *The Irish in the New Communities*, vol. II. Leicester: Leicester University Press.

Harding S. and R. Balarajan (1996). 'Patterns of mortality in second generation Irish living in England and Wales: Longitudinal study'. *British Medical Journal*, 312: 1389–92.

Harrison L. and R. Carr-Hill (1992). *Alcohol and Disadvantage among the Irish in Britain*. Federation of Irish Societies.

Haskey J. (1996). 'Mortality among second generation Irish in England and Wales'. *British Medical Journal*, 312: 1373–4.

Helman C. G. (1994). *Culture, Health and Illness*. Butterworth-Heinemann.

Johansson L. M., J. Sundquist, S. E. Johansson, and B. Bergman (1998). 'Immigration, moving house and psychiatric admissions'. *Acta Psychiatrica Scandanavia*, 98: 105–11.

Kelleher D. (1988). 'The health of the Irish in England' in D. Kelleher and S. Hillier (eds). *Researching Cultural Differences in Health*. London: Routledge.

Kelleher M. J. (1996). *Suicide and the Irish*, p. 16. Dublin: Mercier Press.

Kiberd D. (1996). *Inventing Ireland: The Literature of the Modern Nation*. London: Vintage.

Kunz (1988). 'The Refugees in flight: Kinetic models and forms of displacement'. *International Migration Review*, 7: 125–46 from P. Rack *(1982). Race, Culture and Mental Disorder*, Tavistock.

Leavey G. (1988). 'Not everything makes sense in Black and White'. *Hate Thy Neighbour: The Dividing Lines of Race and Colour*. MINDFIELD edited by S. Greenberg. London: Camden Press.

Lester D. (1972). 'Migration and suicide'. *Medical Journal of Australia*, 1: 92–4.

Liebkind K. (1992). 'Refugee Mental and Cultural Identity'. *Psychiatria Fennica*, 23, Suppl., 47–58.

O'Meachair, G., A. Burns, and N. Clarke (1988). 'Irish Homelessness—The Hidden Dimension'. London: Cara Homelessness Project.

Marmot M., A. Adelstein, and L. Bulusu (1984). 'Immigrant mortality in England and Wales: 1970–8 OPCS studies on Population and medical subjects: no. 47'. London: HMSO.

Merril J. and J. Owens (1988). 'Self-poisoning among four immigrant groups'. *Acta Psychiatrica Scandinavica*, 77, 77–80.

Mullen, K., R. Williams, and K. Hunt (1985). 'Irish descent, religion, and alcohol and tobacco use'. *Journal of Addictions*, 423–54.

Murphy H. B. M. (1977). 'Migration, culture and mental health'. *Psychological Medicine*, 7: 677–84.

Neeleman J., V. Mak, and S. Wessley (1997). 'Suicide by age, ethnic group, coroners verdicts and country of birth; A three year survey in London'. *British Journal of Psychiatry*, 171: 463–7.

O'Connor J. (1975). 'Social and Cultural factors influencing drinking behaviour,' *Irish J. Med. Science*, Suppl. (June), 65–71.

O'Donnell I. and R. Farmer (1995). 'The limitations of official suicide statistcs'. *British Journal of Psychiatry*, 166: 458–61.

Owen. D. (1995). *Irish People in Great Britain: Settlement Patterns and Socio-economic Circumstances*. Centre for Research in Ethnic Relations. Coventry: University of Warwick.

Pearson M., M. Madden, and L. Greenslade (1991). *Occasional papers in Irish studies, 2: Generations of an invisible minority: The health and well-being of the Irish in Britain*. Liverpool Institute of Irish Studies.

Rack P. (1982). *Race, Culture and Mental Disorder*. London: Tavistock.

Releigh V. S. and R. Balarajan (1992). 'Suicide levels and trends among immigrants in England and Wales'. *Health Trends*, 24(3): 91–4.

Sainsbury P. and B. Barraclough (1968). 'Differences between suicide rates'. *Nature*, 220: 1252.

Sashidharan S. P. (1993). 'Afro-Caribbeans and schizophrenia: The ethnic vulnerability hypothesis re-examined'. *International Review Psychiatry*, 5: 129–44.

Skellington R. and P. Moss (1992). *Race in Britain Today*, p. 54. London: Sage Publications in association with the Open University.

Stivers, R. (1978). 'Irish ethnicity and alcohol use'. *Medical Anthropology*, 2; 121–35.

Walsh D. (1987). 'Alcohol and alcohol problems research 15. Ireland'. *British Journal of Addiction*, 82: 747–51.

Whitters A. C., R. J. Cadoret, and R. B. Widmir (1985). 'Factors associated with suicide attempts in alcohol abusers'. *Journal of Affective Disorders*, 2: 19–23.

Williams R. 'The Health of the Irish in England,' in W. Ahmad (ed.). *The Politics of Race and Health*. Bradford: Race Relations Research Unit.

8

Within and Without (The Story of the Welsh) The Impact of Cultural Factors on Mental Health in the Present Day in Wales

Dilys R. Davies

INTRODUCTION

Psychology is a reflexive discipline and as a Welsh-speaking psychotherapist, this chapter reflects my personal interest in exploring issues raised during my experience in a NHS (National Health Service) Trust serving a bilingual community in Wales. The pattern in Wales regarding the structure and provision of psychological services and the referral pattern to those services is that Welsh speakers are poorly represented in the services while few psychotherapists are Welsh speakers. Given the population statistics for the area clearly, there was a differential access to the psychological services. Services providing psychological therapies in other areas of Wales suggest a similar pattern.

Population statistics indicate that in some areas Welsh speakers form the native majority (up to 80 per cent) while in other areas they form an ethnic minority. However, even when they are a minority the numbers are still significant. For example, in one of the most anglicised areas—Cardiff—they make up 6.6 per cent of the population numbering 18,000.The issues revolve around providing adequate and appropriate psychological therapy services to a bilingual population. Precise statistics are not available as none are collected separately for Wales. In England, the Department of Health has established ethnic monitoring of staff and patients. It also suggests that the composition of staff should reflect the local community mix.

What we do not know is how Welsh speakers are represented in the mental health services generally. My own impression from questioning the nursing staff on the general psychiatric ward suggested that more Welsh speakers were represented on the general psychiatric list and more Welsh speakers were reflected in the staff composition. This could reflect similar patterns of mental health care of socially disadvantaged groups generally. In the fields of psychotherapy and psychology these are well-documented areas. However, the most noticeable response regarding these issues of differential provision of and access to service from the service providers—psychotherapists and their managers—was the theme of silence. This was the case even in the instances when the psychotherapist and manager were Welsh speaking themselves. When the issues to do with providing a service appropriate to a bilingual community were brought up they were dealt with by locating the problem in the bilingual population who did not access the services. Similarly, the issue of appropriate service provision was dealt with by referring to the lack of bilingual psychotherapists and by defending the status quo of working in a particular therapeutic style regardless of the community concerned.

One possible reason why this problem is not highlighted is that of invisibility. Welsh speakers do not have physical characteristics that distinguish them from the rest of the population. In terms of bilingualism, Welsh speakers speak English as well as Welsh—the implication being that service providers may as well speak English if it doesn't matter. The themes of invisibility and silence are reflected in the Welsh-speaking population generally including professionals and potential service users. A frequent response given to explain why potential users did not use the services was 'pride', that is not wishing to be seen as not coping or failing in some way—especially not to strangers. Welsh cultural attitudes may also include for example, not wanting to make a fuss or speaking out. The latter is a common attitude when members of the public face professionals as people want the best service and do not want to upset the professional in any way. As I shall outline later in this chapter, such attitudes and expectations may be even more pronounced in Wales. The reason for these attitudes are often culturally determined, reflecting historical/political factors which have been assimilated into our cultural identity.

In this chapter, I shall attempt to address the questions of why the under-representation of Welsh speakers to the psychological services was ignored. A possible reason could be that Welsh speakers do not suffer from emotional stress and thus don't need psychotherapy. However, indirect clinical clues and the evidence of our senses inform us that this is not the case. For a more complete explanation, we shall look at evidence elsewhere. These include first general and specific mental health statistics, and second evidence from other groups.

Differential Access and Service Provision

Surveys estimating the numbers in the general population suffering from mental health problems typically indicate that between 20 and 30 per cent of the population are affected (Albee, 1996). So where are the ethnic Welsh population? Specific statistics that are available for the Welsh speaking population indicate the prevalence of emotional stress. For example, figures indicate a high suicide rate amongst Welsh farmers and a corresponding high incidence of depression.

When we look at the evidence from other groups, the pattern amongst Welsh speakers could fit in with the general pattern of differential access to services amongst other groups in the general population. Access to psychological services generally follows society's 'fault lines' that is along the lines of differential power in society.

Common to all counselling situations are questions of who is able to access such services and the treatment such people receive. There is, however, differential access to different types of mental health treatment. People experience the effects of social inequality, for example, because of their race (Fernando, 1988; Pillay, 1993), gender (Ashton, 1991; Ussher, 1991; Williams *et al.*, 1993), sexual orientation (Rothblum, 1990) or social economic status (Bromley, 1983, 1994). They are particularly vulnerable to distress and are more likely to receive unhelpful responses from services. They are more likely to receive biological and physical treatments than psychological treatments. They are more likely to receive Electroconvulsive Therapy (ECT), psychotropic medication, tranquillizers or confinement, and much less likely to receive psychotherapy. Studies in the US which have focused on ethnic minority service use indicate high drop-out rates from psychotherapy for Black patients (Rosenthal and Franks, 1957). This pattern was confirmed (Yamamoto *et al.*, 1968) in relation to Black and Hispanic Americans being offered talking treatments less often than Whites, and dropping out more frequently at an early stage.

Clients and practitioners also have different expectations of counselling (Richards, 1994). Psychiatric treatment generally is experienced as undermining , yet few alternatives are available. The overall picture is that for people who are poor, who are from ethnic minorities or who are elderly, the less likely they are to receive counselling or psychotherapy. The one issue that such groups have in common is that they are members of groups differing in some aspect from the dominant culture. Research highlights that it is not the numerical issue which is important but rather the fact that they are members of groups who do not hold power in our society. They are further disempowered by the institutions including health systems, which have been developed and are largely organized to meet the needs and requirements of those groups which reflect the power structure of society generally (Clarke and Brindley, 1993).

To address this question of why these issues are ignored in Wales we have to look at two interweaving strands of evidence. The first is to do with the general frame of reference in the theory and practice of psychotherapy. The second strand concerns cultural and social attitudes and expectations of both service providers and the potential users in the bilingual Welsh speaking population.

CURRENT THEORY AND PRACTICE OF PSYCHOTHERAPY

Most probably, human beings have always experienced forms of distress and suffering.

However, how a particular group locates the source of distress, how the symptoms of distress are manifested, and how they are labelled differs according to the historical and cultural context. For example, one can construe that Homer in his account in *The Iliad* of Ajax returning from the Trojan wars wandering in a field speaking to cows was describing the same sort of phenomena that was later labelled as shell shock, then battle fatigue, and more recently as post-traumatic stress. Throughout history and across cultures people have always needed aid and comfort. However, different cultural groups have differing norms and expectations for coping with and dealing with distress and how this is best achieved. Who people confide in and how are others likely to react are all culturally determined. For example this function may be carried out by religion or through traditional ways of comfort and aid by family and friends and the communal sharing of distress. Increasingly, this function has been partitioned off and professionalized, and dealt with by psychotherapy. Whereas fifty years ago there was little psychological involvement in the treatment of emotional distress, over the last decade or so there has been a huge expansion of psychotherapy despite debates about its scientific status and efficacy. It is all too easy to treat distress by psychotherapy, regardless of the source, according to the needs of the service users. The problem can be quickly labelled 'stress' and he or she referred on to the psychological services where there is a ready and growing army of professionals to offer a whole range of psychological therapies. Although psychological approaches should be equally available to all sections of the population, they are not necessarily useful. For example, if a counselling or psychotherapy culture encourages the belief that distress is solely individually determined, this may divert attention from the cultural and social determinants of mental distress.

INDIVIDUALIZATION OF DISTRESS

Even though there is a very wide range of theoretical ideas and practical procedures, many of them markedly incompatible with each other, there are nevertheless some general issues common to most psychotherapeutic approaches. The reductionist view of science prevalent within research in psychotherapy emphasizes an analysis and solution of problems, which ignores wider contextual issues. As Chomsky (1968) and Poole (1972) point out, science is inadequate when it focuses on selected bits of problems rather than treat the totality of problems. Poole defines an adequate science as 'the study of the totality of problems, objective and subjective, by the whole thinker, taking into account all the evidence, both quantifiable and unquantifiable' (Poole, 1972: 108–9).

A common feature of the psychotherapies is that although the presenting symptom or problem may be conceptualized differently within each theoretical framework, they ignore the wider social context of the client's life and the source of distress. It is questioned whether these different therapeutic frameworks actually help clients to understand the source of their unhappiness or merely elevate the notion of illness. Traditional and current psychotherapy and counselling theories (see Dryden, 1990) have not paid much attention to a psychosocial understanding of individuals. Writers such as Masson (1990, 1991) Heath (1992) Smail (1987, 1993) and Szasz (1971) point out the inappropriate therapies and treatments given for conditions of which we do not know the fundamental causes, but which may turn out to be psychosocial in origin. They draw attention to the inappropriate and inadequate view of the nature of the self which ignores political, economic, and cultural sources and which avoids any real analysis and criticism of a social order. Masson criticises Freud for his inherently individualistic view in ignoring external sources of distress, stating: 'Freud is asking us to shift the direction of our attention, from the external to the internal. Freud was perpetuating a tradition that did not begin with him. Its basic characteristics were that it was male-oriented, ethnocentric, sexist, and rigidly hierarchical' (1991: 208).

In psychotherapy, close attention is paid to personal and interpersonal change processes. It concentrates on the significance of events in particular isolated contexts, for example, the patient's unconscious, the transference or shifts in group dynamics, etc. When it does consider wider influences, this is usually confined to a consideration of our immediate relations with each other, such as with family members, and this has led to serious limitations of the explanatory power of the theories it has produced. In the frame of reference of most forms of psychotherapy, the wider context of experience is marginalized or ignored and an overemphasis is placed on personal responsibility. This is reflected also in the institutional and professional cultures of our working environment, and a sociopolitical system which emphasizes individual effort and responsibility. Smail (1993) documents how psychotherapy, psychology, and psychiatry have helped shape a culture of individualism where it has become almost impossible for people to differentiate inside from outside and to attribute the pain they often feel about themselves to its appropriate source. There is a danger of compounding the distress of people by focusing on their role and responsibility. We often wrongly locate the origins or 'cause' of our pain as being located inside us and a reflection of our own inadequacy or personal failing. The 'cures' for this are similarly seen as an individual matter—to be dealt with individually either by our own efforts or by some sort of psychotherapeutic intervention. Change may be offered by different means, e.g., 'insight', 'cognitive restructuring' or 'behavioural techniques'. However, neither the causes or cures of distress are purely a matter for the individual alone. Psychotherapists may alleviate some painful consequences of distress and the descriptions given by therapist can sometimes be helpful, but as writers such as Davies (1994), Richards (1994) and Pilgrim (1994) point out, this is of limited relevance without an understanding of the individual's cultural and social context.

Outlining how the wider society exerts its power and influence over our lives, Smail (1993) describes how our world is structured by powers at varying degrees of distance from us. Those closest to us, which he terms 'proximal powers', are the ones which we are mostly aware of and which preoccupy us most. However, it is those furthest from us (which Smail terms 'distal powers'), which reflect the wider political and economic influences which we are barely aware of (and whose origin we do not even know) that exert the strongest influence on our lives. We all live in an increasingly expanding context in which the location of decisions that affect our lives is plural and complex. The global market place cuts across national boundaries and is more often than not invisible because of its dispersion. Present-day Britain is characterized by the increasing individualization of society under the cultural and economic domination of Americanization. An adequate account of human experience must take into account these distal influences. Smail states: 'The explanation of our conduct is not to be sought in a psychological analysis of individuals, but in a socio-economic, historical analysis of relations between people, and of the ways these have shaped the world we have to live in' (1987: 70).

For many groups who are offered therapy, the wider social and cultural context is ignored as distress may well be located within the individual and the techniques and goals chosen often inappropriate. The pathologizing thing continues as member of those groups then are deceived into believing that there's something wrong with them. Pillay (1993) points out that a greater knowledge of their social and economic reality would be more useful in understanding psychological processes, than assumed culturally-based psychosis in African-Caribbeans and somatization in Asians. Those who label the effects of economic forces and racism as being due to some individual determinant such as neurosis or depression, oppress and pathologize these groups even further. The reason for the distress of Welsh farmers is likely to be due to economic concerns and demographic changes to their communities than it is to any sort of inner conflict or label of depression to be treated by means of psychotherapy. As Sayal states: 'As a clinician, I think it is crucial to relate personal misery to its environment, history and political context. If you rob a person of their history, you rob them of their sense of self' (1989: 6).

MEANING IS SOCIALLY NEGOTIATEDE THROUGH LANGUAGE

When we look at the relationship between the individual and the social context and the process of socialization, theorists from different disciplines from different parts of the world and across time arrive at the same general conclusions. Psycholinguists, psychologists and social philosophers point out that the social context and the individual are inextricably linked and our sense of self or our psychology is social. All the psychotherapies may be viewed as sharing one common feature. The most obvious is that the explanation and treatment of psychological distress are negotiated through the social transactions of two people—the patient and therapist. One of the core processes in therapy is the therapeutic alliance—or that relationship which is established between client and therapist which makes therapy possible in the first place. In psychotherapy, as in any interaction, meaning is socially negotiated. Intersubjectivity requires a frame of reference and this is a social context.

Significant contributions in our understanding of the social context in the development of the individual are based on the work of theorists who may be described as psycholinguists or social philosophers who all point to the social construction of experience. A main theme in G. H. Mead's work is that meaning is socially negotiated. His work was elaborated as part of the 'Chicago School of Symbolic Interactionism' in the 1930s. Schwartz and Jacobs (1979) highlight three main principles from this approach. First, human conduct is a function of the meanings that the actor holds of the world. Second, these meanings arise from social interactions. Third, these meanings are maintained and modified through a process of interpretation within personal encounters. Symbolic interactionists thus study how social reality is negotiated between individuals and how it is understood from individual perspectives within such negotiations.

Husserl (1970) explored the way we confer meaning upon the world. A central tenet in Husserl's work is the idea of perspectives. Although we are all conscious that there is only one world, we also see it differently, interpret if differently, and attribute different meanings to it at various times. As Poole points out, 'Meaning and interpretation belong together inseparably. Anything which visibly has a meaning is in that same instant invested with an interpretation by each and every onlooker' (1972: 6). The meaning attributed to what we select to be significant will vary according to our moral presuppositions, the relative position of our vantage point. Interpretation is always instant, and any act an embodied intention. The world to Husserl is a communalized set of perspectives. The fact that we confer meaning on to the world, instead of it imposing one meaning on to us, implies that we are active participants in this process.

Writing from a social psychological perspective Smail (1987, 1993) outlines how thought, memory, beliefs, perceptions, feelings or a person's 'state of mind' do not exist independently of the environment of which they are partly constituted. According to Smail, the error of psychotherapy has been to consider individual meaning systems as belonging to, and in the control of, people of whom they form a part. The assumption is made that these beliefs and attitudes which order our experience, and the socially determined rules and concepts, practices, and meanings which Smail terms 'forms', are solely located inside a person and somehow subject to operation of his or her will. However, individuals cannot generally be expected to exercise a great deal of control over phenomena such as gender and ethnicity.

Any concept such as 'self' or 'personality' is socially determined. Our personal assimilation and adaptation to these meaning systems is what is meant by our 'psychology'. For example, important to our emotional well-being is one's sense of oneself as male or female. This is inescapable from the forms of masculinity and femininity which are culturally determined independent of us as individuals. Hence, how far I am considered 'feminine' depends on a form of femininity which is outside me. Political movements such as feminism are less likely to make the error of individualization in that feminism does not take as its basic premise that each individual woman needs to change herself. Rather, it recognises that for women to gain a more equitable share of social power requires a change in the forms such as those relating to masculinity and femininity in our culture. Problems often arise when we cannot fulfil the demands of cultural forms. Failures of form may come about through the cultural absence or disintegration of forms capable of giving sense to individual experience. Our experience is unintelligible if we are not taught a language with which to describe it.

Thus, in the most fundamental way what we perceive, believe in, and view of ourselves and our world is based on social and cultural factors. Our attitudes, beliefs, expectations, and perceptions are formed in interaction with others and form the basis of our relationship with ourselves and to our relationship with others and our world. Our individuality or our sense of self is essentially social in origin. Central to this is language.

CULTURAL, LANGUAGE AND PSYCHOTHERAPY

All the verbal psychotherapies, by definition, are dependent on language and of the discourse that occurs between people. Language is not words. There are crucial implications of the social context of language to be considered in the theory and practice of psychotherapy. Some general statements may be made regarding language as a social phenomena. First, the words of a spoken language are formed in a social context and are carriers of social meaning. Second, the boundaries between what is outside or public and inside or private are blurred. Third, it is in this way the valuations of the social milieu reach the core of the individual's psyche. What is outside or external becomes internal. Fourth, language is an integral part of what makes up our psyche or identity.

Bakhtin (1981), Medvedev (1985), Voloshinov (1976), and Vygotsky (1939), all formulated their work at the same time as Freud but stress the social context of experience and view language as social phenomena. For Vygotsky, the organizing principles of thought and feeling rest in the structure of the shared language through which we express those thoughts and feelings.

Voloshinov viewed Freud as a representing a wider intellectual trend which sought to explain and ground human behaviour in fundamentally biological rather than locate it in social and historical terms. Working from Freud's starting point—the patient's language and the talking cure—Voloshinov views the contents of the psyche as being made up of inner speech. What in Freud's terms remains a distinction within the individual becomes, according to this perspective, versions of the conflicts of the social milieu.

The boundary between what is external to us and what we experience as being 'inside' us or part of our 'personality' or 'self' is blurred. Vygotsky is concerned with the activity at the boundaries between people and their environment, with the activities involved in them, making what is 'other' or 'external' to them 'internal'. He proposes a social developmental psychology in which he views man's socially organized experiences as determining the structure of human conscious activity. One of Bakhtin's main principles is that the utterances of spoken language are formed in a social context and are carriers of social meaning. Since language is inescapably social and occurs between people, the valuations of the social milieu reach the core individual experience or the psyche making what is 'other' or 'external' to them 'internal'.

Language is an example of the set of rules which gives a form and meaning to our experience. Our language is thus an intrinsic part of or sense of self or personality. In terms of bilingualism in Wales, the therapist and patient may be speaking the same language but they may not be talking the same language. As we have seen, meaning occurs within a social context which gives it a verbal construction and therefore a social reality. Cultural and historical factors—including beliefs, attitudes etc.—are embedded in language and transmitted over time through the generations. The valuations of the social milieu are transmitted linguistically. The valuation of the language itself is part of that process. As I shall outline later, historically the Welsh language was accorded low status and viewed as useless. Such valuations reach the core of our individual psychology and collective identity. Historical and political consequences are reflected at a personal level in the organization of our cognitive schemata. In other words, if you speak another language, the way your constructs are formed and the way you construct yourself and the world are different because the cultural context in which they are embedded is different. If psychotherapy is about exploring meaning systems, there is a need to represent or symbolize a person's experience, not ignore it.

CULTURAL AUTISM

Because a phenomenon is not verbally named by a society, it does not mean that it does or does not exist. For example, if a society does not acknowledge or give experience a name, this amounts to cultural autism or social muteness. Cultural autism is reflected in individual understanding so that the individual may be rendered mute. For example, although childhood sexual abuse has probably always existed, it is only in the last decade or so that its prevalence has been generally acknowledged and articulated. Once acknowledged, the survivors of such abuse came forward in significant numbers and sexual abuse is now given prominence as a major cause of distress in the field of psychotherapy. A form of cultural autism may be seen in the silence surrounding service provision for Welsh speakers. Cultural autism may also be reflected in the experience of Welsh speakers who comply with the current situation. As I shall describe later in this chapter, in Wales the language itself was oppressed as attempts were made to eliminate it. As Paolo Freire (1996), states: 'To survive the oppression of the language, your voice is oppressed and your power is taken away from you. To survive that you have to comply with the dominant culture.'

CULTURAL RELATIVITY

Cultural factors including attitudes, beliefs, and expectations influence what we see and how we see it. The major philosophical task was seen by Husserl (1970) to be the evolution of a method that would take into account the perspective world and the inter-subjectivity in the cultural and moral communities in which we live. The basic truth of perceptual experience is that what we see is directly dependent upon the perspective from which we see it. Our experience of the outer world modifies that structure and affects the way it works. In a process of selection and exclusion, a world view will be filtered through the hopes and fears, the expectations and the experiences of the individual. The end result is a set of perspectives which have been multiply modified in the transmission. There is, as Poole (1972) and Zukav (1979) point out, not one single truth but truths according to one's perspectives. This is similar to the concepts developed in the 1930s by Allport's concept of perceptual set and in the 1950's by Kelly's personal construct theory. As Zukav comments, '"Reality" is what we take to be true. What we take to be true is what we believe. What we believe is based upon our perceptions. What we perceive depends upon what we look for. What we look for depends upon what we think. What we think depends upon what we perceive. What we perceive determines what we believe. What we believe determines what we take to be true. What we take to be true is our reality. The central focus of this process initially is what we think' (1979: 328).

Poole points out that objectivity is that which is commonly perceived as objectively valid, that is all the attitudes, presuppositions, and unquestioned assumptions typical of any given society. Objectivity implies the acceptance of the dominant social, ethical, and religious view in that society and is defined in terms of the political and social status quo. Thus, anyone who does not see or accept the 'obvious' as the obvious will be taken to have an impaired sense of objectivity. Society's reactions will vary from ignoring the individual to psychiatric treatment. Facts cannot exist in an objective, context-free way, when the facts are about human beings. What we take to be 'facts' in mental health aren't facts at all but are culturally determined. This is seen for example, in how definitions and classifications are not absolute but change across cultures and across time.

Highlighting the cultural relativity of society's definition of what is mentally ill, Albee (1966) points out how in the 1970s, thousands of US citizens were changed overnight from being defined as mentally ill to sane as the American Psychiatric Association dropped its classification of homosexuality as a psychiatric disorder to be treated. In a previous era in the US, run-away slaves were often diagnosed as suffering from 'drapetomania', that is an incurable urge to run away.

What seems right and permissible at one historical point is abhorred at another. How we are labelled effects the way others view and interact with us. We may see or hear things differently. These may be labelled delusions or hallucinations. We may be then viewed as mad or as saints. Society's interpretations of the same behaviour change. For the first two years of the First World War, distress was viewed as cowardice and the consequence was execution by a firing squad. Only later, when British officers were breaking down under those unimaginable conditions, was this distress given the label of shell shock, a syndrome that was treatable.

Ethnocentricity assumes that one description of the world and view of reality is valid and superior to the constructions offered in other parts of the world. If Asian people themselves do not readily and straghtforwardly present with problems that fall neatly into the picture of Western mental illness, and if they have a strong association between mental health problem, stigma and shame, the combined effect might be mental health service 'under-utilization'. However, great caution should be used when speculating about the whole question of mental health service utilization by Asian people. Watters (1996) in a recent review of the topic of Asian mental health makes the point that despite the contradictory and sparse empirical evidence about the topic, a number of unfounded assumptions and rash deductions have been made. One of these is what is termed the homogeneity fallacy which is seen in the search of a consistent pattern applicable to all Asians.

The sociology of knowledge highlights how cultural factors are embedded in and shape what we think we 'know'. Both the process and content of our knowledge is culturally determined. What we assume to be facts are determined by our cultural and historical perspectives. These processes are reflected, for example, in what is defined as science and in our professional institutions. In turn, this gives legitimacy to certain forms and content of 'knowledge'. For example, Sayal (1989) points out that 'facts' are often sweeping generalizations and stereotypes, such as 'passive' Asian woman are subjected to oppressive practices within the family; or that the African-Caribbean woman is strong and dominant. Similarly generalizations are made in mental health such as the assumed culturally based psychosis in African-Caribbeans and somatization in Asians (Pillay, 1993).

Considering the role of psychotherapists in Wales, we can see how by ignoring the cultural context of someone's life involves the imposition of one particular reality on another. The therapeutic situation is one where power resides with the therapist, 'the expert' who can impose his or her view of reality on the client (e.g., Masson, 1990). They may do this unintentionally by simply ignoring the cultural context of the patient's life. Rowe, in her foreword to Masson's book, states, 'In the final analysis, power is the right to have your definition of reality prevail over all other people's definition of reality' (1990: 16). The type of therapy or counselling selected by clients defines reality within the frame of reference of that particular theoretical approach. They present their version of reality as being akin to some kind of 'true' relativity or ultimate truth which is then used as a framework for defining the clients' reality. However, there are a growing number schools of psychotherapy with their corresponding views on the reality and human experience, for example, Karasau (1986) reported 400 different schools. Further, as Rowe states, 'It is a good rule of thumb that if many treatments are in use for the same disease it is because there is no real treatment known for that "disease"' (1991, 370). Heath points out that this form of oppression is rarely intentional, or carried out of malevolent motives: 'I do not need to be malevolent in order to oppress people. I can oppress people with the best of intentions out of ignorance and I may perpetuate my ignorance to protect my power' (1992: 33).

Psychotherapy, rather than being an added resource to a community, can diminish traditional ways of coping with distress. Although there is little doubt that therapists and counsellors believe that they are solely concerned with the humane relief of suffering, according to Smail (1993), they are an example of the way in which our motives can be pure while we are engaged in the pursuit of enterprises of which we are completely unaware. They were claiming a previously non-commercial social function and offering a service for whose effectiveness there was no particularly convincing evidence. Just as with professional grief counselling, it is not that the advice is wrong or misguided, as much of it is common sense, but it breaks down appropriate social conduct and replaces it with commercially available professional knowledge. Once the need for psychotherapy has been created, the demand for it soon increases as people lose confidence in their ability to handle distress as part of a traditional social process.

PROFESSIONALISM

Psychotherapy has became the answer to all sorts of problems and its areas of concern expanded into new areas such as 'disaster counselling' and the development of new concepts such as 'post-traumatic stress disorder'. The person in pain must have someone to turn to and this role is increasingly likely to be met by 'professionals' or 'experts' such as counsellors or psychotherapists whose sincere belief in their therapeutic efficacy is coupled with his or her own personal need to survive in the world. Therapists and counsellors, out of self-interest cannot be expected to call validity of psychotherapy into question in any fundamental way.

The differential patterns of access of Welsh speakers to the psychological services raises questions concerning the reasons why both professionals and managers in Wales have remained silent and not drawn attention to this situation. I would suspect that this is in their own self-interests to do so. Relevant statistics are not gathered and neither is the situation monitored.

The reasons for the silence amongst professionals in Wales could reflect a lack of concern on issues regarding cultural salience and regarding adaption of psychotherapy services along culturally appropriate lines and similarly, a lack of motivation to change the situation. However, when mental health workers ignore the links between the effects of social and cultural factors on psychological distress they serve the interests of only specific social groups or maintain the status quo rather than serve the interests of the client. An adequate service has to serve the community—not exclude it. As far as the psychological therapies are concerned in Wales, the identity of the institution contrasts with the identity of potential users. Therapy fits in with the needs of the institution—including the professional interest of therapists rather than the needs of the community. Psychotherapists function within a context which includes their own professional context, the context of their working environment in the NHS, and the wider socio-economic context.

Regarding the nature of the professional context, there is frequently an uncritical assumption that professions exist merely to provide a disinterested service to the public, based upon a set of specific personal skills and attributes. However, as Pilgrim and Treacher (1992) and Smail (1993) point out that much of the time, professionals pursue their own interests and not those of their clients. They attempt to protect themselves and tend to be or become exclusive and elitist. One of the effects of the professionalism of psychotherapy is a concern for status and respectability, which results in the reinforcement of the status quo.

To this has been added a second factor, which is the current context of the National Health Service (NHS) in Britain. This context reflects the introduction of government policies of a free market economy and the world of business. The business culture introduced a proliferation of managers in the NHS whose role is to carry out policies and directives of their organization—the NHS Trusts. The transmission of a business culture needed the cooperation of people in a project they believe in. Once someone is convinced that his 'motives' are for the best, he or she may happily be recruited to the task in hand. Some of the new managers were people form already part of the business world, others were products of an expanded tertiary education system who were not quite members of established professions and not quite possessing the qualifications for entry but close enough to believe that given the opportunity they could do the job. Whether trying to just carry out their role which is to carry out the Trust's policies as smoothly as possible, or seeking to further their careers, or to confirm their newly-found status, they are not likely to question the organization.

The employment practice encouraged in society generally also affects the employment practices within the NHS such as the introduction of short-term contracts and the emphasis on a flexible labour force. Employees within the new NHS Trusts, including psychotherapists and managers alike, no longer have the security of employment with its implications of continuous work and its related benefits. Concerns about unemployment were usually introduced as the necessity for reorganisation and change. Under these conditions, NHS managers and psychotherapists are unlikely to question existing systems of health care. Ignoring the situation in Wales makes it invisible. The invisibility is maintained through self-interest, through the explicit and implicit collusion with and endorsement of the status quo. This results in nothing being done about it. The passive acceptance by the local community further maintains the status quo

SELECTION BIAS IN THE PROVISION OF PSYCHOTHERAPY

The explanations given about the selectivity of psychotherapy include those to do with therapist expectations, client expectations and the cultural gap that may exist between therapist and client. Pilgrim (1997) points out that the social history of psychotherapy has bound up selection bias in a number of ways and this history engenders and legitimizes the current practice in individual practitioners. Before the First World War in Britain, the problem of shell shock—which was different manifestations of terror—altered the prevailing bio-deterministic view in psychiatry. This was linked to a eugenic model, which reflected the wider influence of eugenics in a British colonial context. Essentially, the common psychiatric view was that the lower orders were products of a weak gene which manifested itself in a wide range of deviance—madness, idleness, idiocy, and criminality. However, during the war, both working-class volunteers and upper-class officers were becoming psychological casualties, and officers were breaking down at a higher rate than the lower ranks. It was unacceptable that, as Stone describes, 'England's finest blood' should be explained by weak genes and thus gave psychological explanations a new legitimacy. The main psychological model at the time was that of psychoanalysis, which originated with Sigmund Freud and focused on the internal dilemmas and conflicts of the middle class. It is in this historical context that the selection bias needs to be understood. The inertia of individual psychotherapist reflects the wider context of cultural inertia within psychotherapy. To change this, therapists would need to accept some political responsibility, for discrimination in mental health is apparent throughout the development of psychology.

Themes of social inequality are reflected at an institutional level in our mental health services such as in the inequality of access to and delivery of psychotherapy services. Explanations for this assignment bias refer to the social distance (e.g., Bromley, 1994)

and cultural gap (e.g., Richards, 1994) between the therapist and the client. There are features of the therapeutic situation which may be at variance with people's cultural experience and expectations. Richards and Bromley point out that in order to develop rapport and a working relationship, there needs to be sufficient cultural similarity between the therapist and the client. For example, research suggests that therapy is more effective and that it is more helpful when helpers share the same cultural and social background as their clients (Sayal, 1989). Richards also describes how access to psychotherapy involves the ability to make optimal use of what psychotherapeutic help is available. To be a 'successful' patient requires a certain amount of what Bourdieu terms 'cultural capital', which includes a readiness to enter the discourse of personal reflection. What may be perceived as unwillingness to engage in this discourse, and has traditionally been termed 'resistance', is sometimes difficult to distinguish from a lack of a shared or cultural understanding of the psychotherapeutic process. The establishment and maintenance of the therapeutic alliance is difficult if the client has internalized culturally derived experiences such as those of inferiority. We are often unaware of the difficulty one person may have in understanding or communicating with another when there is a significant power differential between them.

Therapists working across cultural boundaries cannot hope to develop a positive and empathic alliance with their client group unless they are aware of difference in norms and values (McGoldrick *et al.*, 1982). In some cases, they may so misconstrue the communications of clients and the professional's incompetence at understanding may be turned into attributions about the client's mental illness (Horowitz, 1983). Another implication of a failure to understand those from a different background is that talking treatments would not fit in with the needs of such clients so such clients would drop out of treatment readily. This is the case according to the US studies which have focused on ethnic minority service use. High drop-out rates from psychotherapy for Black patients were noted in early studies by Rosenthal and Franks (1957). This pattern was confirmed by Yamamoto *et al.* (1968) in relation to Black and Hispanic Americans who were offered talking treatments less often and dropped out more frequently from therapy at an early stage.

This raises issues about the discrepancies between the culture of service providers and their clients. Pilgrim (1997) makes the point that if there is a cultural gap between the therapist and the client, the responsibility for its reduction should rest primarily with the service providers as they have more power than the client and they have access to information which relates to the problem, whereas clients are unlikely to anticipate the difficulty. Rather than looking at the cultural deficit of clients in accessing and utilizing psychotherapy, it may be more fair and useful to address therapist inaction and deficit. Some constraints may be outside their control such as the referrer bias. For example, clinicians making referrals to psychotherapists may introduce pre-assessment bias. Also, the proportion of psychologists and psychotherapists from ethnic minority backgrounds is small (see, for example, Bender and Richardson, 1990; Gurani and Sayal, 1987; Webb-Johnson and Nadirshaw, 1993).

THE NATURE OF THE CULTURAL GAP IN WALES

Ethnicity is a problematic notion and has been subjected to a number of definitions (see reviews Anthias, 1992; Hall, 1988, 1989; Omi and Winant, 1989).The term 'ethnicity' at its most general level refers to an identity which emerges from membership of a particular cultural and linguistic group or nationality. Ethnic positioning provides individuals with a mode of interpreting the world, based on shared cultural resources such as territorial, cultural or linguistic resources, and shared collective positioning vis-à-vis other groups (Davis, 1989). Thus while both the Scots and the French are predominantly White-skinned, they belong to different ethnic groups. At any specific time, there may be a consensual view of what characterizes the essential character, needs, and interests of an ethnic group. However, this is always subject to shifts, re-evaluation and transformation. Ethnic identity may be constructed from outside as well as inside the group and different criteria of inclusion may be used by those on the inside and those on the outside (Drury, 1990). The terminological controversies about ethnicity are complicated by the tendency for ethnic identities to emerge from both defensive and offensive groups. For example, the Irish, Welsh, and Scots identity is constructed in part by the commitment of some Celtic people to their cultural traditions, as well as by the derisive stereotypes made about them by some English people. Further, as Pilgrim (1997) points out, the struggle to preserve Celtic traditions and languages has been fought from a reactive or defensive position of exclusion and oppression. By contrast, the English colonial identity was constructed with an emphasis on an assumed superiority. Thus, there is a different political significance if the English self-proclaim their ethnic identity than if those on the colonized Celtic fringe do so. The Celtic people of Britain have fought to preserve their identity in a post-colonial context, and have produced a clear discourse about themselves.

Psychological and psychiatric research data have been accumulated about the African-Caribbean and Asian population, sometimes called 'visible minorities', in Britain. However, there has been a relative silence on the Celtic people in Britain. The Welsh, like the Irish, are White and so are indistinguishable, superficially or 'phenotypically', from their ex-colonizer and thus may be termed 'invisible'. The little work that has been carried out has focused on the Irish (e.g., Kenny, 1985; Greenslade, 1992; and Scheper-Hughes, 1979) (also see Leavey in this volume). It is interesting to note that these writers are themselves Irish or first generation Irish. Kenny (1985) and Greensale (1992) focus on the post-colonial identity and the consequent social and existential challenges facing the Irish. In Greenslade's account (following Fanon, 1970) the Irish faced the historical insult of colonization, loss of language, forced migration, and mass starvation under British rule. They now face an existential uncertainty in the wake of this legacy which is compounded by continued social dislocation from net emigration and their physical proximity to and economic reliance on the ex-colonial power. The latter remains in power in the six north-eastern counties of Ireland.

Kenny (1985) elaborates on a cultural domination hypothesis about Irish psychology by applying the ideas of Bateson (1942) on cultural differences in psychological development. Kenny describes how the relationship between England and Ireland can be understood in terms of three patterns of relating. The colonial relationship enabled the English domination and the Irish submission. The former exhibited their power and the Irish looked on. The Irish became dependent and the English offered them succour.

Colonization entailed the English crushing the autonomy of the Irish and infantilizing them. Kenny describes how these oppressive processes were internalized by the Irish and so they now are self-oppressing in their child-rearing practices and their inner lives. Although Ireland and Wales are at a different points in their historical development, nevertheless there are similarities in their cultural and historical experience of being dominated and also similarities in the present psychological consequences of this legacy.

WELSH IDENTITY BOUND UP WITH THE WELSH LANGUAGE

Historians such as Davies (1993), and Aitchison and Carter (1994) document how Welsh identity has historically been bound up with the Welsh language as other symbols of national identity and criteria of difference with England were progressively eliminated in Wales. For example, political identity was eliminated through the increasing proscription of Welsh from legal and administration affairs and destruction of these systems which the Acts of Union (1536, 1543) was finally to consummate. Aitchison and Carter (1994) in their historical overview, describe how if the Welsh were to survive as a people, they would have to cultivate and sustain their identity by other means. These 'other means' included language and the Welsh language became a significant criterion of difference between England and Wales and one of the badges of Welsh national identity. However, the fact that it was a significant criteria of difference from England led to attempts by the latter to destroy it. The Acts are recognised as a legal attempt to eliminate the language and by implication a different Welsh identity from England.

The formal and complete association of Wales with England was accomplished by the Acts of Union which incorporated Wales into England, making the inhabitants of Wales subjects of the English Crown in the same way as English people. This has been acknowledged as an official attempt to bring about the death of the language. Most detrimental to the language were clauses which made English the only language of the courts of Wales, and which disallowed any person using Welsh from holding a public office.

Aitchison and Carter (1994: 26) quote from Bowen (1908):

And also by cause that the people of the same dominion have and do daily use a speech nothing like or consonant to the natural mother tongue used within this Realm some rude and ignorant people have made distinction and diversity between the King's subjects of this Realm and his subjects of the said dominion and the Principality of Wales. Whereby great discord, variance debate division murmur and sedition have grown between his said subjects...His Highness therefore minding and intending to reduce them to perfect order notice and knowledge of the laws...and utterly to extirpate all and singular the sinister usages and customs differing...his said country or dominion of Wales shall stand and continue from henceforth incorporated united and annexed to and with his realm of England (1994: 26).

Although the phrase 'to extirpate all and singular the sinister usages and customs differing', applied directly to law, it also directly implied a process of cultural assimilation and language erosion. This was reinforced by the provision that 'from henceforth no Person or Persons that use the Welsh Speech or Language shall have or enjoy any Manner Office or Fees within the Realm of England, Wales or Other in the King's Dominion'.

However, although the Act of Union had inevitable repercussions on the language which had become the most tangible symbol of difference and national identity, Aitchison and Carter (1994) point out that the language and the literary tradition which was its highest expression, remained as the most significant hallmarks of Welshness. They point out that one of the explanations of the unexpected survival of Welsh, as compared with Scots Gaelic and Irish, was that the other two Celtic peoples retained elements of separate legal, administrative, and political systems as expressions of identity whereas Wales had nothing but the language.

Historically, to many commentators, the curse of Wales was its distinctiveness—the fact that it was not English, linguistically and otherwise. The distinctiveness, it was argued, lay at the root of the Welsh readiness to riot, a readiness shown in the years between 1839 and 1844. The Welsh language was the essence of the distinctiveness. Insurrection could be expected in Wales, claimed the *Morning Chronicle* in 1839, because there was a linguistic division between the upper and the lower classes. It was the existence of the Welsh language, argued the Rebecca Commission in 1844, that hindered the law and the Established Church from civilizing the Welsh. The attacks upon the language were interwoven with the racism inherent in the prevailing eugenic model of nineteenth-century Europe. The indisciplined Irish proved that the Celts were shaped from inferior stock. As writers such as Freire point out, it is always the dominated group who are labelled as subversive or wicked when they react to domination. At any sign of protest, dominators consider the remedy to be more domination carried out in the name of freedom, order and social peace—that is their peace.

Work in the field of culture and identity point to some recurring themes. Analysing the relationship between groups based on Kelly's (1955) personal construct theory, Bateson (1942) points out that when two different nationalities of communities have had prolonged contact with one another the pattern of their relationship will tend to develop along either of two main processes. Bateson labelled these two processes as 'complementary' and 'symmetrical' differentiation. Symmetrical interactions between nations are those where the behaviour of one side triggers off similar behaviour in the other side, for example competitiveness. Complementary interactions are those where the actions of both sides are very different but yet mutually fit one another like a jigsaw. These interactions are typical if one nation has over time dominated another. Bateson outlines three major complementary patterns under the headings of 'Dominance–Submission', 'Exhibitionism–Spectatorship' and 'Succour-Dependence'. Although the Welsh, Irish, and Scots may have begun with and shown recurrence of symmetrical interactions with the English, the predominant pattern for hundreds of years was complementary.

Kenny (1985) applies Bateson's model to the Irish who, although developing a more symmetrical relationship for the last 60 years since their independence, experienced, like the Welsh, a complementary pattern of relationship to England for hundreds of years. Kenny describes how the Irish were faced with continuing defeat at the hands of oppressors living with an ever present outer authority together with the guilt, shame, sense of inferiority, anger, and frustration that arises from defeat and failure. The English dominated and the Irish submitted. The English exhibited their power and the Irish were the passive spectators. The result of this was helplessness and dependency. This complementary pattern evolved over time through the progressive elaboration of the Dependency–Spectator–Submissive constellation outlined by Bateson. The main method through which this elaboration was achieved was the psychological tactic which Kelly (1955) describes as 'constriction', which deals with the world both at a personal and national level. Here we narrow our range of operations and thus place other options outside our range. In Wales, as historians such as John Davies (1993) and Aitchison and Carter (1994) document, the language itself was subjected to a progressive constriction in the areas in which it was used with a consequent reduction of its status. In the areas of law, administration and government, education and science, and as well as 'genteel' society, its use was eroded. Further, political expediency and low social status together with the social effects of the industrial revolution and successive waves of immigration and emigration led to a decline in the language. Later attempts to eliminate the language led to a further stigmatizing of the language as low class and useless. As we have seen earlier in this chapter, language is part of ourselves as well as being used as a criterion for ethnic identity. Valuations of a language do not just exist in external space but exist within us and form part of our individual and collective psychology. Our reactions to such valuations are likewise experienced individually but they are historical, political, and social in origin.

Welsh language became progressively restricted to being the medium of culture, spiritual life, literature and its associated activities. The domains were never just confined to home largely due to the translation of the Bible and the religious movements of the eighteenth century. Janet Davies (1993) states that if it were not for the Protestant Reformation and the publication in 1588 of William Morgan's translation of the Bible into Welsh, it is likely that the language would not have survived. The history of the survival of the Welsh language up to the start of the twentieth century is entwined with that of religious education. As John Davies points out, the belief was fostered that Welsh should be restricted to being the language of sacred things while English was to be the language of the secular world.

Writers concerned about the psychological effects of colonial domination (see, for example, Fanon, 1970; Freire, 1996; Fromm, 1966; Lukacs, 1965) highlight themes in the psychological processes entailed in and the consequences of domination for both the dominator and dominated. They outline a process which is always initiated by those holding power. This process is perpetuated in different guises from generation to generation of both groups of dominated and dominator alike who are both shaped in its climate. Although the content and methods of domination vary historically, there are features of domination which are a direct result of economic, social, cultural, and political domination.

A central feature of domination is the differentiation of people into Subjects—the dominator—and Objects (or The Other)—the dominated. Writers such as Laing, Freire and Fanon point out the difference between Subject and Object. The term Subject denotes those who know and act, in contrast to Object, who are known and acted upon. Objects respond to changes, passively accept, and adjust to a given reality while Subjects decide for themselves, can act, transform and change their world. Those dominating usually do not perceive their position as one of diminishing others; rather domination is usually seen as an inalienable right or taken for granted. One of the basic elements of this relationship is prescription. Every prescription involves the imposition of one group's choices on another as one prescribes and the other follows the guidelines. For example, in legislations, England detailed prescriptions for Wales. Domination is maintained by different strategies such as manipulation, division, and cultural invasion.

Manipulation

Manipulation is a strategy to bring about conformity and adaptation to the objectives of the dominating group and to preserve the status quo. People can be manipulated by a series of myths which they internalize and in doing so come to accept the dominating group's version of reality and its words. Freire (1996) describes how myths are presented by different forms of communications and gives examples of myths such as the myth of the universal right to education, even though it was not through your own 'word'. The generosity of the elites when what they really do is foster selective 'good deeds', and promote the advancement of people so that they in gratitude should conform is another myth alongwith that of the industriousness of the oppressors and the laziness and dishonesty of the oppressed; the natural inferiority of the latter and the superiority of the former; the myth of defenders of civilization against barbarism or anarchism etc.

One of the methods of manipulation is to reinforce individuals with the notion that personal success is equated with being like the dominators. Freire points out that at a certain point in their existential experience members of the dominated group aspire to a way of life as of their dominators. In order to resemble the dominators and share their way of life they try to imitate them, to follow them, and talk like them. This phenomenon is especially prevalent in the middle class of the dominated group who yearn to be equal to or part of the upper orders. An example in Wales was the behaviour of the Welsh gentry after the Acts of Union. As a consequence of the Acts, if the Welsh gentry—the traditional holders of legal and public offices—wished to participate in public life then that participation would have to be in English.The gentry almost totally severed its links with the language and inevitably, as John Davies points out, the language of 'genteel' society was English. The Welsh language came to be generally viewed as a hindrance to anyone with aspirations to progress up the social ladder. There followed the conviction that Welsh was the language of the barbarous past and English the language of the civilized future. To speak English, preferably with an accent akin to that of the English upper orders, became an ideal to be pursued. Thus Welsh became a language which it was thought children need not acquire, indeed they were better without it since it carried at least an implication of exclusion from the higher reaches of society. Also time could be devoted to more profitable ends, for Welsh language had no apparent economic value. The result was symbolized in educational policies which in practice produced a secular education which was English directed.

Education can either function to encourage conformity and acceptance of a particular world view or as a means to critically engage and participate in the transformation of their world. The interests of the dominating group lie in engendering a passive view of the world and means such as education can be used to make them even more passive because the more people accept the passive role imposed on them, the more they will 'fit' the version of reality prescribed for them—a reality which must remain untouched.

In Wales, English education was seen as the way to suppress any social unrest. John Davies quoted H. L. Bellairs, author of the report on the condition of the South Wales coal field: 'A band of efficient schoolmasters is kept up at a much less expense than a body of police or soldiery' (1990: 389). The dominated group are typically marginalized and are seen as deviating from the social norm. They are regarded as the pathology of the dominant or 'healthy' society and are labelled as 'incompetent' or 'lazy' by the dominating group who seek to make them integrate to its own patterns by changing their mentality.

Education and a form of paternalism in the guise of 'improving' a people can be used as such a means to make people fit better with a dominant culture. An example of this is the *Report of the Commissioners of Inquiry into the State of Education in Wales of 1847*, (the Treachery of the Blue Books). This report on the system of education through the medium of Welsh pointed out the moral laxness of the Welsh. As a result of the report, education through the medium of English was established, and English became the sole language of the schools. Welsh came to be regarded as a language children were better off without. Because teachers' pay was normally based on results and Welsh was not part of the recognised curriculum, the use of Welsh was actively discouraged by teachers—and in many instances, by parents whose motivation simply reflected the belief prescribed for them that their language was of no use. The report's commissioners were unable to understand that a different culture, possibly with different values, could exist within the bounds of UK. With increasing industrialization, progress was defined in terms of material wealth. But the language in the areas of technology and business was English which was thus seen as useful and profitable. Wales was perceived as backward and the reason manifestly rested with the language which isolated the population from the benefits of 'progress'. We see in the report prescriptions for behaviour and the myths of the dominator's ideology such as the myth of the right to education even though it is not through your own 'word' and also myths to do with the industriousness and civilizing influence of the English. The dominating group who are doing the prescribing define themselves as those who know or were born to know. Educational programmes organized by the dominating group are designed according to their own view of reality. Education, with the ideological intent (often not perceived by educators) of unquestioning adoption, resists dialogue and critical thought and treats its students as objects. The students are not called upon to know but to memorize the contents narrated by the teacher. In Wales,

John Davies states, '…in most of the schools of Welsh-speaking Wales, there were pupils whose main experience of education was a mechanical drilling in a language which they did not understand; as late as 1960, it was possible to meet old people who remembered nothing of their schooldays except the learning by rote of a book known to them as "Redimarisi" (Reading Made Easy)' (1990: 455–6).

As we saw earlier on in this chapter, human beings do not exist in silence. Language cannot exist without thought, and neither language nor thought can exist without a structure to which they refer. Fanon points out for the dominating group, 'The words of his own class come to be the 'true" words which he imposes or attempts to impose on others: the oppressed, whose words have been stolen from them. Those who steal the words of others develop as deep doubt in the abilities of the others and consider them incompetent. Each time they say their word without hearing the word of those whom they have forbidden to speak, they grow more accustomed to power and acquire a taste for guiding, ordering, and commanding. They can no longer live without having someone to give orders to' (1970: 115).

Another way of manipulation is through pacts or reforms offered by the dominant society. Almost always these come about in response to the demands of the historical process. As a way of preserving its position, the dominator may accept or carry out reforms before people get too angry, as long as the reforms do not affect their power of decision. In Wales, this has been reflected, for example, in the government's attitude of grudging concessions and reforms in areas such as public administration, education, political and legislative developments, and in public broadcasting. In public administration, there were attempts to gain official recognition for the Welsh language but successive governments proved difficult to be convinced. The positive steps which were won in the first half of the twentieth century were the result of long, hard campaigns. However, as far as public life was concerned, Welsh language continued to have no status. In education, although there were a few concessions to to Welsh people earlier on in the century, it was not until 1944 that a legislation was passed to enable the provision of Welsh-medium schools and it was not until 1956 that the first Welsh-medium secondary school. Full recognition for Welsh education finally came in 1988. Regarding political and legislative developments, efforts to win official status for the language were seen in a series of protests and campaigns which resulted in a series of grudging concessions which eventually led to the Welsh Language Act, 1967 and the 1993 Act bringing, in effect, equality between the Welsh and English languages, but by administrative rather then by a statutory declaration. The same pattern of reluctant concession is seen in the area of public broadcasting. Broadcasting in Britain was begun in 1920 with the goal of a 'national service'. However, implicit in this was the essential Englishness of the BBC spreading the accent, values, and attitudes of the London upper-middle class to every corner of the UK. It is significant that the only Welsh-language programme broadcast from 1927 was from Ireland by Radio Eireann. There followed lengthy protests until adequate provision was made for the Welsh language in broadcasting. This situation was re-enacted a generation later, following the introduction of television. An adequate service in Welsh was only conceded after long campaigns over broadcasting despite constant pressure and dedicated efforts.

Cultural Division

Another fundamental dimension of domination is that by various means, attempts are made to divide people and keep them divided as it is then easier to preserve the state of domination. One means of doing this is by emphasising a focalized view of problems rather than seeing them as dimensions of a totality. In this way rifts in a population may be created and deepened. The more a region or area is broken down into parts without considering these communities as parts of a larger totality, the less people feel a belonging to the totality. This makes it easier to divide people and keep them divided. Sayal (1989) points to the colonial legacy of Black people's respective differences being played off against each other, with one community held up as a negative reference point for another. In Wales, differences within communities such as north versus south, rural versus urban can be magnified, distorted, and played off against each other. Another example of this is the language itself in Wales where a situation has been brought about such that some of the population retain their own language and others do not.

The dominating group, by presenting themselves as protectors of people, divide them further. For example, those who protest may be portrayed as marginals or enemies of society from whose dangerous actions people need defending. Another way of internal division is by the dominating class favouring and promoting certain individuals from the dominated classes—individuals who actually represent the view of the dominating group. These are all ways which exploit, directly or indirectly, people's weak points—their basic insecurity. Regarding the world of work, if people feel dependent and insecure they will be afraid of losing their jobs, or doors closing. If people are divided they will always be vulnerable to manipulation and domination. Dividing in order to preserve their way of life and the status quo is a strategy of dominant groups.

Cultural Invasion

In this phenomenon, the invaders penetrate the cultural context of another group, in disrespect of the latter's culture. They impose their own view of the world upon those they invade, who then lose their originality or face the threat of losing it by curbing their cultural expression.

Cultural invasion can bring about domination and can also be its result. In cultural invasion, the values and ideology and the reference point is the world view of the dominating group which is imposed upon the world of those whom they invade. Another culture is superimposed rather than attempts made to learn about people's world or respect the particular view of the world held by people. This is the case whether or not the actions were well intended or whether or not individuals from the dominant culture are aware of the significance of their actions. Whether subtle or direct, cultural invasion is thus always an action against the persons of the invaded culture who are put in the role of spectators of this process. Both they and their reality are objects of the actors' action.

Cultural invasion may be imposed through education or different forms of transmission where they need not even go personally to the invaded culture. In Wales, cultural invasion was evident in educational and broadcasting policies as well as by successive waves of immigration from England. Since the 1960s, this has been characterized by the growth of second homes in Wales. Since the 1970s, more people from English urban areas, attracted to rural living and inspired by the self-sufficiency movements, moved to Wales where land was cheaper. Another group were those who had no economic role but sought places to retire frequently in the rural areas and along the coasts. This resulted in the Anglicization of many Welsh-speaking areas by the 1970s. By the 1980s, fears grew that the Welsh-speaking rural communities would be utterly swamped as the vast majority of the newcomers had little interest in adapting to a Welsh culture and language. Rather, the pattern was domination on a local scale with the new immigrants assuming a leadership role in local institutions and councils. In the field of education, by 1970, as the result of English immigration into the Welsh-speaking areas of the west and the north, most natural Welsh schools were facing major linguistic problems, increasingly using English to accommodate the newcomers most of whom had little interest in learning Welsh. 'English colonisation of the Welsh countryside was on a scale sufficient to change the ethnic character of many communities' (John Davies, 1990: 631).

Cultural invasion, the imposition of one world view upon another, implies the 'superiority' of the invading group and the 'inferiority' of those who are invaded, as well as the imposition of values by the former. For cultural invasion to succeed, it is necessary that those invaded become convinced of their intrinsic inferiority and the superiority of the other group. The values and goals of the latter thereby become the pattern for the former. As Fanon points out: 'The more invasion is accentuated and those invaded are alienated from the spirit of their own culture and from themselves, the more the latter want to be like the invaders, to walk like them, dress like them, talk like them' (1970: 134). They come to see reality with the outlook of the invading group rather than their own and the more they mimic the invaders, the more stable the pattern and position of the latter becomes. Overwhelmed by a different culture which dismisses their own culture and expressiveness, a frequent response by individuals caught up in this is fatalism, indifference, and silence. One consequence of domination frequently observed is that of the passivity of the dominated who Freire describes as being submerged in the 'culture of silence' or 'structure of mutism'. Although they may see themselves as disadvantaged, their perception of themselves as oppressed is impaired by their submersion in the reality of oppression.

When we explore the constructs found in a culture, the attitudes and attributes are not meant to imply static, fixed attributes of persons or groups but a repertoire of constructions evolved over time through the relationship between two groups. Over time, this is manifested in our relationship to ourselves as well as in our relationship to others. According to Kelly (1955), we experience ourselves and our world through constructs or bipolar dimensions that we have developed through our experience in which each group takes up position on opposite ends of a bipolar construct, e.g., either dominating–submitting, active–passive, etc. The same concepts may be seen in the work of Freire, Fannon and Fromm, who analyse the pattern of relationships between dominant and dominating groups. This may be seen as what psychotherapists such as Ryle (1990) terms a reciprocal role process. This involves not just the relationship between two sets of constructs belonging to two separate groups but includes the concept, the notion that the constructs of one group are internalized by the other group and become their own. Regarding our relationship to ourselves, writers such as Fromm, Fanon, Freire and Anna Freud, use different terms but all describe the same psychological process which is the direct result of the experience of being dominated. One way of coping with feeling powerless and dominated is to identify with the internalizing aspects of the dominator in order to feel and restore one's sense of effectiveness. This results in an internal split or duality within the self. This is what Anna Freud termed 'identification with the aggressor', Fromm 'internal duality', Fanon 'adhesion' to the dominator, and Freire 'housing' the other. In this way, people maintain an illusion that they are not helpless and do have some power in their lives.

Earlier on in this chapter we saw how the self is formed in the sociocultural relations of the social structure. According to writers such as Fannon and Fromm, a situation of domination maintains the self in a position of identification with or 'adhesion' to a reality which seems all powerful and overwhelming. Part of the oppressed self is then located in the reality to which it 'adheres'. In this way the structure of thought of the dominated group has been conditioned by the situation which has imposed its shape on them so that the self of the dominated is both dominator and dominated. The attitudes, beliefs, values, and actions of the dominating group are internalized and thus felt as part of the self. The self is then split—shaped by and existing in a contradictory experience with the resulting ambiguity or duality. This adhesion—

or partial adhesion—of people to the dominating group makes it difficult for them to locate it outside themselves.

It is because of this ambiguity, according to Althusser (1971), that many professional people who have been 'determined from above' by a culture of domination become intermediaries or managers carrying out the directives of those who are in power. Because they have been conditioned by a culture of achievement and personal success, to recognize their own situation as objectively unfavourable would seem to hinder their own possibilities of success. However, because these patterns of domination are instilled within them they are insecure and anxious in their professional role. According to Friere (1996), they then tend to rationalize this anxiety with a series of evasions and rationalizations rather than any critical analysis or constructive action. From this perspective, many Welsh-speaking managers in the psychotherapy services in Wales may be seen in such dual roles, performing the role of intermediaries in carrying out the directives of a system which disregards the cultural context within which they work.

From the work on culture and identity, inter-related types of cultural constructs and themes emerge. These themes, which are the consequences of domination, operate at an individual, interpersonal, and group or national level.

FATALISM AND DOCILITY

Erich Fromm points out that when superficially analysed, this fatalism is sometimes interpreted as a trait of national character such as docility or passivity. However, he points out, fatalism in the guise of docility is the result of a historical and sociological situation, not an essential characteristic of a people's behaviour.

PASSIVITY

Freire, Fanon and Fromm describe how a consequence of domination is that people will feel downtrodden, fatalistically accept and react in a passive and alienated manner. Commenting on this legacy in Ireland, Kenny points out that the Irish have been left with components of despair, dependency, self-abnegation, withdrawal, shame, guilt, loss of pride, loss of confidence, and sense of worthlessness. These same themes are found in historical accounts of our legacy in Wales which document passivity, servility, lack of awareness, faint heartedness, and lack of pride. John Davies

(1993) points out that commentators such as Michael Daniel Jones saw this resulting from English control of the land, industries, and commerce and the dominance of the English language over the courts and schools. Saunders Lewis (1962) points to our lack of national awareness, our deficiency of national pride. He considered that the purpose of politics was the defence of civilization. He wrote that civilization 'is more than an abstraction. It must have a local habitation and a name. Here its name is Wales.' (cited in John Davies ,1990: 591). He viewed civilization as being threatened when people were without property and responsibility.

DEPENDENCY
This is the result of a process where people at a certain point in their existential experience are dependent on others. The dominated group, having internalized the image and adopted the guidelines of the dominating group, becomes adapted to and resigned to the structure of domination. The result of passivity and the giving up of responsibility is dependency and helplessness as people lack confidence in themselves. Seligman's (1975) notion of learned helplessness is pertinent here. When we find that none of our coping mechanisms make any difference to our dilemma, we don't do anything or give up, i.e., become depressed.

FEAR OF RISK TAKING
Due to the conditioned fear of going against external and internalized power structures, people fear risks and experimentation with reality, and prefer security. A hidden premise here which is usually not made explicit is that it is better to be a subject of domination than risk any other course of action.

LACK OF RESPONSIBILITY OR INITIATIVE
This is a consequence of fatalism and a reaction to an impossible external environment where people no longer see it possible to act constructively and change the situation. All responsibility is pushed on to the dominating group or authority figure. This leads to feelings of self-doubt, helplessness and hopelessness. Any action which may be construed as trying to change the situation will be viewed as unwarranted confrontation.

FEAR AND MISTRUST
Domination results in what Fromm terms a 'dominated consciousness full of doubts, fears and mistrust' (1966: 147). This is seen in

their ambiguity to their own people as they mistrust the oppressor 'housed' in them. Continually frustrated and fearful of directly confronting the source of their frustration, Fanon describes how people can give vent to their anger and attack the dominator indirectly by forms of 'horizontal violence', against their own people often for the pettiest reasons.

SENSE OF INFERIORITY AND LACK OF CONFIDENCE

Because they have been continually told that they are inferior, that the 'other' knows things and is able to run things, eventually people become convinced of their own unfitness. They have a diffuse belief in the other group's invulnerability and power. This results in insecurity and a lack of confidence. John Davies documents that historically, Welsh speakers were imbued with self-contempt and describes how Saunders Lewis viewed the chief aim of movements towards self government in Wales was 'to take away from the Welsh with their sense of inferiority'. Self-depreciation derives from the internalization of the opinion that the dominators hold of them.

Interpersonal Styles of Communication

Considering interpersonal cultural constructs or styles of communication resulting from domination, Kenny outlines four types of constructs which are an elaboration of Bateson's cultural analysis of the submission–dominance constellation.

SUPERFICIAL COMPLIANCE

One way to cope with a dominant authority is to appear at least superficially compliant. An aspect of this is group conformity. By focusing attention on what one must be seen to be doing, there is a gulf created between such activities and one's inner personal reality.

INDIRECT COMMUNICATION

This technique had a strong survival value in the face of oppression where it was important to learn to be evasive and develop a mental dexterity. This may be re-labelled by the dominating group in such terms as deceit and dishonesty. Another example is the difficulty in being self-assertive even when there is a justifiable complaint. Rather, people will complain to one another about somebody else and not like the idea of facing the person directly. This also applies to relationships with friends and to positive events. For example, it may be difficult in directly communicating positive feelings so that things tend to be understated if stated at all. Indirect communication also involves covert retaliation/aggression such as gossiping and backbiting.

AVOIDANCE OF SELF-REVELATION

This is when people feel unable to communicate aspects of themselves directly to others. Kenny points out that this is an elaboration of the submission construct and a reflection of the taboo against exhibitionism, especially against exhibiting superiority or too high a self-regard. The effect of this strategy is to block self-expression through self-censorship. This also means that inner feelings remain unexpressed and, therefore, unacknowledged in relationships.

ELABORATION OF THE INNER WORLD

The fourth construct is a corollary of the first three constructs which are about communication with the external world. This construct involves a creative application of spectatorship to inner processes. Here we find an elaboration of fantasy, magical thinking, poetry, music, etc. We have seen how in Wales, the language, and thus identity, became constricted and associated with the world of literature, poetry, and spiritual life. According to Kenny, this may also be a strategy for self-reassurance—the creation of a personal 'reality' which could not be touched, got at or invalidated. However, the more the focus is on inner reality, the more the external reality comes to be regarded as something about which not much can be done and for which you do not feel responsible for.

Below is a summary of some of the dimensions found within this type of cultural heredity. They are characteristic features of the pattern of relationship between Wales and England outlined earlier in this chapter. This is an adaption and elaboration of the work of Kelly, Kenny, and Bateson to include the concept of duality or reciprocal roles.

These are some of the constructs which we can abstract from the above analysis of Welsh identity in the context of this type of cultural legacy. These are not exhaustive by any means. They represent in summary form some of the basic cultural channels through which we tend to process our psychological and cultural phenomena. Such cultural options become enshrined so that they

Table 8.1: Biopolar Constructs

Spectator	Actor
Object	Subject
Accept	Impose
Obey	Prescribe/Lead
Submissive	Dominating
Failure/Defeated	Successful
Inferiority	Superiority
Dependent	Independent
Helpless	Powerful
Passive	Active
Superficial compliance	Involvement
Conforming	Innovative
Evasive	Direct
Ashamed	Proud
Self-depreciating	Self-affirming
Low self-esteem	High self-esteem
Self-doubt	Self-confidence
Worthless	Worthy
Useless	Useful
Silent	Speaking out

are seen almost as 'facts'. Kenny describes how although it has been 60 years since Ireland finally became independent of England, there has been very little change in these types of bipolar choices. When people criticize the Welsh or Irish it is generally the negative pole of some of these constructs that are picked out and re-labelled. For example, passive can be viewed as 'lacking initiative' or 'lazy' and 'evasive' may be re-labelled as 'deceitful'. These constructs are formed in our relationship to others. We also internalize the views that powerful 'others' hold of us becoming, as Fromm and Friere describe, as dual beings. These views are then adopted as part of our selves. Given below is an example of such a reciprocal role patterns.

These constructs and reciprocal roles become functionally autonomous, as if they have a life of their own, and people find it very hard to shake out of these moulds. This is the nature of the cultural gap between monolingual English psychotherapists and bilingual Welsh speakers in Wales. The words we use not only describe the world we live in but also dictate what we can see and

Table 8.2: Reciprocal Role Patterns

Relationship to others		*Relationship to self*
OTHER	SELF	SELF
Dominating	Oppressed	Self-oppressing
Contemptuous	Despised	Self-contempt
Controlling	Controlled	Passivity/Helplessness
Powerful	Defeated/Weak	Self-defeating/Hopelessness
Autonomous	Crushed	Depressed

how we see the world, and therefore, how we act. These constructs are therefore self-fulfilling prophecies if they are not questioned.

CONCLUSION

In this chapter I have tried to begin to address the question of the differential access to and provision of services to Welsh speakers in Wales by exploring two interweaving strands of evidence. The first is to do with the general frame of reference in the theory and practice of psychotherapy. Invisibility and silence are the themes found in psychotherapy theory, research, and practice in Wales. This is due to factors such as the general neglect of social and cultural issues and individualization of distress in psychotherapy and professionalism. The second strand concerns cultural and social attitudes and expectations of both service providers and the bilingual Welsh-speaking population.

Although some of the psychotherapies have their origins elsewhere, e.g., psychoanalysis, they are mainly American-based and reflect the individualistic values of that culture. They locate distress as being within a particular individual and treatment of that distress within the interaction of therapist and client. Writers such as Heath (1992) and Smail (1987) point to ways forward in therapy. A more equitable therapeutic endeavour would include an awareness of the pervasive effects of cultural and social issues manifested in the often debilitating effects on the individual's sense of self, in institutions, and in interpersonal relationships including therapeutic relationships. There are many ways of offering more appropriate forms of help and promoting a better therapeutic outcome. In many instances, the most important positive developments in working practices have been outside the statutory services in areas such as self-help groups, crisis lines and intervention services, e.g., White City Project (Holland, 1992), The Newpin Project (Newpin, 1992) and Shanti Project (Mills, 1992).

A great deal of work has now accumulated on cross-cultural counselling. Draguns (1996) summarizes developments in this field aimed at overcoming the challenge of a 'cultural gulf' which can exist when clients do not come from a 'cultural mainstream'. An explicit assumption being made in cross-cultural counselling is that interventions have been conceptualized and practised in such a mainstream. Draguns (1996) lists the following ways of attempting to help ethnic minorities:

1. Culturally sensitive workers from the mainstream start with their dominant understandings of working with clients from their own racial or ethnic group and then tentatively test out how far these do or do not work with clients from outside their group (Berry, 1969).

2. The second response is to start by developing a full understanding of the values, norms, and healing practices of a particular minority with the explicit aim of respecting and even co-opting these practices rather than imposing the models of the 'mainstream' (Nwachuku and Ivey, 1991; Nathan, 1994)

3. Another response has been to identify obstacles to effective and helpful interventions, with a view to overcome or remove these impediments. For example, there is cultural variability in attitudes towards self-disclosure to strangers and to members of the opposite sex. There are also differences in expectations about levels of directives from designated authority figures.

4. This response Draguns describes as 'cultural accommodation' (Higginbotham *et al.* 1988), which contains and extends all the above three items. It involves planning mental health services by collecting data on the culturally diverse population to be served, negotiating with particular groups about their needs and preferences and then converting this audit into practical steps. The latter would entail developing culturally sensitive services which were approachable and accessible, and which contained personnel and interventions that were acceptable to clients and prospective clients.

These strategies to provide mental health services with the goal of 'cultural gulf' reduction are pragmatic attempts to respond as widely as possible to diverse individual expressions of distress. Pilgrim (1997) points out that they do not explore too deeply the ethnic patterning of distress nor do they debate the possible merits of separatism or collective struggle. Its emphasis is on the interpersonal rather than the social or political. Cross-cultural counselling has been developed more extensively in the USA where, as a nation built on immigration, socio-political stability has depended on the success of multi-culturalism. Despite questions about the completeness of cross-cultural counselling as a basis for analyzing the relationship between ethnicity and mental health, it provides advantages compared to the generalizations and assumptions leading to insensitivity to cross-cultural difference such as an awareness of differences in norms and values and therapists' failure or deficiency in understanding a different background.

Invisibility and silence are also the themes regarding psychotherapy research in Wales. In Wales, the issues of differential access and provision for psychological help need to be carefully monitored and statistics gathered so that empirical work on these issues may be carried out. In a recent comprehensive review of Irish mental health, Jones (1997) highlights the need for a multi-faceted research programme on mental health. This is not only because of the inherent inadequacy of single factor, reductionist approaches arguments, but also because of the need for research which reflects upon the meanings attached to emotions in their cultural context as well as their causal antecedents (e.g., Scheper-Hughes, 1979). This involves both quantitative and qualitative methodology. In other word, personal accounts of people and ethnographic observations of their culture are a necessary element of culturally appropriate research into mental health.

Psychotherapists working with Welsh speakers have not drawn significant attention to the problem of differential access. I suspect that this is in their own self-interest not to do so. There has to be a willingness to change on the part of service providers. Kenny views that dominant groups such as England resist change and the resistance to change or to anything that interferes with their understanding of the world and the status quo is explained by their experience of being a dominant class. He gives the example of the situation in the Falklands and Northern Ireland and suggests that the English need the Irish to help maintain their self-image as a world dominating force who also may exhibit paternalism. Kenny describes how, even after 60 years of independence, the Irish are still undergoing a psychological weaning process from the English who, in turn, have seriously ambivalent feelings about the hitherto dominated group taking full responsibility for itself. Kenny suggests that change is resisted because of the human tendency to hold on to the familiar and the secure, no matter how painful and destructive the continuance of such a vicious circle may be.

Both Friere (1996) and Kelly (1955) remind us that it is not possible to escape from cultural controls merely by ignoring them. Similarly, Kenny (1985) points out that once a situation of domination has been established, it engenders an entire way of life for both groups who are caught up in it as both are submerged in the situation. Domination by its very nature requires a dominant pole and a dominated pole. In terms of cultural options, writers on cultural identity point out that trying to reverse positions along the bipolar dimensions is insufficient by itself. When a person psychologically switches from one end of a dimension to the other, he or she is still trapped within the confines of that dimension.

According to Bateson and Kelly, change is possible through a process which is the opposite of constriction i.e. dilation which can help achieve more symmetrical relationships. There are several ways that this may be achieved. One way is by departing from dyadic relationships and its established pattern of constructs by introducing new elements into the relationship such as forming a triad which will generate new constructs. Kenny suggests that the way forward for Ireland is through its membership of the European Union which he hopes will lead to the genesis of new constructs to replace the old ones of dependency and lead to the development of psychological autonomy. Triadic relationships, thus, may offer the Celtic countries a way forward.

The process of dilation in terms of the Welsh language and identity may well be on its way in Wales, both quantitatively and qualitatively. It seems that the constriction may have been abated and dilation may have been brought about by the instigation of statutory and educational policies which have recognized the status of the language. For the first time, census figures suggested a growth rather than a decline in the language. In 1991, the numbers claiming a knowledge of the language were marginally more numerous than in 1981, especially amongst the younger age group, which reflects the increase in Welsh-medium education. The status and use of the language has also been promoted by political means culminating in the Welsh Language Act of 1993. Although there was much the Act did not do (for example, it did not amend employment laws to allow employers to designate posts as requiring the ability to speak Welsh), it did repeal legislative obstacles and established the principle that in the conduct of public business and the administration of justice, the Welsh and English languages should be treated on a basis of equality. It promotes the status and the use of Welsh in the delivery of services. It places a duty on public bodies to prepare Welsh language schemes which provide the administrative means for implementing language policies. The Act also established a statutory body—the Welsh Language Board—with the function of promoting and facilitating the use of the Welsh language. As we have reviewed in this chapter, language is not just words. It is not good enough to merely translate forms, to have a token greeting in Welsh or even to just have the good manners to write back in the chosen language of clients. Neither is it reasonable to put the responsibility onto the client to make requests for services in their preferred language. An adequate mental health service in Wales would closely examine these issues and seek culturally appropriate alternatives to silence and invisibility.

REFERENCES

Aitchison J. and H. Carter (1994). *A Geography of the Welsh Language 1961–91.* Cardiff: University of Wales Press.

Albee G. (1996). 'Searching for the magic marker', *Paper presented at the J. Richard Marshall Memorial Conference of the Psychotherapy Section of the British Psychological Society*. Nottingham, 27 April.

Allport G. W. (1962). 'Psychological models for guidance'. *Harvard Educational Review*, 32: 373–81.

Altuusser L. (1971). *Lenin and Philosophy*. London: New Left Books.

Anthias, F. (1992). 'Connecting race and ethnic phenomena'. *Sociology*, 26(3): 421–38.

Ashton H. (1991). 'Psychotropic drug prescribing for women'. *British Journal of Psychiatry*, 158: 30–5.

Bakhtin M. M. (1981). *The Dialogic Imagination: Four essays.* Texas: University of Texas Press.

Bakhtin M. M. and P. N. Medvedev (1985). *The Formal Method in Literary Scholarship: A critical introduction to sociological poetics.* Harvard: Harvard University Press.

Bateson G. (1942). 'Regulation and Differences in National Character', in G. Watson (ed.), *Civilian Morale*. Boston: Houghton Mifflin.

Bender M. P. and A. Richardson (1990). 'The ethnic composition of Clinical Psychology in Great Britain'. *The Psychologist*, 3: 250–2.

Berry J. (1969). 'On cross-cultural comparability'. *International Journal of Psychology*, 4: 119–28.

Bromley E. (1994). 'Social class and psychotherapy revisited'. *Paper presented at the Annual Conference of the British Psychological Society*, Brighton.

Bromley E. (1983). 'Social class and psychotherapy' in D. Pilgrim (ed.). *Psychology and Psychotherapy*. Routledge and Kegan Paul: London.

Chomsky N. (1968). *American Power and the New Mandarins*. Penguin: Harmondsworth.

Clarke D. and H. Brindley (1993). 'Black women and HIV: Developing health services to share the challenge'. *Clinical Psychology Forum*, 58: 6–9.

Davies D. R. (1995). 'Themes in psychotherapy with the unemployed'. *British Psychological Society Psychotherapy Section Newsletter*, 17: 36–46.

Davies J. (1990). *Hanes Cymru*. London: Allen Lane, The Penguin Press.

——— (1993). *A History of Wales*. London: Allen Lane.

Davis S. (1993). *Threshold—a local initiative from women and mental Health*. London: Springer.

Draguns J. (1996). 'Humanly universal and culturally distinctive: Charting the course of cultural counseling' in P. B. Pederson, J. G. Draguns, W. J. Lonner, and J. E. Trimble (eds). *Counseling Across Cultures*. London: Sage.

Dryden W. (1990). *Individual Therapy: A Handbook*. Milton Keynes: Open University Press.

Fanon F. (1970). *Black Skin, White Masks*. London: Paladin Books.

Fernando S. (1988). *Race and Culture in Psychiatry*. London: Tavistock.

Freire P. (1996). *Pedagogy of the Oppressed*. Harmondsworth: Penguin.

Fromm E. (1966). *The Heart of Man*. New York.

Greenslade L. (1992). 'White skin, White masks: Psychological distress among the Irish in Britain' in P. O'Sullivan (ed.), *The Irish in New Communities*. Leicester: Leicester University Press.

Gurani P. D. and A. Sayal (1987). 'Ethnic minorities and Clinical Psychology. Some further comments'. *Clinical Psychology Forum*, 7: 20–3.

Hall S. (1988). 'Marxism Today'. *New Times*, October.

——— (1989). *New Ethnicities: Black Film: Black Cinema*. London: ICA Documents, 27–31.

Heath G. (1992). 'Is there therapy after Masson?' *Clinical Psychology Forum*, 45: 32–6.

Higginbotham H., S. West, and D. Forsyth (1988). *Psychotherapy and Behaviour Change: Social, Cultural and Methodological Perspectives*. New York: Pergamon.

Holland S. (1992). 'From social abuse to social action: A neighbourhood psychotherapy and social action project for women' in J. M. Ussher and P. Nicholson (eds). *Gender Issues in Clinical Psychology*. London: Routledge.

Horowitz A. (1983). *The Social Control of Mental Illness*. New York: Academic Press.

Husserl E. (1970). *The Crisis of European Sciences and Transcendental Phenomenology*, trans. D. Carr. Evanston. IL: Northwestern University Press.

Jones A. (1997). 'High psychiatric morbidity amongst Irish immigrants: An epistemological analysis'. *Unpublished PhD thesis*. Milton Keynes: Open University.

Karasu T. B. (1986). 'The specificity versus non-specific dilemma: Toward identifying therapeutic change agents'. *American Journal of Psychiatry*, 183: 687–95.

Kelly G. (1955). *The Psychology of Personal Constructs*. Norton: New York.

Kenny V. (1985), 'The post-colonial personality'. *Crane Bag*, 9: 70–8.

Laing R. D. (1960). *The Divided Self*. London: Tavistock.

Lukacs G. (1965). *Lenine*. Paris.

Masson J. (1990), *Against Therapy*. London: Fontana.

——— (1991). *Final Analysis*. London: HarperCollins.

Mead, G. H. (1934). *Mind, Self and Society from the Standpoint of a Social Behaviourist*. Chicago: University of Chicago Press.

McGoldrick M., J. Pearce, and J. Giordano (1982). *Ethnicity and Family Therapy*. New York: Guilford Press.

Mills M. (1992). *SHANTI: A Consumer-based Approach to Planning Mental Health Services for Women*. London: Women's Counselling Services.

Nathan T. (1994). *L'Influence qui guerit*. Paris: Editions Odile Jacob.

Newpin (1992), *Annual Report, 1992*. London: National Newpin.

Nwachuku, U. and Ivey, A. (1991). 'Culture specific counseling: an alternative training model'. *Journal of Counseling and Development*, 70: 106–15.

Omi M. and H. Winant (1987). *Racial Formation in the United States*. London: Routledge.

Pilgrim D. (1994). 'Some are more equal than others'. *Paper presented at the British Psychological Society Annual Conference*. Psychotherapy Symposium, Brighton, April.

——— (1997). *Psychotherapy and Society*. London: Sage Publications.

Pilgrim, D. and Treacher, A. (1992). *Clinical Psychology Observed*. London: Routledge.

Pillay H. M. (1993). 'The DCP workshop on race and culture issues of equality and power in psychology'. *Clinical Psychology Forum*, 61: 24–5.

Poole R. (1972). *Towards Deep Subjectivity*. London: Allen Lane.

Richards B. (1995). 'Psychotherapy and the injuries of class'. *British Psychological Society Psychotherapy Section Newsletter*, 17: 21–35.

Rosenthal D. and J. D. Franks (1957). 'The fate of psychiatric clinic outpatients assigned to psychotherapy'. *Journal of Nervous and Mental Disease*, 127: 330–43.

Rothblum E. M. (1990). 'Depression among lesbians: An invisible and unresearched phenomenon'. *Journal of Gay and Lesbian Psychotherapy*, 1: 67–87.

Rowe D. (1991). *Breaking the Bonds*. London: Fontana.

Ryle A. (1990). *Cognitive-Analytical Therapy: Active Participation in Change*. Chichester: Wiley.

Sayal A. (1989). 'Black women and mental health'. *Clinical Psychology Forum*, 22: 3–6.

Scheper-Hughes N. (1979). *Saints, Scholars and Schizophrenics*. Berkeley, CA: University of California Press.

Schwartz H. and J. Jacobs (1979). *Qualitative Sociology*. New York: Free Press.

Smail D. (1987). *Taking Care: An Alternative to Therapy*. London: J. M. Dent and Sons Ltd.

——— (1993). *The Origins of Unhappiness*. London: Harper Collins.

Stone M. (1985). 'Shellshock and the psychologists' in W. F. Bynum, R. Porter and M. Shepherd (eds). *The Anatomy of Madness*, vol. 2. London: Tavistock.

Szasz T. (1972). *The Myth of Mental Illness*. London: Routledge.

Ussher, J. M. (1991). *Women's Madness: Misogyny or Mental Illness*. London: Harvester Wheatsheaf,

Voloshinov V. N. (1976). *Freudianism: A Marxist Critique*. New York: Academic Press. Originally published in 1927.

Vygotsky L. S. (1962). *Thought and Language*. Cambridge, MA: MIT Press.

Watters C. (1996). 'Representations of Asians' mental health in psychiatry' in C. Samson and N. South (eds). *The Social Construction of Social Policy*, London: Macmillan

Webb-Johnson A. and Z. Nadirshaw (1993). 'Good practice in transcultural counselling: An Asian perspective'. *British Journal of Guidance and Counselling*, 21(1): 20–9.

Williams J., Watson, G. Smith, H. Copperman, J. and D. Wood (1993). *Purchasing Effective Mental Health Service for Women: A Framework for Action*. Canterbury: University of Kent/MIND Publications.

Yamamoto J., Q. C. James, and N. Palley (1968). 'Cultural problems in psychiatric therapy. Archives of General'. *Psychiatry*, 19: 45–9.
Zukzv G. (1979). *The Dancing Wu Li Masters: An Overview of the New Physics*. London: Random House.

9

Indian and Western Medicine: Rival Traditions in British India

*Poonam Bala**

The central theme of this paper is the dynamics of the interaction between Indian and Western medicine, and the state policies in India under the British rule during the nineteenth and early twentieth centuries. In discussing the State and medicine in British India, an allusion to the above relationship in earlier periods is valuable. For, the period was one in which the indigenous medical systems, namely, Ayurveda and Unani, flourished well under royal patronage, and brought encomiums to their practitioners.

INDIGENOUS MEDICINE IN PRE-BRITISH INDIA: A PROFILE

The history of medicine in India commencing from sixth century BC represents a history of accommodation and change, frequently associated with invasion or changes in the ruling ideology. The halcyon portrait of the Ayurveda, synergetically related with religion and politics in ancient India, as portrayed in many books of history and countless lores, appears to be dubious. It is known that medical practices as contained in the Ayurveda were met in ancient India by State opposition in the form of political and social condemnation by the ruling orthodoxy. This opposition found

* Associate, Centre for Health Promotion, Faculty of Medicine, University of Toronto, 100 College Street, Suite 207, Banting Institute, Toronto, Ontario M5G 11, 5, Canada.

expression in the legal and priestly literature produced at the time. The pragmatism of developing medical science represented a challenge to the priestly authorities, and hence to their scriptural declarations. And in order to resist the potential threats to the ruling ideology, the priestly and religious states declared medical practitioners as heretics. This attitude also had an impact on the practising Ayurvedic practitioners. In order to evade State censorship of medical science, physicians conceded to the law-giver by producing medical texts with an underlining of religious ideas. To quote Chattopadhyaya (1976), 'To add apparent conviction to its loyalty to the norm of orthodox piety, special chapters are added to the text (*Charaka Samhita*, for instance) for loudly proclaiming the theory of soul and its salvation.' And in order to evade State censorship of medical science, the Ayurvedic physicians conceded to the law-givers by producing medical texts with an underlining of religious ideas. Nevertheless, some of the great practitioners earned reputation through royal patronage during the ancient and subsequent medieval periods.

Thus, when medical practice could not be resisted, there were attempts to appropriate it and present it within a religious format. This process led to a curious accommodation, within Hindu texts, of medical practices which were otherwise against religious observances. However, the impact of religion on medicine may not have been as hampering for medical practice as is usually claimed. For, we know that the late ancient and medieval Indian rulers sought out the best practitioners in their attempt to accommodate the two forms of medicine. Both Ayurveda and Unani passed through phases of conservation and advancement in medical knowledge. Several medical compilations were compiled and translated for the royalty. Also, with a dependable clientele base, Indian medical practitioners flourished well and amassed huge fortunes. At the end of the ancient period, the Ayurvedic system of medicine represented a codified body of medical knowledge and theory, redacted and edited by Ayurvedic physicians, by a useful compilation of significant drugs.

In medieval India, too, the Ayurveda passed through phases of conservation and advancement in terms of medical knowledge. The religious underlining in the Ayurvedic texts, however, did not appeal to the early Muslim rulers. As a result, the Muslim royalty only recognised Unani medicine and its practitioners (called *hakeems*) brought from Persia. And it was only in later years that the Brahmins (priests) gave way in order to incorporate the scientific essentials of a new system of medicine. The conservative nature of ancient medicine at this stage proceeded towards a state of dynamism due to the influence of Unani medicine. Added to this was the rising status of medicine under the Muslim rulers who made constant efforts to systematize medical knowledge at the time. The medical knowledge had, by this time, proved to be significant to the Muslim royalty. In the years to follow, the two systems were integrated and accommodated without one threatening the other. Physicians at this time are known to have been encouraged and paid from *purshigan*, the royal treasury.

To conclude on the status of indigenous medicine in the ancient and medieval periods, it may be said that both Ayurvedic and Unani system of medicine were encouraged by the State. Common patronage was facilitated by similar methods of diagnosis and treatment. This represented the initial phase of dynamism in indigenous medicine which continued well into the subsequent periods.

Given the dynamic character of indigenous medicine, we shall look into further changes in it, brought about in the British period.

MEDICINE UNDER BRITISH RULE

With the advent of British rule in Bengal, the above relationship began to change. In this section, I shall examine the dynamics of the interaction between indigenous and Western forms of medicine, and indigenous reaction to British policies towards indigenous medicine.

The first two decades did not witness any significant change in the attitude of the British to Indian medicine. Yet, the State appointed Indians as subordinate health workers in hospitals manned by British physicians. Those attaining professional skill were later attached to regiments and civil stations as native doctor: in addition, indigenous physicians are also known to have found employment with the East India Company in 1762 by which time as many as nineteen native doctors were in employment. According to Crawford (1972). Ayurvedic physicians were employed on the cruisers of Bombay marine in the early nineteenth century. The increasing demand for native doctors, coupled with the appreciation of Ayurvedic medical treatises by the Court of Directors of the East

India Company, led to the foundation of a school for native doctors, called the Native Medical Institution (NMI) in Bengal in 1822. This was the first orgainzed effort by the British government for the communication of medical instructions to the indigenous population. Discourses included instructions in Ayurvedic medicine, with parallel instructions in Western medical science. Students trained at the NMI were, according to the orders of the then Governor-General, to be appointed in the Native Corps. Following this move, a Sanskrit College was established in Calcutta in 1824, and in 1827, more teachers were appointed to lecture in Sanskrit to students of Ayurveda and to acquaint them with the works of eminent medical authorities of ancient India—Charaka, Vagbhata, and Susruta amongst several others. Rudimentary treatises on anatomy, surgery, and medicine were translated from English into the Indian vernaculars for inclusion in the medical curriculum at the school and college. Needless to say, the British regime initiated their medical policies in India not by expunging Indian tradition but by patronizing it.

In 1833, Lord William Bentinck, the then Governor-General of India, appointed a Public Instruction Committee to review the conditions of the then existing medical education and training, and to suggest measures that would be expedient to adopt with a view to the better instruction of the people, including the arts and sciences of Europe. William Bentinck's decree of 1835 for the demolition of the existing NMI and its replacement by a medical college led to the closure of the NMI. Medical classes at the Sanskrit College were accordingly discontinued. The order of 1835 also decreed that a new medical college be established for instructing Indians on the pattern adopted in Europe and that instructions should be given through the medium of English which, incidentally, became the court language in the same year. Thus, in 1835, the Calcutta Medical College was established in accordance with the pattern of curriculum and instruction in Europe. This marked the end of the first attempt at synthesis of Indian and Western medical forms. This also ushered in an era of official patronage and recognition of the Western system of medicine.

The above assault on Indian tradition by the British engendered a reaction amongst the Indian nationalists (details follow later) and spurred a series of movements by cultural nationalists who made several attempts at resuscitating the Ayurveda by political propoganda and by institutional support after provincial governments were set up.

Nevertheless, despite withdrawal of support, the British regime continued to maintain interest in the traditional forms of medicine, in the form of employment of indigenous physicians, and utilization of a significant indigenous drugs in order to enrich the Western pharmacopoeia. During the late nineteenth century, there was a proliferation of Western medical schools and colleges. The fact that training in Western institutions ensured the elite a State-recognised status and better chances of entering the service of the State—the railways and the like—it attracted more Indians into Western medical discourses. And in Bengal, those best placed to engage in a prosperous private practice were those who could well afford English education. This represented the socially advantaged group comprising the Brahmins, *Kayasthas*, and the *Baidyas*, collectively called the *Bhadralok*. And as Western medicine became more formalized and standardized, and as English became the medium of instruction, those sections of the population with English education, were progressively advantaged. The *Bhadralok*, thus formed a rival group with the rest of the Indian population. Several members of this elite group of Bengal were involved in propogating the spread of English education. With the expansion of Western medical science, there emerged a series of new bureaucratic statuses occupied by practitioners of indigenous medicine, some of whom gained knowledge of European medicine with, what Leslie calls, various degree of eclecticism. Indian practitioners possessing a knowledge of Western medical science claimed a superior status to other indigenous practitioners resulting in conflicting situations between the orthodox Hindus and other *vaids*. The founding of a Native Medical Society in 1832, with the object of confining medical practice to *vaidyas* stands as the earliest record of the association of indigenous practitioners, which diverted them from getting acquainted with Western medicine. This led them to support traditional forms of medicine, as follows.

INDIGENOUS MEDICINE SANS OFFICIAL PATRONAGE IN BRITISH INDIA

Despite the continued expansion of Western medical schools and colleges in India, Indian medicine continued to be taught and practised in the traditional manner in the '*tols*', the traditional homes of professional physicians. *Kaviraja* Gangadhar Ray is known to have contributed to the sustenance of indigenous medicine in British India. He trained several students in his '*tol*' at Berhampore (Bengal) and wrote Sanskrit commentaries on Ayurvedic texts, the most famous being that of Charaka, called *Jalpakalpataru*. Following him, Gangaprasad Sen of Calcutta also attempted to bring indigenous medicine at par with occidental medicine. He is known to have exported Ayuvedic drugs to Europe to compete with its Western counterpart in the market place. He also introduced a consultation fee which either equalled or surpassed those of British physicians and drew public attention to Ayurvedic drugs by publicizing them. This almost became a hereditary family profession continuing several generations after the two *vaids* (or *Kavirajas*). It may be surmised at this stage that Western medicine was unable to supplant indigenous medicine which continued to thrive well with the support of Ayurvedic practitioners. In 1919, Bills were moved in the Legislative Assemblies in support of the same and for rendering financial assistance in setting up new schools of Indian medicine. Practitioners of Indian medicine raised several issues on the employment of *vaids* and *hakeems* by municipalities, seeking pecuniary aid from the government. In 1878, Indian physicians opened a dispensary in Calcutta and successfully propagated knowledge of Indian medicine through inexpensive books on the same. They highlighted the importance of the Ayurvedic pharmacopoeia, and founded several pharmaceutical concerns to manufacture and sell indigenous drugs. This enabled the *Kavirajas* to earn considerable wealth so that they were at one time, what Gupta claims, 'among the richest men in the country'.

While one set of orthodox physicians patronized indigenous medicine, another group of *vaids* made efforts to establish a medical college where parallel instructions in Ayurveda and Western medical science could be imparted to the Indian population. The Gobinda Sundari Ayurvedic College, founded by *Kaviraj* Ramachandra Mallick, and the Vishwanatha Ayurvedic College founded (founder's name not known) towards the early twentieth century, exemplify this move. Yet another class of physicians were involved in the national movement towards the early part of the nineteenth century. Since medical knowledge of the ancient

Hindus was linked with the culture of the past, the move to resuscitate Ayurveda could be seen as part of the rising national consciousness among the Indian population. The movement accorded a prominent place to the revival of Sanskrit language and literature, which represented the perennial fount from which Indian vernaculars were derived. What follows is a discussion on the indigenous response towards revival of indigenous medicine as a corollary to the expansion of occidental medical science.

MEDICAL REVIVALISM AND THE NATIONAL MOVEMENT

In India, the rise of the anti-imperialist movement was a gradual outcome of the contradictions between the colonial imperatives and the basic interests of the vast majority of the Indian population. It was also goaded by exponents of Hindu cultural nationalism who assumed that the degeneration of India and the subsequent destruction of its nationality were greatly enhanced by the inroads that Western civilization had wrought upon the traditional cultural systems of the country. The movement was based on the belief that Hindu population constituted a religious and racial unity and the Vedas, which were the outgrowths of Aryan intellect, were superior to anything the world had previously known. Yet another factor contributing to the intensification of the national movement was the introduction of English as the medium of instruction in all disciplines throughout the country. The establishment of the Calcutta Medical College, followed by similar institutions in Madras and Bombay Presidencies further strengthened this policy.

The recognition that contemporary traditional practices do not reflect the significant achievements of the ancient civilization as a result of their decline, largely due to the imposition of an alien culture and the subsequent demand for State patronage or governmental interference from new regimes for their resuscitation, figures as an important feature of most of the revivalist movements in South Asian history.

The revivalist movement for Ayurveda was initiated by advocates of Ayurveda with a view to restoring and promoting indigenous forms of medicine, as opposed to Western medicine. The movement aimed at achieving recognition and status by seeking State patronage and founding more institutions. The movement found expression in 1907 with the bringing together of a professional group of indigenous practitioners in the form of the All India Ayurvedic Congress, which formed the leading organization of *vaids* in India during the period.

The movement achieved success in gaining support from the Indian National Congress which demanded State patronage for Ayurveda, and in 1920, passed a resolution in favour of popularization of school, colleges, and hospitals for instructions and treatment in accordance with indigenous medical science. In the subsequent year, Shaymadas Vachaspati, a reputed Ayurvedic scholar, founded a national university in Bengal, called Gaudiya Sarvavidyayatnam, as part of the Non-Cooperation Movement. An Ayurvedic wing was started in protest against the Western-oriented education of the day. In the same year, Mahatma Gandhi laid the foundation of an Ayurvedic College in Calcutta with an extensive hospital attached to it. Chandrakishore Sen, a *Kaviraj*, opened a dispensary in Calcutta where he sold indigenous medicines at inexpensive rates. There were also attempts at publishing inexpensive books to propagate the knowledge contained in the Ayurvedic texts. In 1884, an Ayurvedic company, N. N. Sen and Company, was formed to promote Ayurvedic drugs. This was followed by Sadhana Ausadhalaya and Kalpataru Ayurvedic Works, to name a few.

In Bengal, as in the rest of India, the strength of indigenous medical groups had become apparent by the late nineteenth century, which went alongside the increase in the number of Western medical practitioners and also institutions of Western medicine. By this time, the hostility to indigenous medicine had increased substantially, and by the turn of the century, both Ayurveda and Unani medical men saw Western medicine as major threat to their status. Differences became more apparent with the rise of the national movement in India.

A major assault on indigenous medicine followed in the aftermath of the registration acts in each province so that 'no doctor of indigenous medicine could be legally recognised to give testimony in legal disputes or to perform any other legally required function'.

The above move intensified the feelings of Indian nationalists in favour of Indian medicine. Advocates of the Ayurvedic revivalist movement were, however, divided in their opinion on the educational and professional standards of Ayurveda in comparison with Western medicine. One group favoured reliance on ancient medical texts, thus, encouraging '*shuddha*' or 'pure' Ayurveda. The other group advocated complete integration with Western or modern medicine. The recognition that 'pure' Ayurveda could not handle public health problems led the proponents of integrated medicine to frame a system of Ayurvedic education embodying concurrent instructions in oriental and occidental medical sciences. From the time of World War I and the Montagu-Chelmsford Reforms of 1919 that gave Indians a larger role in governing the country, Ayurvedic movement was increasingly linked with politics. One of the features of the reforms was the introduction of 'dyarchy' or dual power in the provinces where, apart from the control exercised by imperial authorities, subjects as health and education were delegated to provincial legislatures. The increasing entry of Indians into the legislature opened up opportunities for them to voice their demands in favour of pristine heritage of India.

From 1900 onwards, the State was pushed into making decisions on indigenous medicine. The provincial governments, set up in the early part of the twentieth century, gave Ayurveda some measure of support in the form of founding more educational institutions throughout the country. As the available evidence shows, in Punjab, the provincial government employed *vaids* and *hakeems* for extension of medical relief. Several local state governments set up Boards of Indian Medicine as government institutions regulating indigenous practitioners. As a sequel, a government school of Ayurveda was set up in 1887. In 1908, a committee was set up by the local government to look into the curriculum of Ayurveda in these schools. Following its recommendations, education in indigenous medicine was fortified by including studies in anatomy, physiology and surgery in the curriculum. Medical schools and colleges for Indian medicine expanded in subsequent years. Gradually, with more patronage of princely States, and caste and religious associations, additional schools and dispensaries began to emerge in different parts of the country so that at the time of independence, in 1947, there were as many as 57 urban Ayurvedic and Unani schools with hospital wards for clinical instructions, laboratories, and dissection halls.

Indigenous medical practitioners also established a State Faculty of Ayurvedic Medicine in Bengal for regulating the standard of instructions in Ayurvedic medicine as well as to grant certificates and diplomas to graduates of Ayurvedic schools and colleges.

CONCLUDING REFLECTIONS

The aforesaid account leads to the following conclusions. It can hardly be gainsaid that the Ayurvedic system of medicine continued to provide medical relief to a vast majority of the Indian population and thrived well with a dependable clientele base. In ancient India, the ruling ideology discouraged medical practice in anticipation of potential threat to its teleological harmony, but later accepted its presentation within a religious format. Both Ayurveda and Unani flourished well during the subsequent period in medieval India, facilitated by the similarity in humoral diagnostics and therapeutics. It may also be said that Ayurveda in British India enabled its practitioners to do well and amass good fortunes. In response to the introduction of Western medical science in India, three categories of patrons of indigenous medicine may be isolated. One, there were those Ayurvedic enthusiasts who obtained support through the national movement, and who identified Ayurveda with the pristine culture of India. Then there were the provincial governments who supported indigenous medicine and its practitioners. Lastly, some of the indigenous physicians themselves took the lead in voicing their opinion in favour of Indian medicine.

The impact of the spread of English language and its subsequent introduction in all arts and sciences in India was confined to the socially advantaged section within the society. This applied to the Presidencies—Bombay and Madras—where Western medicine was formalised through recognised medical colleges granting medical degrees.

In the twentieth century again, we found that Ayurveda was given all kinds of encouragement. Continued competition with occidental medicine resulted in medical 'oligopoly' instead of the oft quoted monopoly. We have seen how indigenous medicine claimed similar official status through establishing indigenous institutions and universities, and by establishing a State Faculty. In the presence of a pluralistic medical situation, where both Indian and Western medical forms co-existed with equal magnanimity, it can be said that Western medicine in British India was faced with a peculiar situation in which it had to compete instead of the with traditional medicine and hold its own.

NOTES

1. The term Indian medicine has been used synonymously with indigenous medicine which includes, unless specified in the text, the Ayurvedic and Unani medical system.
2. '*Kaviraja*' means practitioner of Ayurvedic medicine. Similarly '*hakeem*' is used for practitioner of Greco-Arab or the Muslim system of medicine.
3. Western medicine was officially introduced in India as a State medical system in the early nineteenth century.

Ancient period refers to the period when the Ayurvedic system of medicine was codified and redacted alongwith other medical works. It includes the period from sixth century BC to the seventh century AD. Medieval period refers to the period of Muslim rule in India, starting from about the twelfth century. For details on policies and their impact on the medical systems during these periods, see Bala, Poonam. (1985), 'Indigenous medicine and the State in Ancient India', *Ancient Science of Life*, V(i), pp. 1–4.

See also Bala, Poonam (1982). 'Ayurvedic System of Medicine: Its Fate in Medieval India' *Bull. Ind. Ins. His. Med.*, XII, pp. 22–7.

See also Bala, Poonam. (1982), 'The Ayurvedic and Unani Systems of Medicine in Medieval India', *Stud. His. Sc.*, VI(4), pp. 282–9.

REFERENCES

Bala, Poonam (1990). 'State Policy Towrads Indigenous Drugs in British Bengal' *J. European Ayurvedic Society*, I, pp. 167–76.

——— (1991), *Imperialism and Medicine in Bengal: A Socio-Historical Perspective*. New Delhi: Sage.

Brass (1972). 'The Politics of Ayurvedic Education: A Case Study of Revivalism and Modernization in India' in S. H. Rudolph and L. I. Rudolph (eds). *Education and Politics in India: Studies in Organization Society and Policy*. Cambridge, Mass: Harvard University Press, pp. 342–71.

Chattopadhyaya D. P. (1976). *Science and Society in Ancient India*. Calcutta: Research India Publications.

Crawford D. G. cited by C. Leslie (1972). In E. Friedson and J. Lorber (eds). *Medical Men and their Work: A Sociological Reader*. Chicago: Aldine.

Crawford op. cit., p. 48.
Delhi Records 6, Home Department Proceedings, July 1919. Medical Branch, National Archives of India.
——— See also Jeffery, Roger (1988). *Politics of Health in India.* Berkeley: University of California Press.
Each province had branches of the Ayurvedic Congress to present the needs of indigenous practitioners.
Gupta, Brahmananda (1976). 'Indigenous Medicine in 19th and 20th-century Bengal' in Charles Leslie (ed.). *Asian Medical System: A Comparative Study.* London: California University Press, pp. 368–78.
Gupta, op. cit.
Jaggi. O. P. (1977). 'Indigenous System of Medicine during British Supremacy in India'. *Stud. His. Med.*, I(4): pp. 320–47.
McCully B. T. (1966). *English Education and the Origins of Indian Nationalism.* Gloucester: Peter Smith.
Medical Proceedings, 2 January–26 February 1835. Pt. II, National archives of India.
Metcalf B. D. (1985). 'Nationalist Muslim in British India: The Case of Hakim Ajmal Khan'. *Modern Asian Studies,* 19(I): pp. 1–28.
Quinquennial List of Registered Ayurvedic Practitioners from 1352 to 1356. B. S. Calcutta (year of publication not known).

10

A Historical Disorder: Neurasthenia and the Testimony of Lives in Latvia

Vieda Skultans

Neurasthenic illness in Latvia embody many of the contradictions and difficulties of life under Soviet rule.[1] In trying to understand the Latvian experience of neurasthenia I address two interrelated theoretical issues. First, I examine the implications of viewing autobiographies of illness as alternative histories. I look at the ways in which the medicalization enterprise is restricted if a whole life is brought into consideration. When life histories translate injury into collective trauma, they succeed in hindering the transformation of planned state violence and terrorization into medical knowledge.[2] And second, if Latvian illness narratives are 'evocative' transcripts of resistance, where does this leave medical

Acknowledgements: I am grateful to the British Academy and to the Economic and Social Research Council (ESRC) for funding the fieldwork on which this paper is based.

[1] I use the present tense advisedly because although Soviet rule ended formally with the declaration of independence in 1991, its legacy in terms of personal suffering remains. Diagnostic practices also have yet to change. Any uncertainty over tense reflects the indeterminacy of social change.

[2] The planned use of terror falls into three periods. During the first year of Soviet occupation in 1940–1, some 15,000 people were arrested and killed. They were, for the most part, people in senior positions. During the post-war period arbitrary arrests continued. Partisans and anyone suspected of aiding them were targeted. On 25 March 1949, one-tenth of all farmers were deported to Siberia, thus paving the way for the collectivization of farming. (For a history of these events, see Andrejs Plakans).

anthropology?[3] If Latvian informants succeed in dismantling and dismissing attempts to medicalize their pain, in what sense, if any, can its study be called medical? To address these questions, I compare the Soviet psychiatric writing on neurasthenia with its implementation in everyday medical practice in Latvia. In particular, I focus on its life stories, which are an important marker of difference between lay and medical understandings of suffering and illness.

Calloway (1992) has claimed that 'neuroses have had a relatively low profile in Russian and Soviet psychiatry' (p. 167). I would suggest that it was their ubiquity which rendered them invisible. A recent article on neurasthenia ends with the dramatic statement that: 'Neurasthenia is extinct in the West because its cultural work is done' (p. 542). Neurasthenia was alive in Soviet Latvia because its cultural work was so widespread. However, the uncertain political allegiance of Latvians to the Soviet Union introduced ambivalence and cognitive dissonance to this work. Doctors and psychiatrists had the difficult task of bridging political and conceptual differences. Perhaps Latvian doctors were ready to diagnose themselves as suffering from neurasthenia for this very reason.

Everyday medical accounts of neurasthenia attempt to reconcile two contradictory perspectives: one focuses on individual inadequacy, the other on the difficult social circumstances and hardship of lives. In conversation, doctors acknowledged the contribution to the development of neurasthenia of the impossible conditions under which lives are lived. Medical histories, on the other hand, scrutinize patients' past lives for signs of character weakness. However, informants themselves opened up the discussion of ill health by introducing yet another dimension, namely, the historical and collective nature of their experiences. My work rests on some sixty-three and thirty subsequent interviews with people

[3] I borrow the term 'evocative transcript' from Caroline Humphrey who reworks Scott's thesis on hidden transcripts in the context of the Soviet Union. She argues that the social circumstances for the production of hidden transcripts were not to be found in Socialist Mongolia. In particular, there was no sharing of a social space by an enduring group. The production of a hidden transcript was subverted 'by the knowledge that virtually everyone had a double life' (p. 25). The term 'evocative' simultaneously captures the universality and ambiguity of these transcript. Medicine in Latvia makes extensive use of such evocative transcripts.

responding to a newspaper advertisement calling for neurasthenia sufferers to write to me about their experiences of illness. These autobiographies are transformed by a historical consciousness: individual injuries contribute and testify to a collective national trauma. The autobiographical narrative of one particular provincial doctor—Kristina—illustrates the way in which a life history bridges the personal and collective and two-way movement across this bridge. History frames Kristina's life and explains the damage inflicted on her health: thus history both takes away and gives back meaning. However, Kristina also uses her life story to construct an alternative history which challenges Soviet history. Clearly, such uses were not anticipated by Soviet psychiatric theory.

SOVIET THEORIES OF NEUROSES

Soviet psychiatry was charged with the heavy duty of explaining not only politically incorrect behaviour, but also disaffection and discontent. Doctor-patient conflicts testify to the difficulties of explaining away the persistence of human unhappiness. Time and history—so important for dialectical theory—play no part in Soviet psychiatry: their conclusion would have undermined its ideological aspirations. Rather, Soviet psychiatric ideas occupy a timeless realm in which puppet characters shadow-box with society. However, the implementation of theory was constantly endangered by the unhappy voice of memory.

Official psychiatry pronouncements have a more optimistic ring: 'The formation of new socialistic consciousness is associated with the overcoming of the conflicts between personal and social—in the new socialistic understanding the individual and the social form a single entity' (p. 50). The challenge of welding together social and individual interests was met by developing a diagnostic system with a strong emphasis on somatic character types. The work of Pavlov provides a theoretical basis for this enterprise. Myasischev's theory of four character types derives from Pavlov's tripartite description of the nervous system: strength, mobility, and balance. These yield the classification of human types set out in Table 10.1.

The classical provenance of this classification—acknowledged by Myasischev himself—needs no emphasis. However, the fact that he

Table 10.1: The Theory of Four Character Types

Strength	Balance	Mobility	Humoural type
+	+	+	Sanguine
+	+	–	Phlegmatic
+	–	?	Choleric
–	?	?	Melancholic

Source: Adapted from Myasischev (p. 196).

does not bother to follow it through in a systematic way, leaving certain dimensions unaccounted for, suggests that there are other implicit but more important principles of categorization at work. Indeed, towards the end of the book we find a more basic dualistic typology which categorizes human character into the social versus the individualistic or egoistic (p. 207). This accounts for why neurasthenia and hysteria, both characterized as typical of a weak nervous system, are not further differentiated in terms of mobility and balance. The simplified dichotomy is of more importance for psychiatric thinking and practice than the classification spelt out at greater length. It offered a means of translating political threat into psychiatric language.

One of the principal axes along which egoism and the commitment to the collectivity are measured is the attitude to work. 'Incapacity for work deprives individuals from earning a living but equally importantly, excludes them from the working group' (p. 12). Thus attitudes to work also play an important diagnostic role: 'We do not obtain proper criteria for assessment of the functional disturbances unless we consider the patient's attitudes towards his task and how this changes during work and in working conditions' (p. 14).

Thus, although a Pavlovian-derived typology provides the theoretical infrastructure for an overall theory of neurosis, it is the orientation of society towards the collectivity, and the work collectivity in particular, which informs the exigencies of everyday psychiatric practice. The theoretical exegesis of neurotic disorders also rests upon pragmatic considerations concerning the individual's relationship to the collectivity rather than on a humoural-based typology. Myasischev has developed a schema which relates the type of neurosis to the locus of conflict. In this schema, there are three categories of neuroses: neurasthenia, hysteria, and obsessive–

compulsive disorders. Each category is linked to a particular kind of conflict between the individual and society (see Table 10.2).

Table 10.2: Relation between Type of Neurosis and Locus of Conflict between Individual and the Society

Neurotic Illness	Locus of Conflict	Society
Neurasthenia	Individual's abilities	Social and self-imposed expectation
Hysteria	Individual wants	Social expectations
Compulsive Disorders	Wants	Moral imperatives

As the table shows, in the case of neurasthenia, the conflict and mismatch is between the individual's physical and psychological abilities and social and self-imposed expectations. The individual finds himself, or more often herself, unable to fulfil these expectations. The symptoms of neurasthenia are: 'Irritability, an unstable or depressed mood, a tendency to become fatigued or tired easily with complaints of headache, loss of memory and poor appetite' (p. 193). Official Latvian psychiatric thought closely follows this account of the aetiology and symptomatology of neurasthenia. For example, Imants Eglitis writes of 'an exaggerated excitability and tendency to tire, emotional and somatic lability' (p. 164).

Thus, all neurotic disorders are perceived as conflicts whose source lies in a mismatch between social expectations and norms and the individual's abilities to meet those norms. They are situated at the interface between the individual and society. However, their power to monitor relations between individuals and the collectivity is restricted by the ancient language of somatic character types which deprive voices of their meaning.

The role of the psychiatrist as educator, one who teaches correct attitudes towards self and society, derives from this underlying dualistic typology. Indeed, Myasischev acknowledged, 'The field of the struggle with the neuroses is a borderline field between education and medicine' (p. 270). Soviet psychiatry has generally been acknowledged to be collectivist in orientation (p. 234). In keeping with this orientation, the task of Soviet psychiatrists was seen as one of restoring individual confidence (p. 165) but at the same time, directing the patient towards socially required standard of behaviour (p. 599). Although the relationship between the psychiatrist and the patient was described as being more intimate and friendlier than in the West, the role of the psychiatrist was also described as active and educative (p. 440). Dispensaries rather than hospitals were thought to be more appropriate for the monitoring of psychiatry illness (p. 297, pp. 433–44). Dispensaries were also thought to be more effective in restoring patients to full social functioning. Soviet psychiatry was characterized by the relatively large numbers of psychiatrist and small numbers of hospital beds (p. 298, p. 154). All these features contributed to the powerful role of Soviet psychiatry in 'educating' its peoples.

Latvian Psychiatric Practice

Psychiatric practice in Latvia diverges in some ways from Soviet psychiatric principles in that hospital treatment and community care are given equal importance. There are ten psychiatric hospitals in Latvia providing a total of some 6000 beds. This yields approximately 2.5 beds per thousand inhabitants, an extraordinary high ratio by any standards.[4] The ratio of psychiatrists per head of population is also high, but particularly so in the capital. Psychoneurological departments attached to polyclinics also treat psychiatric disorders. There are twenty-five such psychoneurological units in Latvia and each unit is responsible for some 300,000 people. Within Riga, there is the City Psychoneurological Dispensary with thirty psychiatrists, each allocated responsibility for a designated area of the city with some 30,000 inhabitants. In addition, there are ten emergency ambulance centres in Riga, each of which has a psychoneurological brigade. It appears then that Latvia is well provided for in terms of both in-patient and outpatient psychiatric facilities. No doubt this was related to its socially educative role, particularly important in a country where political allegiance could not be counted upon.

In Latvia, the diagnosis of neurasthenia is elusive and paradoxical. Prior to my research I had been assured by psychiatrists and doctors of its ubiquity: it was, I was told, the most commonly used diagnosis. Yet, in the course of my fieldwork I found it exceptionally difficult to pin down. This elusiveness appeared in the letters

[4] The comparable Bristol, UK, figures are 0.20 beds per thousand inhabitants.

which I received early in 1992. Of the sixty-three letters only a few discussed their illness. The diagnosis of neurasthenia meant little to them. Most were not sure what was they suffering from. For example, a letter from Liepaja beings, 'It is difficult for me to judge whether I am suffering from neurasthenia—I will leave, that for you to decide'. People's focus on the past, on their life histories rather than their illness experience, makes any such decision difficult. I found commonalities of history and memory rather than of symptoms and illness categories. Informants did complain of anxiety and fear. Some spoke of an inner fever. For many, these feelings were particularly strong at night, when they would wake terrified, feeling suffocated, and with hearts racing. Common phrases were 'I am short of air', 'I don't have enough air' or 'My heart is on strike'. These expressions of distress have strong political resonances and pay little regard to the medical specialities of the neurasthenic experience.

Neurasthenia is equally elusive in psychiatric hospital and clinics, not being considered sufficiently serious to warrant psychiatric treatment. The diagnosis appears to have been used principally within general medicine, and particularly within the psychoneurological specialisms of community health clinics or polyclinics. Here neurasthenia accounts for about a third of all diagnoses. It also figures significantly in the work of the emergency services, which I shall discuss later. However, literature on neurasthenia is sparse. The standard psychiatric textbook devotes an incomplete paragraph to it. Arthur Kleinman found something very similar in China. He writes of 'the limited space devoted to neurasthenia in current Chinese textbooks of medicine' (p. 178) attributing this reluctance to a professional anxiety about its scientific status.

A LOCAL HISTORY

The semantic complexity of neurasthenia reflects Latvian history. Its sedimented layers of meaning have been deposited by successive occupying powers and cultural hegemonies. Neurasthenia was a common diagnosis in the early part of the century, as witnessed by one of my narrators born in 1910:

> In 1929, I volunteered for the army in the hope that I would be sent to Riga, where I would be able to go to night school. Instead, I was sent to

Gulbene [a small provincial town in north-east Vidzeme] and on top of that I got a very strict sergeant. Before enrolling I wondered how I would feel, because I needed a lot of sleep, but in the army I didn't suffer from lack of sleep, but I still didn't feel well. I went to the doctor, he couldn't find anything wrong. He drew a cross on my chest with his stethoscope and left a red 'wound' as though drawn with a knife. The doctor was amazed—a country boy and he feels unwell. 'You have neurasthenia.' He wrote out a prescription for some drops—strychnine. I said, 'But that's a poison'. He said, 'Yes, but it should be drunk in small measure'. He gave me three days off. After a while I went back and got five days off. My companions were surprised—a neurasthenic. Returning from the doctor I gave my records to the medical assistant. She said, 'Well, yes neurasthenia has been dragged over here from America.' 'Is it catching?' I asked. 'No', the assistant replied. Later I was transferred to another division and then felt better.

Ernest's recollections illustrate many of the features attributed to neurasthenia in the nineteenth century: it is associated with study and city life. For example, the doctor evinces surprise that despite being a country boy he is yet so sensitive. Neurasthenia has a certain cachet. The American provenance of the illness is very clearly recognized. The American derived layer of meaning of neurasthenia informs Ernest's letter and it is also evident in the illness of other older informants.[5]

Neurasthenia continued to be a common diagnosis during the independence period. It is described as: 'One of the most commonly encountered illnesses of the nerves, which belongs to the functional group, that is those whose occurrence is not reflected in organic or perceptible changes, but whose essence consists in weakness in the functioning of nervous processes. The chief characteristic of neurasthenia is increased irritability of the nervous system and weakened endurance for work'. However, Harijs Buduls, a well-known psychiatrist of the independence period, devotes very little of his writing to neurasthenia—a mere

[5] George Beard's study of neurasthenia was published in 1880. The symptoms of neurasthenia derived from the inadequate working of the nervous system rather than any pathological changes in its structure. Neurasthenia was thus a disease with a physiological base which although associated with the stress of modern life and overwork, was nevertheless distinct from modern mental illness. It affected women rather than men and bedrest was advocated as a cure. It affected upper-class women and, therefore, had a certain social cachet.

paragraph. He discusses neurasthenia in the course of a short chapter on the psychopathic personality. 'Many psychopaths have many characteristics of the neurasthenic with an exaggerated sensitivity, quickness to tire, lack of direction, and some other disturbances of somatic and psychic function. Psychopathy has many points of contact particularly with a form of neurasthenia which has psychological manifestations and which is called psychic asthenia' (pp. 125–6). The link with a particular type of asocial personality and the limited prospects of cure or indeed improvement provide an important bridge with later Soviet ideas.

Thus in Latvia, Soviet Psychiatry met ground that was already well worked and one might have supposed it to have been receptive to it. The Soviet neuropsychiatric version of neurasthenia was not that different from the older Latvian versions. Why was it not superimposed unobtrusively onto existing ideas? Moreover, in Soviet Latvia, all psychiatrists received postgraduate specialist training in Russia, principally in Moscow but also in Leningrad. They were, therefore, well versed in Soviet psychiatric theory.[6] And yet Soviet ideas about neurasthenia did not take root in Latvia and lost what ground they had hitherto occupied. The reasons for the paradoxical status of neurasthenia—its simultaneous omnipresence and invisibility—lie outside the realms of psychiatry.

EVERY RESISTANCE OF MEDICALIZATION

Lay thought attributes the breakdown of health to history and the burden of historical consciousness and memory. A recurring phrase refers to 'all these mad times' an 'all these chaotic times'. The impact of such times on health is perceived as direct, brutal and inevitable. People use a language of physical assault and violence to describe their experience of health and illness. They talk of health being spoiled, damaged, destroyed, and beaten. The heart and the head are often singled out as sites of violence. Events can only be resisted up to a point before health finally succumbs to their impact. The relentless grip of memory also is thought to make people ill. Thus,

[6] Arthur Kleinmann has documented a similar process influencing Chinese psychiatry and refers to 'the importation of a tripartite Russian classification of neurosis in which neurasthenia figures importantly along with hysteria and obsessive–compulsive disorders' (p. 33).

lay accounts rework psychiatric theory reinterpreting the nature of the conflict between individual and society. Rather than recognising individual inadequacy, they turn the medical account on its head and lay the blame for illness at the doors of society and history. Latvian history shapes lives and with it , health and illness. Latvian doctors have the difficult task of mediating between these opposed interpretations of illness and finding a common ground between lay and psychiatric language.

Doctors share with ordinary people the belief in collective damage to health. In conversation, doctors and psychiatrists admit that the majority of Latvians are suffering from neurasthenia. The estimates of neurasthenia sufferers varied from 60 per cent to 90 per cent. Some even claimed that it was a universal condition:

> In principle virtually everyone suffers from these problems of neurasthenia. Either these or related problems, because all these social circumstances leave a heavy imprint on people. (Dr I. A., Riga, August 1992).

It seems that lay ideas about the universality of neurasthenia have also been assimilated by the medical profession and that they are responsible for the sweepingly high estimates of neurasthenia prevalence. A paradoxical corollary of this is that doctors tend to avoid the diagnosis and have a generally pessimistic view of the prognosis (p. 16).

Although Latvian doctors are aware of the difficult circumstances of people's lives and of their histories, they operate with a model of psychoneurotic illness which focuses on individual inadequacies. Social factors play an ambivalent role within medical and psychiatric practice. Although in conversation about their work and their patients, doctors and psychiatrists make constant references to social circumstances, these are not incorporated into official categories. Indeed, it is the acknowledged ubiquity of a distressing past and stressful present circumstances which help to create a feeling of helplessness; nothing can be done:

> Of course, of course. Many people cannot be helped either then, or now. There are people who've lived all their lives in a communal flat. We can't give them a flat. There are people who live three or four to a room. There is no way we can help them. You ask me about drugs. We have no drugs. Very often we have no antibiotics. OK. We have no psychotropic drugs, nobody will die because of that, but at present we do not even have antibiotics; that's how far it's got.

Such attitudes are reinforced by the fact that many doctors have lived through and continue to live in circumstances which are similar to those of their patients. This casts them in the role of mediators. The crucial role of psychiatrist in instilling Soviet ideological goals and political conformity is well documented. Their role as mediators between ideological practice and the miseries of daily life is even more important and less well-known. Thus, the multiple meanings and ambiguity of neurasthenia permit idiosyncrasy in diagnostic practice and promote the social work of neurasthenia.

At the onset of my research I had wanted to exclude the overtly political dimensions of psychiatry. However, I found as the work proceeded that I had to change my position about this at the insistence of my narrators. First, narratives constructed illness in political terms; second, perceptions of the everyday practice of psychiatry were inevitably coloured by its political involvement. Most people were aware of the way in which compulsory psychiatric treatment had been used against dissenting political figures such as Peteris Lazda and Gederts Melngailis. Psychiatrists could recount many such incidents. For example, Dr Kirsentals, director of the City Psychoneurological Dispensary, described the way in which political dissidents would be rounded up in ambulances and confined to a psychiatric hospital before any state celebrations. Certainly all psychiatrists were aware of the reputation of their profession. I asked Dr A. S. Kirsentals how she felt about the earlier political role of psychiatry:

> I will tell you straight: I am ashamed to be a psychiatrist. Although I like my work, I am ashamed that my colleagues can do something so base and dishonest. Because I think to exploit this specialism for dishonest purposes, where it is so difficult to prove anything objectively.... In surgery it is not so difficult to see that a bone is broken by making an X-ray, but here it is impossible to prove whether a person is speaking the truth or whether he is making it up and therefore I simply have nothing to say. I am ashamed.

However, not only were the dissenting words and behaviour of major political figures treated as psychiatric problems, but smaller acts of rebellion and criticism of everyday practices could be met with a psychiatric response. For example, Dainis found that his exasperation at not being able to find a flat and his accusation that the executive committee was taking bribes led to his forced psychiatric hospitalization. Nina, who worked in a state bank, found that her complaints about dishonest practices at work gave rise to compulsory psychiatric treatment. Her letter complained that: 'In our society, nervous people are often made out to be mad'. Dzintra, a history teacher, found that her lessons were perceived as anti-Soviet and she also was compulsorily confined. I could give more examples. The rights and wrongs of any one case cannot be established in retrospect, but these examples demonstrate the general reputation of psychiatry. As one psychiatrist discussing the reluctance of people to consult her profession put it: 'The old imprint is still there'.

Among my original sample of sixty-three letter-writers, five were doctors (8 per cent) who wrote about themselves rather than in a professional capacity.[7] One consequence of this readiness for self-disclosure is that there is far less of a professional distance between doctors and their patients in Latvia than there is in Britain (pp. 14–18). This greater intimacy puts doctors in a difficult role. Doctors use both medical and lay ideas of neurasthenia: as an illustration, the doctors who replied to the neurasthenia advertisement wrote about themselves and their accounts were similar to lay people's. For example, Anna is a psychiatrist who offered to talk about her own neurasthenia. She spoke about her life and emphasized its commonality with others:

> I don't for a moment think that I am the only one who hasn't succeeded. No, I've always told myself that I'm not the only one like that, the whole Latvian nation is like that.

Illness narratives offer a political critique in parallel with descriptions of personal injury. There is a shared language of damage, injury, and exploitation which is applied to society as well as individuals. The principal complaints were of dishonesty, disorder, and unpredictability:

> I feel I'm being strangled. I cannot stand all the irregularities. There are no rules.
>
> I feel like a taut bow the whole time. There are irregularities at work. All the corners of the heavens have been spoilt.
>
> It is an unfulfilled life. Everywhere everything is dishonest, dirty. I cannot bring any order into my life.

[7] Kleinmann found a similar over-representation of health professionals in his clinic sample of one hundred neurasthenia patients (p. 138).

All that disorder is eating away at me. My son is stealing, but is there anyone in this society who isn't stealing?

That's been imported here [i.e., from Russia]. No contract can be made. Everything is through bribes. There is no clarity. We are like meat in a mincing machine.

Nina's narrative makes a direct connection between dishonesty at work and the erosion of health:

I worked in the state bank as an inspector. That was a thankless sort of profession. I came into contact with all sorts of dishonest people as you know in our Soviet period. I had to sort out the irregularities but the system wouldn't allow that. And that's why I had the conflicts at the bank. They simply took revenge on me so that I wouldn't be able to poke my nose there and even today they dislike me. Dealers, you know, were speculating, they were carrying out all sorts of malpractices and the appropriation of state funds took place before my very eyes, but I wasn't allowed to identify it. Well, that traumatized me the whole time... I want to work honestly, but we weren't allowed to work honestly. You're probably familiar with these things? You read the Latvian press, don't you? All that wears down the nervous system.

Underpinning these extracts from letters and subsequent interviews is a socio-historical model of illness, which draws upon life histories to explain the erosion of health.

A Doctor's Life Story

Kristina is a doctor whose accounts of her illness, her life, and her understanding of history are inseparable. Her life story is offered as testimony. In her letter she wrote: 'Perhaps you will be able to use my life story' and I would like to do so. Her life story is unique to her and yet, at one and the same time, records both a shared history and a collective experience and memory.

Like many older narrators, Kristina's life story is dichotomized by the war into a before and an after period. Her account of her pre-war childhood is typical in it emphasis on books and unchanging spiritual values:

I don't remember much. But I remember those years as very sunny. Those early years are linked to my father's shop, to books. I imbibed a love for books that is still with me... I'm so tired in the evenings but I definitely have to read something. That's stayed with me all my life. So those first four years were very happy. My parents cared for us, brought us up properly.

Kristina singles out a birthday to mark the boundary between the Latvian period and the Soviet occupation. Her emphasis on family celebrations and rituals is typical of many narratives which contrast a sacred cyclical time with disorder and unpredictability. The following incident with the dough and the hens emphasizes the disorder and wastefulness of events.

When the Russians came in, I remember that our parents were very frightened. And it happened like this that the deportations were on 14 June 1941 and my mother's birthday is on 14 June. And the day before we had moved...and we moved on 13 June. And the next day, 14 June, was my mother's birthday and we were planning a small family celebration, nobody could foresee.... We'd asked some very close friends and I just remember that in the morning while we were still sleeping my mother ran somewhere very anxiously. She came running back very alarmed and was crying...I still remember what she looked like with untidy hair. She grabbed her head and said, 'Rich, everything is lost there won't be any celebration, all our friends have been taken and deported'. She mentioned the Zilnieks family in particular and so.... Then in her panic she took the dough which she'd prepared for the *piragi* and poured it out for the hens. Father shouted, 'What are you doing? You could have baked the *piragi* and taken them to the station to those unfortunate people. As I remember it, there was tragedy in the move to that house and also life developed in a tragic way. My mother said that she built the house with enormous care and effort, but that she didn't spend one happy day there.

Kristina dates her ill health from the time of her father's imprisonment:

He was six years in prison. He sat out his sentence to the last day, until 1951.... He was in Ventspils prison, after that he was in Riga prison, and after that he was sent to the Archangel district in Voisk. He was there for about four years. And then he was released on 30 April 1951. And he returned to Ventspils on condition that he did not register in Ventspils, or live there or work there. He was considered a criminal and Ventspils being a port, he was not allowed to register there are work there. Well, that period of time destroyed my nervous system (Latvian *sagrava*, literally crumbled or ate away). My father was really intelligent, he didn't know how to do farm work. My mother had lived in the country with her foster parents, she was different. She could cope with any situation, but my father wasn't like that. And then when he returned from deportation, he wasn't given any work. And then at one time he worked in Zura agricultural school as a horse groom. But he didn't get on well because he didn't know how to....

And then I remember that my mother used to go there specially to show him how to harness a horse. He said, 'Yes, yes, It's all clear'. But when my mother left he harnessed the horse and the horse unharnessed itself. Quite simply he was unhappy because he wasn't allowed to work where he wanted to work. Then I think he was probably made redundant....

An episode during the German occupation involving a soldier and his dog is held responsible for her contracting meningitis.

Well, and then in the autumn of 1944, I fell ill with infectious meningitis. Well, I don't know what the cause was, but a few weeks earlier I was learning the piano with a private teacher and I went to her for lessons. And I had a red dress, bright red, with little white spots. And I was going with my notes to the piano teacher and I remember it as though it were today: there was a German officer lying in the grass and next to him a big Alsatian dog was eating from a tin. And suddenly he attacked me. He did shout at the dog in his own language but he didn't come to my help, until my mother ran out. My dress was torn. He hadn't bitten me, only scratched me, but I was terribly frightened. And it turned out.... Well, every army has its policy, it turned out that he'd been specially trained to attack the colour red. And he saw me with the red dress and that upset him and that's why he attacked. Later the officer apologized to my mother, so she recounted. I was terribly frightened and two weeks later I fell ill with meningitis. And I was very ill and I remember that my father went on his bike to some German first aid post for brontusil. And he brought it home and with its help I got better. And then soon after my father was arrested and then there was all that uncertainty about my father and my mother was floundering about. She was left without means and with four small children. I was nine, my brothers were seven and five, and my little sister was two and had no means of livelihood. I was the oldest and I was exceptionally emotional. And all my mother's troubles, all her anxieties about how to feed the family, I took upon myself even though I was a small child. And I remember the following episode at school.... The teacher comes up to me and calls me. She calls once, she calls me twice and I don't hear her and then she starts shaking me.... What am I thinking about.... And I am so startled as though from a sleep and I say to the teacher: 'I'm sorry but I'm thinking about where to get hay for my mother's cow'. And I wasn't listening to the lesson, I was living in my own world. And the teacher wanted to scold me but when I told her she wasn't cross with me, she understood.

But then I remembered after the meningitis I had terrible headaches and I was terribly anxious and my period of convalescence coincided with all those terrible events when my father was arrested....And then I remember that I often had headaches and the stuttering started.[8] ...And it become especially bad during the period that my father was arrested, when I was just going to school. I started going to school during the German period; I finished the first class, but after the war I was in the second and third class and those were the most terrible. And I wrote to you in my letter about the episode.... They were terrible times.... They were our very own Latvians. I have to say there is a category of people that know how to adapt to whatever government is in power. And there was a teacher there, her name was Trage; by the way, she was my father's childhood friend, they had gone to school together. They knew each other well but she knew how to adapt to those in power. And then there was another teacher Kupce, who was also known to my father, because my father was the director of the book shop. Everybody knew him as an intelligent man but the new government despised him as an enemy of the state and his children had to be despised too. And I remember, there was a Russian language lesson and there was a little poem. ...Well, I hadn't heard the Russian language and as a child I didn't know its accents and I said it was wrong.[9]... And the teacher grabbed me...I had a plait in a doorknocker and two bows.... And I remember it as though it were today, how she caught me by that plait and dragged me along the corridor to the staff room and said, 'You criminal's child. You won't cripple the Russian language'. And then she didn't take me inside the classroom, but made me stand in the corner near the door. And then all the children went past and laughed and each called me different names. And that was a terrible trauma for me, for the whole of my life. To this day I see myself standing there and relive what I was feeling at that moment. At that moment I wanted to die and I thought, if only something would happen which would stop me from having to live in this terrible world.

[8] In Latvia, stuttering is usually classified as a form of neurosis.

[9] Although officially there was no one state language—the constitution (c1.36) refers explicitly to the right to use one's native tongue—in practice there was pressure to use Russian and, in particular, to conduct official business in Russian. Russian was introduced as the language of clerical, administrative, and business affairs as early as 1940. For example, the Communist Party in Jelgava used Latvain in 1940, but by the beginning of 1941 it was Russian. Throughout the Soviet period, all major congresses and official ceremonies of the Communist Party not at national and district levels were held in Russian. In May 1947, the Ministry of Education of USSR ordered the introduction of the Russian language in all schools. In March 1950, further instructions for the expansion and improvement of Russian language teaching were introduced. See L. Zile (1991), 'Latijas Rusifikcija'. In: *Latvijas Vesture*, vol. 1, pp. 31–6.

And during that period of study what tormented me most was a neurocircular dystonia of a cardiovascular type... that's the so-called heart neurosis. And by the way, that happened when I was just 11 years old, when I was in school. At the time when all the teachers were calling me a criminal's child, terrorizing me, that's when the heart neurosis started. And it manifested itself in a stenocardian fashion, I had a severe pain in the region of the heart being just 13 years old.

My mother worked in a hospital and her wages were 310 roubles in old money, in today's money that would be 31 roubles.[10] And my mother—so that we four children would not die of hunger—kept a cow, some pigs, and then during the summer we would grow vegetables, pick nettles, mother would boil them and add a handful of bran and gave them to the pig and the cow, so that we could survive. And I was the oldest and I saw and understood all that.

Although I asked Kristina for her medical history, hers is not a narrative of health and illness. Rather illness is introduced in her autobiography for rhetorical purposes to lend weight to her perspective and evaluation of past events. Illness makes its first appearance at the beginning of the second period of Soviet occupation. Her father's arrest and his being branded as a criminal reverses the earlier order in which he was a respectable bookseller. Kristina describes her health as disintegrating in a way which mirrors the disintegration of society.

Kristina's memory of the German occupation is set in a military and violent context. Her illness—meningitis—is equally dramatic and violent.

The problem of the early Soviet period—the fatherless families, the shortage of food, and the difficulties which many Latvians encountered in learning to speak Russian—were long-term and they led to chronic health problems, namely headaches. However, the humiliation experienced in the Russian lesson finds a precise symbolic equivalent in stuttering. Like many children whose parents were imprisoned or deported Kristina was taunted by teachers and children alike. The common jeer that she was a criminal's child strikes at the heart and she describes herself as suffering from a cardiac neurosis.

All these difficulties and problems are heightened by Kristina's own understanding and perceptiveness. However, not all her

[10] Currency devaluation took place in 1961.

memories are of repression and violence. She recalls episodes which speak of accommodation and the overcoming of difficulties:

Well, what I remember from my childhood is that we survived mostly on fish—Ventspils being a port—and milk. We got the milk in this way. My mother's foster mother's sister turned out to be a Communist. ... And when the *kolhozes* [collective farms] were founded she said ... I still remember her words: 'Latvian *kolhozes* won't suffer if I give away one cow to some poor children.' And then she gave us a cow from her byre, which was to have been handed over to the communal farm in a week's time. She gave us a cow. And you could write a whole story of how we brought the cow from Piebalgia. First of all we took it by lorry to Tukums, then by foot. And then in Tukums my mother agreed with some railway workers that the cow would be loaded on to an old carriage. There were some old carriages there for transporting timber for the sawmills in Ventspils and.... That was in 1946. At that time I was not quite ten. And I was with her and we were all so tired that we all fell asleep. Even the cow stopped fretting and we woke up when the train was being already being uncoupled and the carriage was lifted from the rails and taken to the saw mill. And I remember that two men went to receive the carriages and one of them called out: 'Hey, there's a cow here, and a woman and a child!' Then we went on foot from the saw mill—it's some four or five kilometers. And then the children were very happy.

Kristina's autobiographical and illness narrative can almost be read as a political allegory. Her personal memories share many common elements with other narratives. For example, there is the reference to a 'sunny' pre-war childhood, inferred rather than remembered, and the coming together of personal and national destinies on 14 June, being a birthday and the day of deportations. The arbitrariness and unfairness of her father's arrest and deportation are described. There is the moral chaos following the Russian occupation when even respectable, established firms like the Rapa bookshop do not keep their word. In the immediate post-war years, there is the threat of famine felt particularly acutely by her mother, but also through empathy by Kristina. For her father, there is the difficulty of finding a place for himself after his return to the homeland and for Kristina there is the trauma of finding herself called a criminal's child. Kristina dates the origins of her nervous ill health to that early period of her childhood and the chaotic times the family were going through. She is very ready to attribute neurasthenia to herself, but she does not talk directly about illness.

Instead what she gives me is a social history of the past 50 years as it is filtered though her personal experience and memory.

I felt I must have missed out on some of the illness-related aspects of her account and asked Kristina to recall her symptoms. This war her reply:

I don't feel exhaustion. On the contrary by nature I am very energetic despite the fact that I have a heavy load at work. I have three gardens. I grow sugarbeet, but I manage everything on my own: work, cleaning the house, the garden.... I grow potatoes, sugarbeet, I also grow some vegetables to sell because it's quite hard for three people to survive on one salary. So I don't think that I'm suffering from nervous exhaustion. I have quite the opposite, a kind of tension and anxiety. About my work conditions. The work situation is such that there are a lot of difficulties with transport. We have one ambulance and it very often goes wrong, there are no spare parts. But we still have to get to the patients. Children fall ill regardless. Often there is no petrol. And particularly in winter there are enormous problems, when the parents telephone and call you to the patient but you have no transport. Earlier people used to come themselves to fetch you, the *kolhoz* where they worked would help; there used to be a rule that the collective where the patient worked had to provide transport when a child was ill. Now we have such petrol difficulties and there is a petrol famine, that the *kolhoz* can't supply it either. And that's why we're all so anxious and nervous about what's going to happen tomorrow, what the future will be like.

Kristina succeeds in the turning what was intended to be a medical discussion into one about problems at work and lack of petrol, almost as though the existence of neurasthenia could be inferred from the existence of such problems and social injustices.

The practice of medicine in Soviet Latvia disclosed the uneasy fit between ideology and reality. Neurasthenia, positioned on the meeting ground between individual and society, exemplifies this uncertain relationship. In conceptualizing and situating neurasthenia in this way, Soviet psychiatry paved the way for the metamorphosis of neurasthenia to fit Latvian experience. Thus, where there is a mismatch between individual resources and social expectations, the argument can be developed in one of two directions: one can either question the adequacy of individual resources or one can question the legitimacy of historical happenings and social expectations.

How do these findings relate to the theoretical agenda set out at the beginning of this chapter? What effect do life stories have on the creation of medical knowledge? Latvian resistance to Soviet occupation was embodied in evocative transcripts of ill health. Evocation is a most appropriate term because it emphasizes the universality of the experience of ill health and yet acknowledges the rich potential for ambiguity in the language of illness. However, the narratives themselves are not primarily about illness. Rather, the polyphony of the narrative enables the most commanding voice—that of collective experience—to call the others to its bidding. Thus, the voice of personal distress and certainly the medical voice are subservient to the grand historical narrative: the distressed voice of the individual is enlisted to promote the collective narrative. Illness is used to flesh out and give weight and meaning to historical events. The spirit of testimony point to the social and collective nature of these narratives.[11] Their anxiety is as much about individual survival. So where does this leave the medical anthropology enterprise? The answer must be that it leaves it initially perplexed but ultimately enriched. Anthropologists, although this may not be how they would view it, have concentrated on medicine's success stories. An example that is particularly relevant to my concerns is Allan Young's study of post-traumatic stress disorder: he displays psychiatry's successful colonization and medicalization of past time (p. 7). This road was blocked to Soviet psychiatry by its insecure hold on the historical past. Failures to establish medical knowledge are less easy to identify and document. Only by listening closely to our informants, by entering into dialogue with them as well as our colleagues, can we acknowledge such failure and move on to the wider pastures which lie beyond the confines of medical anthropology conceived.

REFERENCES

Bloch S., P. Reddawa (1977). *Russia's Political Hospital: The Abuse of Psychiatry in the Soviet Union.* London: Victor Gollancz.

Buduls H. (1928). *Psichiatrija.* Raga: Valters and Rapa.

Calloway P. (1992). *Soviet and Western psychiatry.* Keighley: Moor Press; Eglitis II (1989). *Psihiatrija.* Riga: Zvaigzne.

[11] For a discussion of the way in which different cultural groups use testimony, see Annette Wieviorka's article *On testimony.*

Field M. G. (1967). 'Soviet psychiatry and social structure, culture and ideology: a preliminary assessment'. *Am. J. Psychothery,* 21: 230–43.

Humphrey, C. (1994). 'Remembering and "Enemy" the Bogd Khaan in twentieth century Mongolia', in R. S. Watson (ed.). *Memory, History, and Opposition under State Socialism.* Santa Fe: School of American Research Press.

Kleinman A. (1982). 'Neurasthenia and depression: A study of somatization and culture in China'. *Cul. Med. Psychiatry,* 6: 117–90.

——— (1986). *The Social Origins of Distress and Disease Depression, Neurasthenia and Pain in Modern China.* New Haven and London: Yale University Press.

Kolb L. (1966). 'Soviet psychiatric organisation and the community mental health care concept'. *J. Psychiatry,* 123(4): 433–9.

Lebensohn Z. M. (1962). 'The organisation and character of Soviet psychother'. *Am. J. Psychother,* 16: 295–301.

Lutz T. (1995). 'Neurasthenia and fatigue syndromes' in G. Berrios, R. Porter (eds). *A History of Clinical Psychiatry: The Origin and History of Psychiatric Disorders.* London: Athlone; p. 533–44.

Myasischev V. N. (1963). *Personality and Neuroses* [trans. Wortis J. *et al*], Wasington, DC: Joint Publications Research Service.

Plakans A. (1995). *The Latvians: A Short History.* Stanford: Hoover Press.

Pocrabinek A. (1980). *Punitive Medicine* [trans. A. Lehrman]. Ann. Arbor: Karoma Publishers;

Skultans V. (1995). 'Neurasthenia and political resistance in Latvia'. *Anthropol Today,* 11(3): 14–18.

Svabe A., A. Bumanis, and K. Dislers (eds), (1937). *Latviesu Konversacijas vardnica.* Riga: A Gulbis.

Velmers O. (1992). 'Medicine in Latvia'. Unpublished paper.

Wieviorka A. (1994). 'On testimony' in G. H. Hartman (ed.). *Holocaust Remembrance. The Shapes of Memory.* Oxford: Basil Blackwell, 23–41.

Young A. (1995). *A Harmony of Illusions: Inventing Post-traumatic Stress Disorder.* Princeton: Princeton University Press.

Ziferstein I. (1972). 'Group therapy in the Soviet Union'. *Am. J. Psychiatry,* 129(5): 595–9.

——— (1976). 'Psychotherapy in the USSR' in S. A. Corson, E. O'leary (eds). *Psychiatry and Psychology in the USSR.* New York and London: Plenum Press, pp. 143–79.

Oup Apl 347

1-6-02